EXPLORATIONS IN BACKYARD BIOLOGY

EXPLORATIONS IN BACKYARD BIOLOGY
Drawing on Nature in the Classroom, Grades 4-6

R. Gary Raham

Illustrated by the Author

1996
TEACHER IDEAS PRESS
A Division of
Libraries Unlimited, Inc.
Englewood, Colorado

TEACHER IDEAS PRESS
A Division of
Libraries Unlimited, Inc.
P.O. Box 6633
Englewood, CO 80155-6633
1-800-237-6124

Production Editor: Stephen Haenel
Copy Editor: Jan Krygier
Proofreader: Ann Marie Damian
Design and Layout: Pamela J. Getchell

The Ogden Nash poems appearing on page 89 ("The Fly") and page 161 ("Bugs") are from *Verses from 1929 On* by Ogden Nash. Copyright 1942 by Ogden Nash. First appeared in the *Saturday Evening Post*. By permission of Little, Brown and Company.

Library of Congress Cataloging-in-Publication Data

Raham, Gary.
    Explorations in backyard biology : drawing on nature in the classroom, grades 4-6 / R. Gary Raham.
       xix, 205 p. 22x28 cm.
       Includes bibliographical references and index.
       ISBN 1-56308-254-3
       1. Nature study--Activity programs.   2. Natural history--Study and teaching (Elementary)   I. Title.
    QH54.5.R34   1996
    372.3'57--dc20   96-10792
                                                            CIP

Contents

Part II
The Hunters and the Hunted

Part III
Animal Communication

Part IV
Your Backyard in Balance

Figures

Preface

Explorations in Backyard Biology: Drawing on Nature in the Classroom, Grades 4-6 explores new worlds of adventure in the life sciences for both students in upper elementary-level classes and their teachers. Students read short features on fascinating creatures as near as their own backyards, are invited to expand their interest with exciting classroom and field activities, and are shown how to use drawing and writing skills to record their experiences in a naturalist's notebook. Teachers are provided in-depth material on each topic of discussion and are introduced to references that will help satisfy their own curiosity.

The first chapter refers to some amazing studies in split-brain research that show how our brains are organized for problem solving and demonstrates how drawing skills can be used to tap creative resources often underused. It then shows how scientists of all persuasions have used drawing and writing skills to tease out some of nature's mysteries and invites students to create their own naturalist's notebooks to facilitate similar discoveries.

Students and teachers then explore four large areas of natural history: size, scale, and the world of the very small; predator-prey relationships among animals; animal communication; and the ecology of living communities, including their human members. The last two chapters in particular emphasize the interactions and interconnections in living systems and the effects of human activities on the health of our planet.

Explorations in Backyard Biology may be used to supplement other science programs teachers are using by providing self-contained projects that can be integrated with other curricula or used as springboards for science projects. However, I hope teachers will use it on an ongoing basis to combine something children naturally like to do—drawing—with an area some students (and teachers) may find difficult—science. Drawing on nature can be fun and exciting!

Acknowledgments

I would like to thank Vicki Jordan, science teacher at Wellington Junior High, and Linda Morrow, teacher at Eyestone Elementary, both in Wellington, Colorado, for reading and commenting on portions of the manuscript. I also appreciate Vicki trying out my "Quick Key for Creature Identification" on Wellingtonian arthropods and their student discoverers.

Herb Saperstone, a geologist and video script writer with Scott Resources in Fort Collins, also provided valuable insights as did Dick Scott, Ph.D., retired paleobotanist, who was able to comment on the project in its entirety.

The student articles "Spider Talk" and "A Robot with the Right Bee-Havior" originally appeared in *Highlights for Children,* a magazine whose own motto is "Fun with a Purpose." I would like to thank Kent Brown and his staff for permission to use the articles and for his encouragement over the years in writing for children.

Betty Edwards's *Drawing on the Right Side of the Brain* struck a sympathetic chord with many people, including myself, who feel that art is often undervalued as a route to understanding how the world works. Some of the activities in chapter 1 are patterned after exercises in her book.

Dougal Dixon has proved on several occasions that creativity and science are far from mutually exclusive. The Slobber and the Hiri-Hiri characters in chapter 11 are products of his imagination and appeared in his book *After Man: A Zoology of the Future.*

Thanks also to Shirley Parrish for copyediting several chapters and to my family, who have learned to put up with an odd assortment of creatures from time to time and who have served as occasional models, sounding boards, and experimental subjects, not to mention sources of unending support.

Introduction

Explorations in Backyard Biology invites you to practice a few drawing skills, to indulge your curiosity, and to share the fun of discovery with your students. If you already have some background in science, so much the better, but the information you need to work with the topics at hand is provided, along with suggested references for more in-depth study.

If you suffer from drawing angst, please try out some of the suggested exercises in chapter 1 ahead of time and see if you can't banish any drawing insecurities that might have lingered from your own childhood. Drawing skills *can* be learned. The difference between artists and nonartists is that artists are compelled to draw all the time, and they stumbled across the observational tricks described in chapter 1 by accident. Although you may not be a compulsive artist, you will be surprised how much your drawings will improve using these techniques. You will also be surprised at how well drawing will improve your powers of observation—a critical skill in science.

Once you and your students have had some fun with chapter 1 and have started your naturalist's notebooks, chapter 2 provides a good framework for understanding the small worlds many of Earth's creatures inhabit. The remaining chapters can be juggled a bit to coincide with other projects you might have or to accommodate the availability of certain animals or opportunities for field trips. The last two chapters are perhaps best studied last because they help to unite human concerns with those of the rest of nature.

Student articles have been designed to be short (800 to 1,100 words) with a high-interest approach kids can relate to. These segments can be easily copied as a reading assignment. Activity directions have also been written so that they can be copied for student use, or you can modify them to more closely match your own circumstances. If you use this book primarily as a resource for science projects and independent work, you may want to let students look at some of the supplementary material as well.

May your pencils stay sharp, may the bugs cooperate, and may you and your students have lots of fun drawing on nature!

Chapter 1

DRAWING AS A TOOL IN SCIENCE
The Naturalist's Notebook

TWO BRAINS ARE BETTER THAN ONE

Wouldn't it be great to have an extra brain? Maybe one brain could concentrate on homework while the other planned parties or talked to friends. Or maybe one could be like the afterburner in a jet, kicking in when you really need extra thinking power. Truth is, you have two brains, but one of them is a little bashful and can't talk.

Viewed from the top, as in figure 1.1, a human brain is clearly divided into two parts (called *hemispheres*) and looks a bit like an oversized walnut. This view is somewhat misleading for two reasons. First, nerve fibers crisscross from one side of the brain to the other. What you see with your right eye, for example, is processed by the left side of the brain and vice versa. Likewise, the right side of the brain controls the nerves and muscles for the left side of your body. Second, a bundle of 50 million nerve fibers, called the *corpus callosum*, connects the left and right sides of the brain, much like a cable that links a computer to a printer.

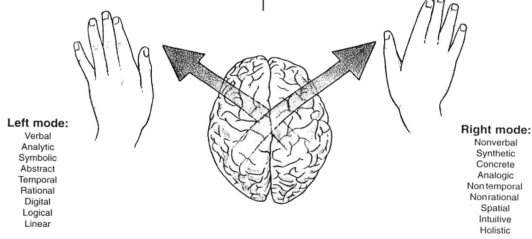

Left mode:
Verbal
Analytic
Symbolic
Abstract
Temporal
Rational
Digital
Logical
Linear

Right mode:
Nonverbal
Synthetic
Concrete
Analogic
Nontemporal
Nonrational
Spatial
Intuitive
Holistic

Fig. 1.1. Crossover of brain functions. Top view of human brain with eyes toward the top of the page. Because nerve fibers cross from one side (hemisphere) of the brain to various sites on the other side of the body, the left side of the brain controls vision and muscular activity on the right side of the body and vice versa.

1

From *Explorations in Backyard Biology.* © 1996. Teacher Ideas Press. (800) 237-6124.

Different Brains, Different Talents

Despite the brain's interconnections, the two halves have different abilities. This fact became clear in the 1860s because of the work of Dr. Paul Broca. Broca had a patient who could understand what was said to him and communicate, after a fashion, with hand gestures and facial expressions, but the only words he could say were "Tan Tan." When the patient died, Broca discovered damage in a hen's egg-sized area of the left side of his brain, which is now called *Broca's area* (see fig. 1.2). Many language skills are centered here.* Damage to another left hemisphere area causes people to speak in nonsensical sentences.

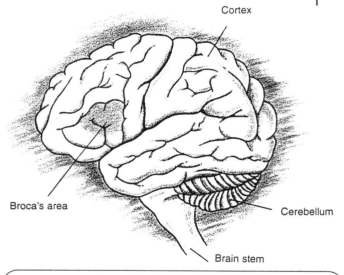

Fig. 1.2. The left side of a human brain. The shaded region (called Broca's area after its discoverer) controls language functions in most people. A small percentage of left-handers have language skills located on the right side of the brain.

Some of the different abilities of the left and right sides of the brain are harder to detect. This is illustrated by the story of Dr. W. P. van Wagenen who, in the 1940s, had to cut his patients' brains in half to save their lives! His patients suffered from severe epileptic seizures that started on one side of the brain and then moved to the other. No medication helped. As a last resort, he thought he might be able to keep the seizures from spreading by cutting the corpus callosum, which you can see in figure 1.3. He didn't know how much damage this would cause, but he knew his patients would die otherwise. To his surprise, cutting this thick bundle of nerves stopped the seizures and *caused no obvious damage* to his patients.

Twenty years later, studies of similar patients showed that cutting the *corpus callosum* does have some effects, and these effects imply that in many ways each of us has two separate brains. A split-brain patient called Vicki viewed pictures with only one eye (and thus one brain hemisphere) at a time. Pictures shown to her right eye (analyzed by the left, language-centered part of the brain) could always be identified right away. However, pictures shown to her left eye (analyzed by the right brain) produced strange results. When her left eye was shown a picture of a woman on the telephone, Vicki could only describe the picture as that of a woman. When asked what she was doing, Vicki said, "skipping rope." But if Vicki closed her eyes and let her left hand (controlled by the right brain) write the answer, it correctly described the woman as using a telephone!

---

* Between 5 and 12 percent of people in the Western world are left-handed. In most left-handers verbal functions still are found in the left hemisphere. But in some cases, where left-handers have left-handed mothers, verbal functions are in the right hemisphere.

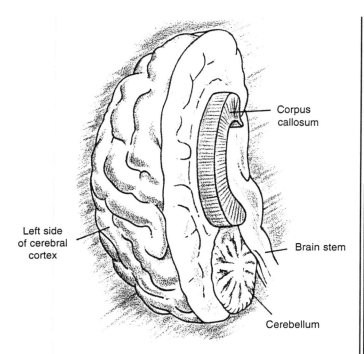

Fig. 1.3. Brain structure (cross section). Lateral, cutaway view of the brain seen from the right rear. A broad arc of nerve fibers called the corpus callosum connects left and right brain hemispheres.

When her left and right eyes viewed different commands (right eye: laugh, left eye: clap), Vicki laughed and clapped simultaneously but could only describe seeing the command to laugh. The left side of her brain literally didn't know what the right side was doing.

Left- and Right-Brain Skills

Research with many such patients over the past 30 years or so has shown that the left brain is very good with symbols and abstract concepts. It likes interpreting language and numbers, figuring things out step by step, and drawing conclusions based on logic. These are skills you are often asked to use in school. The left brain is usually bossy, too, and wants to be in charge. The right brain likes nonsymbolic things that you can see and feel directly. It doesn't talk well but sees the likenesses

between things, doesn't always require a lot of facts, makes leaps of insight, and is creative. Drawing is something the right brain likes to do. These differences are summarized in table 1.1.

Table 1.1. A Comparison of Left-Brain and Right-Brain Skills

The Left Brain . . .	The Right Brain . . .
is very VERBAL, using words to name, describe, and define things.	is NONVERBAL. It has an awareness of things, but there is a minimal connection of objects and ideas with words.
is ANALYTIC. It likes to figure things out in a step-by-step way.	is SYNTHETIC. It likes to put things together to form wholes.
likes to use SYMBOLS to represent objects and ideas. A skull and crossbones stands for poison. A plus sign stands for the process of addition.	relates to CONCRETE OBJECTS that exist at the moment.
deals with the ABSTRACT, using small bits of information to stand for the entire concept.	works by ANALOGY. It sees the likenesses between things.
likes to keep track of TIME, doing first things first, second things second, and so forth.	is NONTEMPORAL (unconcerned with time).
is very RATIONAL. It likes to draw conclusions based on reason and facts.	is NONRATIONAL. It doesn't need to make judgments based on reason and is often willing to suspend judgment.
likes NUMBERS and counting.	thinks SPATIALLY, trying to see where one thing is in relation to another.
admires things that are LOGICAL, like mathematical theorems or well-stated arguments.	is INTUITIVE and makes leaps of insight often based on guesses and hunches.

Although we don't always realize it, we do our best work when we give both of our brains a chance to do what they do best. Let the right brain roam free without time limits to creatively solve tough problems, but then rein it in once in a while to put things in order and get things done. The difficult thing is to keep the bossy left side from doing things the right side is better at.

In *Explorations in Backyard Biology* you'll get to use both sides of your brain in creating a naturalist's notebook and learn some exciting things about nature in the process. We'll start with a few activities that will make your bashful right brain come out and shine.

ACTIVITIES

Learning to Recognize Right-Brain Thinking

You may already love to draw. If so, these exercises will definitely be fun. But even if you feel a little self-conscious about drawing, these exercises will help you recognize the state of mind that artists possess when they draw. You will also learn some tricks of observation that make drawing much easier.

The Face That Made a Vase

Look at the silhouette drawing of the vase in figure 1.4. Now look at the white shapes on either side of the silhouette that create the shape of the stem and bowl. They look like a side view of two identical faces facing each other.

Read the directions that follow to begin to create your own faces-vase drawing.

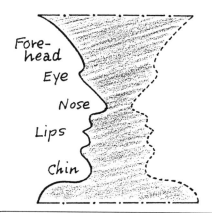

Fig. 1.4. The face/vase illusion. Two face profiles, "nose-to-nose," create the silhouette of a goblet or vase when connected by horizontal lines. Make your own by following the directions in the text.

1. If you are *right-handed,* draw the profile of a face on the left side of your page facing right. You can copy the face profile from the vase in figure 1.4 if you want, but it's probably better to draw a profile from memory. Make it a silly one if you want, with a big nose and pointed chin. If you are *left-handed,* draw a left-facing profile on the right side of the page, if that feels like a more natural thing to do. (For some left-handers hemispheric dominance in the brain is the opposite of right-handers.)

2. Draw horizontal lines at the top and bottom of your profile. These create the top and bottom of the vase.

3. Trace over your first profile lightly and name all the parts of the face: forehead, nose, upper lip, etc. Your left brain will like this activity of naming symbolic shapes.

4. Now, starting at the top of your drawing, draw your first profile in *reverse* to create the opposite side of the vase. To make the vase look correct, this second profile needs to be just like the first in everything except the direction it's facing. This will be harder to do at first *and requires a different way of thinking.* Try and see what you do differently to make the drawing look right.

Do this exercise before reading further.

How did you solve the problem? Did you find yourself scanning back and forth between both profiles, looking at the shapes between lines and the angle one line made with another? Did you stop thinking about drawing noses, chins, etc., and just concentrate on making the shapes and curves correctly? Did class time seem to go by more quickly? If so, you tapped into the right-brain way of doing things.

The Upside-Down Trick

In this next drawing you're going to get a better chance to access your right brain. You'll do it by copying the drawing of Einstein in figure 1.5.

"Achh!" your left brain says. "I can't do that. Too much detail! The eyes will come out different sizes and all cockeyed and the nose is too complicated and...." Shhhh. Quiet this left-brain babbling by turning Einstein upside down. Now, it's not Einstein anymore, just a bunch of interesting shapes. As before, read through the following directions before starting.

1. Turn the picture upside down and *keep it that way* so the left brain doesn't get involved in making premature judgments. Find a place to work quietly by yourself. Let your teacher worry about keeping track of the time.

2. Look at the upside-down drawing for a minute. See how all the lines fit together. Where one line stops, another starts. Consider the shapes between lines and the angles certain lines make with another.

Fig. 1.5. Einstein. Here's a "brain." Turn him upside down and he'll be easy to draw.

3. Start the drawing at the top and work your way down from one line to another, kind of like putting together a jigsaw puzzle. Avoid naming or thinking about the part of the face you're drawing—that's just your left brain trying to butt in. Think "this line curves this way, then crosses over and makes this weird shape..." and so on.

4. As you get into the drawing you'll find yourself becoming interested in how the lines and shapes fit together. You'll lose track of time. Your left brain has finally gotten tired of this nonsense and turned off. Your right brain is humming contentedly and has nothing to say! Remember, all the information you need to draw Einstein is right there in front of you. All it takes to draw a "brain" is the right brain.

Drawing Something by Drawing Nothing: Negative Space

Left brains don't like dealing with empty spaces. They can't name them, categorize them, or come up with ready-made symbols to describe them. Right brains like them just fine and find them quite useful for drawing.

Fig.1.6. A dinosaur and its negative space. (*A*) A drawing of a dinosaur. (*B*) The negative spaces (in black) that define the dinosaur's shape. Negative spaces are often easier to draw than positive spaces that our left brain likes to name.

Look at the two drawings in figure 1.6. Figure 1.6(a) is a traditional drawing of a dinosaur. Figure 1.6(b) shows the space around the dinosaur between the positive drawing and the edge of the paper. The colored-in areas are called negative spaces. If you cut out these shapes and pasted them on a colored piece of paper the same size, you could re-create the shape of the dinosaur. Photocopy the picture and try it!

You can use negative space to help get complex drawings right in terms of perspective and proportion. First, let's create a viewfinder with a hole the same shape as the paper on which you do your drawing. Let's assume you draw on standard, 8½-x-11-inch paper.

1. Take a piece of heavy paper or cardboard and trim it to 8½ x 11 inches.

2. Draw diagonal lines from opposite corners. They will cross in the center of the sheet. Draw a small rectangle at the center of the sheet by connecting the horizontal and vertical lines at points on the diagonals. This rectangle will be proportional to (the same shape as) the larger piece of paper. A rectangle about 1 x 1¼ inches is a good size (see fig. 1.7).

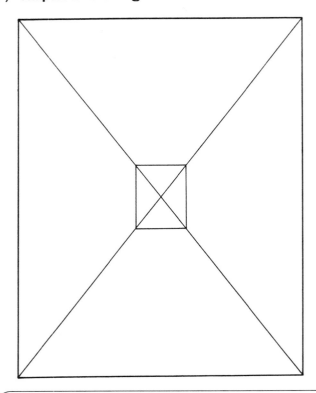

Fig. 1.7. Viewing rectangle diagram. A viewfinder made by taking a piece of cardboard the same shape as an 8½-x-11-inch piece of paper; drawing diagonal lines corner to corner; picking a point on one of the diagonals; dropping vertical and horizontal lines until they intersect the other diagonals; and cutting out the resulting small rectangle.

3. Cut out the small rectangle with scissors or a utility knife. You now have a viewfinder. Have someone hold the paper you plan to draw on far enough away so that it just fills your viewfinder when you look through it. The shapes of the viewfinder and paper should just match.

4. Look at an object you want to draw through the viewfinder—maybe a three-quarter view of a chair. Get far enough away so that the object just touches *at least two edges* of the viewfinder. Make sure your drawing paper is turned the same way as your viewfinder.

5. Now look at the negative spaces between the object and the edges of the viewfinder. Take the time to wait until you see these areas as shapes.

6. Imagine that the object itself vanishes. All you have left to draw are the funny shapes made outside where the object was—the negative spaces. Your right brain will find this a fun way to draw.

The Naturalist's Notebook

Once you practice a bit at the artist's "tricks of the trade" introduced above, you should see improvement in your own drawing abilities. You'll also find that you notice many more things about the objects you draw than you ever would have otherwise. Drawing can become a valuable tool in science, both by sharpening your powers of observation and by enlisting the powerful creative abilities of your right brain.

Therefore, as you explore "Monsters in the Mud Puddle," "The Milkweed Universe," and all the other exciting creatures and places described in this book, you will be asked to make drawings, notes, and observations in a notebook. This notebook will be something of a cross between a diary and a scientist's formal records. Many explorers of the last century kept such naturalist's notebooks, and their observations were of great value to modern scientists. Some of you could make discoveries new to science, perhaps in your own backyards, but even if the discoveries are only new to you, you'll find the effort exciting and worthwhile.

Happy hunting!

From *Explorations in Backyard Biology.* © 1996. Teacher Ideas Press. (800) 237-6124.

CREATING A NATURALIST'S NOTEBOOK

The split-brain research described earlier in this chapter, as well as subsequent research, has provided fascinating insights into the way the human mind works. We think of ourselves as individuals with a unified sense of self, whereas it might be more accurate to describe our concept of self as a theory generated by the verbal left brain to make sense of what all the other brain subsystems are doing.

There's no denying that the left brain's integrative and executive functions are crucial to our day-to-day functioning in the world. Just as nations flounder without clear leadership, we as individuals would become lost in a sea of sensations and random impulses without some left-brain navigation. But right-brain innovation is too often downplayed or ignored in our Western world culture, and it's time we as educators look for ways to regularly exercise our right-brain talents. The naturalist's notebook is a great way to get kids to access their creative side on a regular basis.

What Is a Naturalist's Notebook?

A naturalist's notebook is a kind of diary, but one that includes both sketches and words, and one whose topic of interest is the natural world. This "natural world" may include, but need not be restricted to, forests, grasslands, streams, lakes, deserts, and other places that may be hard to visit, depending on your time and budget. Cities and urban areas are natural worlds, too, containing a variety of living things you can discover, armed with a little information and a lot of enthusiasm.

Naturalist's notebooks rode in many knapsacks and saddlebags in the last century. John James Audubon filled his with thousands of sketches of birds. John Wesley Powell took along an illustrator on his journeys down the Colorado River and made daily records of his adventures. Stephens and Catherwood traveled in the Yucatan, drawing and describing the ruins of Mexico's great civilizations. But naturalists also abounded in the population at large. Nature lay just out the back door for many people. Large parts of the world remained underexplored and exotic, with new species turning up regularly.

You may have created field notebooks in college—somewhat formal cousins of the notebooks described here. All scientists learn to record in some way their observations and the results of their experiments. After all, human memory is fallible, both in how much it remembers and in what it remembers. But in some disciplines the drawing aspect of journaling has been downplayed and ignored, partially because of the ease of taking pictures. This is a mistake! *Creating* the image of your interest brings valuable dividends of its own.

Why Make a Naturalist's Notebook?

Perhaps the best reason to create a naturalist's notebook is because it's fun. Kids love to draw at an early age, but some get turned off by age 10 or 12 when they don't have the success they think they should have at rendering objects in a realistic manner. If you were one of those students, see if you can rediscover the joys of drawing by practicing the activities I described earlier for students and/or looking up *Drawing on the Right Side of the Brain* by Betty Edwards. She discusses this concept in more detail and offers other tricks to get your right brain in gear.

A naturalist's notebook is also a great way to remember experiences and a painless way to get students into the habit of making careful observations and asking lots of questions. It makes science something you can do for recreation and not just a recitation of boring facts. Every time you work with living things, either in the field or the classroom, you are guaranteed to learn something new.

Using drawing to teach science promotes visual thinking, which can be a powerful adjunct to our left-brain verbal skills. As we all know, everybody with 20/20 vision doesn't always *see* what he or she looks at with the same accuracy. Seeing something depends on whether it has emotional content for the viewer, what the viewer's point of view is, and how much the viewer knows about what he or she is looking at. If you can transmit your excitement and knowledge of life science to your students, and I can tweak the way they look at overlooked parts of nature, we can make them "see all that they can see."

How Do You Make a Naturalist's Notebook?

A bound book of unlined pages that isn't too large to carry around in the field makes a good notebook and gives the student something nice and substantial that he or she can keep and add to after the coursework is done. If this is impractical, use single sheets of unlined three-hole-punched paper and a clipboard and add them to a three-ring binder later. Don't let kids redo the drawings and rewrite notes later, however. This defeats the purpose of recording what you see when you see it. As time goes by, they will get better at their drawings and have more to say about what they see.

Any #2 pencil will work for drawing, but students could be encouraged to try drawing with pencils of different hardnesses, charcoal pencils, colored pencils, or even fiber-tipped pens. Eberhard Faber makes an ebony, jet black, extra-smooth pencil that I like. FaberCastell Pink Pearl erasers are good, but standard pencil erasers work well, too. At this stage it's not necessary to get too hung up on materials. The most important thing is to get students in the habit of keeping their sketching materials handy and using them. Both you and they should become unself-conscious drawers again!

Notes on the References

Drawing on the Right Side of the Brain by Betty Edwards is a good book to have on your shelf. It has become a classic for tapping into right-brain skills and is fun to read.

The Sierra Club Guide to Sketching in Nature by Cathy Johnson provides more detailed information for naturalist-artists on tools and techniques for fieldwork. She has especially good tips for working in color.

Experiences in Visual Thinking by Robert H. McKim suggests many good activities for increasing visual awareness. Its approach is somewhat more academic than Betty Edwards's book.

The two books by Richard M. Restak parallel series that appeared on public television during the 1980s. In particular, Restak's *The Brain* has a good summary of split-brain research. *The Brain: A User's Manual* by the Diagram Group provides background information on neuroanatomy and brain function.

If you like to cruise the Internet, look up *Lab-Top Book for Writing in Science*. John Shaw also advocates that art and science departments look for creative ways to work together.

Part I

The Underloved and the Overlooked

Chapter 2

LET'S GET SMALL

THE POWERS OF TEN

How tall are you? How wide is your hand? How long is a dog's ear or your teacher's nose? These are all measurements easily made with a ruler—at least if you can get your dog and your teacher to stand still. Cats, crickets, parakeets, mice, moths, and most of the living things we interact with on a day-to-day basis are also easily measurable. If you become a backyard biologist, however, you will eventually discover creatures much smaller than those that usually become a part of your life. Some will be barely visible if you have good eyesight. Others will have to be magnified 10, 100, or even 1,000 times. A few microbes are so small that they can't be seen with visible light at all. Explore "The Powers of Ten" by "thinking small" and you will begin to get a feeling for the tremendous range of sizes in living things.

Explaining Exponents

The "powers of ten" are actually numbers called *exponents* that are written above and to the right of the number 10. The number 10^2 is shorthand for the product of 10×10, or 100. The number 10^3 stands for the product of $10 \times 10 \times$ 10, or 1,000, and so on. When exponents are negative numbers, they represent a fraction. 10^{-3} means $\frac{1}{10^3}$, which is $\frac{1}{1000}$ or .001. Ten to the zero power (written as 10^0) equals 1. For most practical purposes we exist in a world of 10^0 meters (10^0 m), where 1 meter can be used to measure most of the things we interact with every day—and a lot of things we don't (see fig. 2.1). Chairs, cats, lamps, and teachers

You

1 m

Chipmunk

Compsognathus

Fig. 2.1. The World of 10^0. Most of the objects we see and use every day can be measured with a meterstick. Notice that a portion of the chipmunk is enclosed within a square box having sides .1 meter long. The chipmunk will appear again in the illustration for objects in the realm of 10^{-1} m. Look for a one-tenth size box in all the illustrations that follow.

13

From *Explorations in Backyard Biology*. © 1996. Teacher Ideas Press. (800) 237-6124.

teachers can all be measured easily with a meterstick. One of the smallest dinosaurs, by the way, *Compsognathus,* was about .6 meters tall (the size of a chicken).

To comfortably measure the largest living things on Earth we would need to use a measuring device 10 times longer than a meterstick (see fig. 2.2). With this we could measure the 15-meter length of a *Tyrannosaurus* skeleton or the 25-meter length of the largest animal to have ever lived: the blue whale. This world of the first power of ten, 10^1, seems to be the upper limit for animal life on Earth. Plants like the giant sequoia tree, which are 80 to 100 meters tall, reach to the realm of 10^2 m.

Measurement on a Smaller Scale

By thinking on a smaller scale, we can get to know even more of the world's life-forms. Creatures that are about one-tenth of a meter in size, a metric unit called a *decimeter* (dm), live in the world of 10^{-1}m (see fig. 2.3). A chipmunk is about 1.5 dm long, as are the largest insects in the world, the African Goliath beetles, with wing-spans greater than a sparrow's! The smallest bird, the tiny bee hummingbird, is about .5 dm long, about the same size as the smallest mammal, the pygmy shrew. Both of these animals would fit comfortably in your hand, which is about a decimeter wide. Measure it and see!

Divide a decimeter by 10 and you have 1 *centimeter* (cm), which is almost half an inch. This world of 10^{-2} is the realm of the smallest animal with a backbone: a fish called the dwarf goby (see fig. 2.4). The smallest bird egg, that of the bee hummingbird, measures 1.15 cm. Both the smallest frog and the smallest reptile are less than half as long as a safety pin.

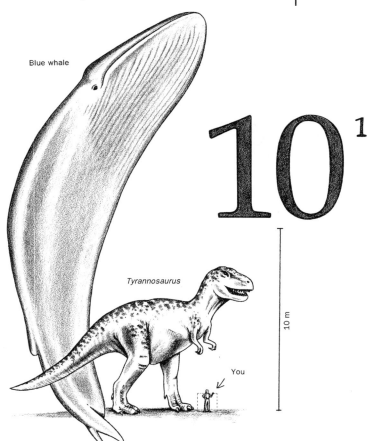

Blue whale

10^1

10 m

Tyrannosaurus

You

Fig. 2.2. The World of 10^1. The largest animals on Earth, both past and present, could be measured with a "10-meter stick." This size seems to be the upper limit for active, mobile creatures on planet Earth.

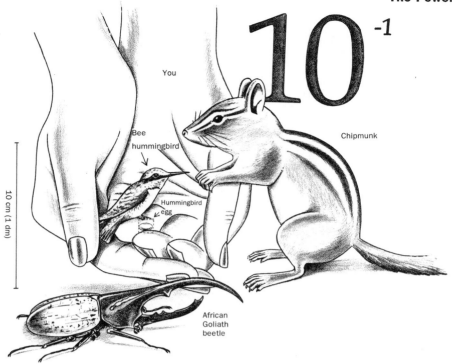

Fig. 2.3. The World of 10^{-1}. Ten centimeters (1 decimeter) is a comfortable length for measuring birds, bugs, and furry rodents.

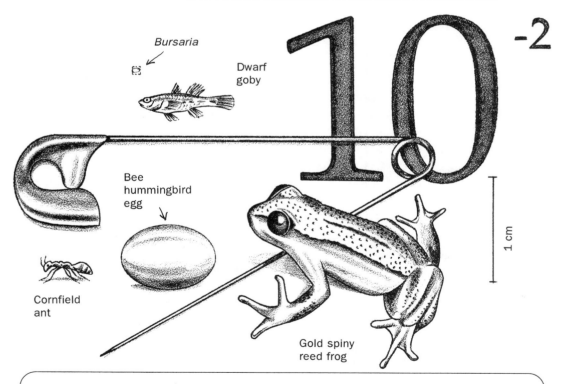

Fig. 2.4. The World of 10^{-2}. A centimeter ruler could measure everything you are likely to see with your naked eyes. The largest single-celled animals are just barely visible as tiny moving specks in pond water.

From *Explorations in Backyard Biology*. © 1996. Teacher Ideas Press. (800) 237-6124.

One-tenth of a centimeter is a *millimeter* (mm), the smallest division on your metric ruler. The largest single-celled protozoans, like *Bursaria* (see fig. 2.5), rule this 10^{-3} universe. Here you will also find the largest insect eggs, 3.2 mm long, the smallest spider, .8 mm, and the smallest centipede, 4.8 mm. Many ticks, mites, and fleas—common parasites of humans and other mammals—fall into this size range as well. Cornfield ants, widely distributed in the United States and perhaps the most abundant species of insect worldwide, are about 5 mm long and snack on the sweet secretions of root aphids.

wasps, the smallest insects, are 200 microns long, as are many common protozoans. This is also the size of a typical grain of sand. Rotifers, the smallest multicellular creatures, range in size from 80 to 500 microns long. The smallest plant seeds, belonging to an orchid, measure 100 microns as do the smallest insect eggs. The human egg cell measures 140 microns wide.

Shrinking further into the microscopic world, we reach 10^{-5} m, which equals 10 microns. Ordinary human cells, like the white blood cells that flow through your capillaries, are about 10 microns in diameter (see fig. 2.7). While most bacteria are about 3 microns long, the largest species measures 45 microns, both comfortably in the 10^{-5} m world. A free-living plant cell called *Gonyaulax* is about 40 microns in diameter, but sometimes populations of these cells reach such large numbers that they create visible "red tides" in the oceans. Toxins produced by these cells can kill fish and other marine life.

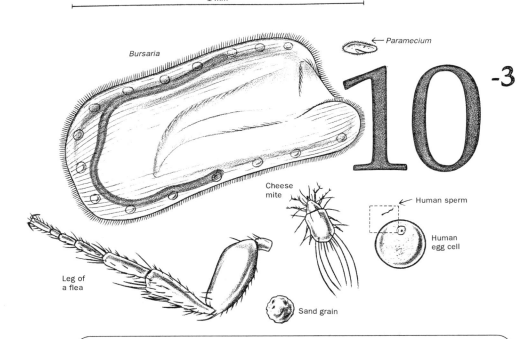

Fig. 2.5. The World of 10^{-3}. A millimeter is the measure of things considered very tiny in our world, such as a grain of sand or a cheese mite. In fact, the other meaning of the word *mite* is "a very little particle or quantity."

The world of 10^{-4} (see fig. 2.6) is truly a strange world we can only appreciate with ample magnification. The measure 10^{-4} m is equal to 100 micrometers (*microns,* abbreviated μm). Certain species of parasitic

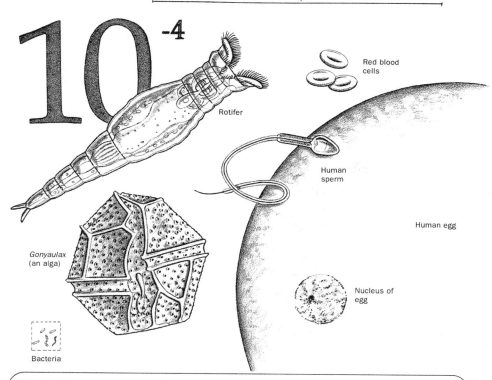

100 µm

10^{-4}

Red blood cells

Rotifer

Human sperm

Human egg

Gonyaulax (an alga)

Nucleus of egg

Bacteria

Fig 2.6. The World of 10^{-4}. This microscopic world was not discovered until 1674 when the Dutch lens maker Antony van Leeuwenhoek took the time to look at water from Berkelse Mere, a lake near his home in Delft, Holland, with one of his magnifying lenses. "The sight of all kinds of twisting and spiraling little animals 'twas wonderful to see . . . . "

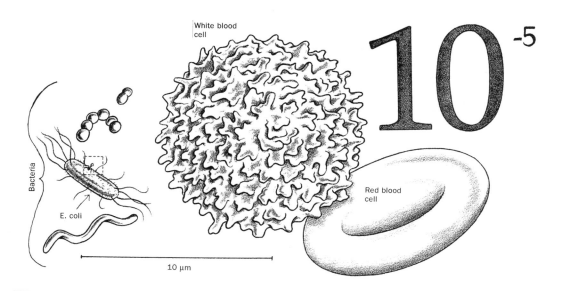

White blood cell

10^{-5}

Bacteria

E. coli

Red blood cell

10 µm

Fig. 2.7. The World of 10^{-5}. Light microscopes at their highest magnification can just make out the shapes of bacteria—rods, spheres, or tiny spirals. Red blood cells look like unfinished donuts in this world and white blood cells look like escapees from a science fiction movie.

The measure 10^{-6} m is one-millionth of a meter or 1 micron. This realm lies at the limit of magnification using compound microscopes because our eyes can only detect visible light, which has wavelengths in the half micron range (see fig. 2.8). The head of a human sperm cell is 2 microns wide as are the common vitamin K-producing bacteria, *E. coli,* that live in your intestines.

nm long. The smallest known viruses consist of a few genes wrapped in a shell of protein no more than 20 nm in diameter.

Life on Earth exists over a size range of 10 orders of magnitude, from the 20-nanometer viruses to the immense 100-meter sequoias! Small creatures, representing the vast number of Earth's living things, rarely capture our attention unless they make us sick or cost us money. But the micro world around us is an exciting, surprisingly bizarre place, every bit as strange as an alien planet. This book can serve as a guide to this miniature world, and the admission ticket is nothing more than a curious mind and a willingness to "think small."

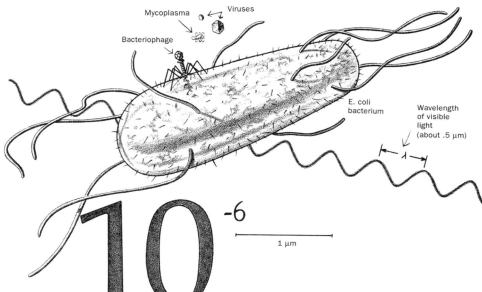

Fig. 2.8. The World of 10^{-6}. In the world measured by a single micron, light itself is too coarse to reveal the details of objects. Beams of electrons show what some bacteria and viruses look like.

The smallest creatures dwell in the world of 10^{-7} m (equal to 100 *nanometers,* abbreviated nm). The bacteria in your intestines have strange-looking viral parasites called bacteriophages that are about 240 nm long (see fig. 2.9). Plants also suffer from parasites like the tobacco mosaic virus, which is 300 nm long. Typical flu viruses that invade people during winter months are 115 nm long. The smallest self-reproducing creatures, bacteria called *Mycoplasmas,* have irregular shapes between 150 and 300

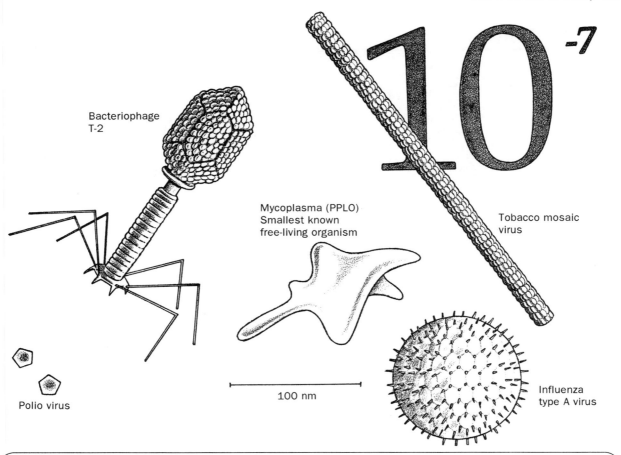

Bacteriophage T-2

Mycoplasma (PPLO) Smallest known free-living organism

Tobacco mosaic virus

Polio virus

100 nm

Influenza type A virus

Fig. 2.9. The World of 10⁻⁷. This strange realm is inhabited by viruses and mycoplasmas. Viruses can reproduce themselves with the help of other organisms, but have none of the other characteristics we associate with living things.

ACTIVITIES

That's the Size of It

Go to the chalkboard and draw a square meter using chalk and a meterstick. Three other students should draw squares of 1 decimeter, 1 centimeter, and 1 millimeter, respectively.

With your class, count off in fours. All the ones search for objects that fit in the square meter, twos look for objects that fit in a square decimeter, and so on. Which group could find the most objects? Why?

That's the Measure of It

Create your own measuring scale using a body part or some common classroom object. Measure the following things using your new scale:

The height of your chair

Your height

The width of your desk or table

The height of the doorway

List the advantages and disadvantages of your unit of measurement.

Dinoschool

If you can find or make a scale drawing of your school building, draw your favorite dinosaur to the same scale. How many could lie down in the building at the same time? Could your dinosaur look over the roof? What size door would he need to get in?

Microscopic Jungles

Collect eight sealable plastic bags. Label them 1 through 8. Each bag will hold a different sample. After adding the material in each bag as described below, seal the bag. (Throw the bags away, unopened, once you have made your observations.)

♦ Fill bag #1 with a sliced-up piece of fruit.

♦ Fill bag #2 with slightly crushed grapes and add enough water to just cover them.

- Fill half of bag #3 with water from a lake, pond, or river, with both surface and bottom material.
- Fill bag #4 with enough hay to cover the bottom and add water to cover.
- Fill bag #5 with some dried beans and enough water to cover them.
- Fill bag #6 with some cottage cheese or cream cheese spread over its bottom.
- Fill bag #7 with some head lettuce leaves and add a little water.
- Fill bag #8 with two pieces of stale bread and just enough water to moisten it.

Keep the bags out of direct sunlight. If a bag swells and looks like it might pop, have your teacher bleed some air from it.

📖 IN YOUR NOTEBOOK

Over the 7 to 10 days that your jungles "age," record in your notebooks all of the changes you see. Leave at least one page for every bag so you have room to keep records and make sketches. Pay attention to things like texture, color, and the way different things grow (in streaks, blobs, fuzzy patches, dark spots, etc.). Measure the size of growths when you can. Following your teacher's directions, look at your gardens with magnifiers or microscopes and draw what you see.

TAKING THE MEASURE OF LIVING THINGS

Some Background Information

The exploration of size ranges and their measurement, while fun, represents more than just a "gee whiz" survey of Earth's life forms. It forms the basis for scientific observation and description. Understanding measurement *will* take some hands-on work with rulers and other measuring tools. Following are some aspects of size and measurement that you may want to discuss with your students.

Size and Scale

In our world of 10^0 meters we're used to all the physical laws of nature working in a certain way. If we put one foot in front of another, pushing against the ground as we go, we know we can walk or run from one place to another. If we dive into the water and use our arms like paddles or oars, we can move through this liquid medium with some degree of efficiency. At smaller sizes the rules aren't quite the same. Viscous forces, like the "thickness" of water, become more important than the inertial, mass-driven forces that act at our scale. Also, the forces at work between molecules that create phenomena like surface tension on a film of water become a large factor. Let's look at the example of the fly and the pelican.

Flies eat fish just as avidly as pelicans. Why can't a fly catch his fish the same way? A pelican's mass and speed allow her to dive through the water quickly enough to snare an unsuspecting fish. The surface tension of the water doesn't hinder her progress significantly. The fly, on the other hand, would find the surface of the water to be a quite formidable wall, and even if he broke through, forward and backward motions of his limbs would result in almost no net motion in the water. Why? His mass is not sufficiently large to allow him to glide any appreciable distance between strokes. A fish can glide up to five body lengths between limb strokes, but a bacterium can "glide" only the width of an atom against the forces exerted by water molecules; a fly can't do much better.

An animal's size thus determines how it moves around its world. Any creature over a millimeter or two in size is going to find muscle power, like our own, to be the most efficient means of locomotion. The water flea, *Daphnia*, uses muscle power to speed through water at 7 mm/sec. Creatures between 20 microns and 2 mm, like protozoa and a few flatworms, use cilia. These short, hairlike extensions act like flexible oars. They generate forward motion with a rigid backstroke but bend on the return stroke to decrease friction. All of these animals move about 1 mm/sec. Bacteria and other small cells use longer, threadlike structures called flagella. Flagella generate a wave or corkscrew motion that allows motion through water, although at a speed of only .1 to .2 mm/sec.

In a similar fashion, other modes of locomotion like flying and jumping are affected by scale. A motivated student might want to explore why the shape of a plane's wing wouldn't work on a dragonfly and vice versa, a size-related topic covered in some detail in the reference *On Size and Life* by Thomas A. McMahon and John Tyler Bonner. Another very readable book on the same topic is *Diatoms to Dinosaurs* by Chris McGowan.

The Joy of Metric

The student article provides a good opportunity to explore the metric system of measurement, one used universally by the science community and much of the rest of the world. With each larger or smaller unit related to its immediate neighbor by a factor of 10, it is easy to convert from one scale of size to another. Adopted by the French National Assembly between 1791 and 1795, its use has grown steadily to the present. Originally, the meter was defined in terms of a fraction of the Earth's circumference and, later, by the distance between two ruled lines on a bar of platinum-iridium alloy in a temperature-controlled vault. Today, it is precisely defined in terms of the wavelength of a particular color of light emitted by the elemental gas krypton under specified conditions.

Of course, all units of measure are arbitrary. The English system may have been based on the length of the foot of Charlemagne. The Greek's basic unit was the finger (equal to about 19.3 mm), with 24 fingers equaling the Olympic cubit. The Romans calculated 5 feet to the pace, and 1,000 paces equaled a Roman mile.

Notes on the Student Activities

That's the Size of It

Chances are students will have a much easier time finding things to fit in the square meter because that is a size frame they are used to dealing with. Some students may surprise you, though, by finding lots of examples for the smaller squares.

That's the Measure of It

Things to look for in a measuring unit or device: Is it portable so you can measure many things? Is it uniform? If students pick a nose as a unit of length, point out that size will vary from person to person. Is it the right size to measure the object you are interested in?

Dinoschool

Have fun with this one. It might make a good outside project for a dinosaur nut, or some students could work on drawing the scale model of the school while others draw their dinosaurs to the proper scale. Several dinosaur dictionaries are on the market that provide typical sizes of dinosaurs.

Microscopic Jungles

In general, bacterial colonies will be small, round, and shiny. Each colony is a mass of cells descended from one bacterium that fell on a good food source. Molds appear fuzzy, threadlike, velvety, or cottony. Fruiting bodies, holding spores, may look like black or colored specks on a cottony mass.

Protozoans, probably in bag #3 or #4, may be visible only as tiny specks in the water. Growth of microscopic plants (algae) will turn the water green or bluish green.

If you have access to a dissecting microscope, have students calibrate the field of view at different magnifications with a metric ruler. For example, put a ruler on the stage at 10X magnification and line up a millimeter mark even with the left edge of the field near the middle. Count the number of marks across the middle of the field, estimating any last fraction of a mark. It might be 23 mm (2.3 cm).

With tweezers or pipettes place samples from the jungles on the stage and have students estimate the sizes of what they see. Repeat the calibration process for 40X magnification. A typical field might be 5.5 mm wide. Have students calibrate this field in microns (1 mm equals 1,000 microns). The size of protozoans is often easier to comprehend at this magnification than with a microscope because you can see them in three dimensions, twisting and turning as they move through the water.

Although the emphasis in these exercises is to become aware of size differences and how to measure them, students should also become excited with the wealth of small creatures all around them. They'll want to know the name of every beast they see. Try to have on hand some common references like *How to Know the Protozoa* by T. L. Jahn and *How to Know the Freshwater Algae* by G. W. Prescott (see the "References" section at the end of this book), but feel free to emphasize that the microscopic world is underexplored and they might well be looking at unrecorded species. As Dorian Sagan and Lynn Margulis say in *Garden of Microbial Delights*, "We understand individual microbes about as well as a Venusian observing city traffic through a telescope would know about us." The size difference between our worlds is a vast gulf to cross, but well worth the trip.

Notes on the References

Cosmic View: The Universe in 40 Jumps is an innovative children's book authored by a Dutch schoolteacher, Kees Boeke, in 1957. He used his own school and country to talk about both very large and very small sizes. Look it up, if you can, and try adapting his technique and updating it with examples from your time and place.

One Million by Hendrik Hertzberg is a "gimmick" book in the sense that it consists of a book of 1 million dots, 5,000 to the page, to give a person a concrete sense of what 1 million means. Call-outs throughout the book give interesting and amusing facts regarding all the big numbers along the way.

On Size and Life by Thomas A. McMahon and John Tyler Bonner and *Powers of Ten* by Philip and Phylis Morrison are adult references you may find helpful. The latter book pays tribute to Boeke's *Cosmic View*. *The Science of Life* by H. G. Wells, Julian S. Huxley, and G. P. Wells includes one of the first treatments of size differences in the living world.

One of the most valuable books in the "Identification Culturing Guides" section of the "References" listing is *Garden of Microbial Delights*. It is well illustrated, a relatively easy read, and modern in its approach. The authors also give plenty of practical references for the amateur naturalist.

Chapter 3

MICROWARS

ANIMAL-TRAPPING FUNGI

Potato plants take carbon dioxide from the air and, with the help of the energy of sunlight, turn it into starchy roots that people dig up and eat. Potatoes are either eaten or rot away (or are thrown out before they smell bad). In our everyday world these two sentences describe the typical roles of plants, animals, and fungi: producers, consumers, and decomposers.

As you saw in chapter 2, however, when you look at the world from the perspective of a different size, our common perceptions don't always apply. Green plants, in general, *do* produce their own food, but occasionally plants like the Venus's-flytrap will catch animals to supplement their diet. In a similar way, on a smaller size scale, fungi, which usually decompose dead animals and plants, can take an active role as predators.

A Whole New World

Imagine yourself in the world of 10^{-3} meters. You are 1 millimeter tall, standing on some healthy topsoil at the edge of a garden. Grass stems are like trees and a sand grain is the size of a basketball. Look down and around you at the mountainous piles of soil particles, the fallen "logs" of dead grass stems and the "water bead" lakes of dewdrops. What do you see? Perhaps some eight-legged mites the size of small dogs skitter past. Algal cells as big as your hand may glisten in the sunlight, or an amoeba nearly as big as you may ooze through a space between sand grains. But almost certainly you will see worms. Not earthworms—they would be as big as freight trains—but roundworms called *nematodes:* transparent worms with tapered ends anywhere from a tenth to several times your length. They'll be moving fast, bending or flipping with the flexing of strong muscles, feeding as they go on spores, fungi, or bits of animal or plant tissue that might be lying around.

You may notice near you a network of coiled, transparent ropes nearly as thick as your arm stretching away into the distance. Three-celled loops sprout from the strands here and there. Don't touch them! Watch what happens when the end of the roundworm gets snagged in a loop. After a second or two, the cells that form the loop expand like balloons, nearly pinching the worm in two. The worm thrashes and twists like a hooked fish, perhaps for as long as an hour or two, but he finally grows still. He has been captured and poisoned by a fungus called *Arthrobotrys dactyloides*. If you watch long enough, you will see a finger-like projection grow from the ring into the animal. Eventually it will extend and coil to fill the entire body. Within a day the worm will be fully digested by the fungus (see fig. 3.1).

25

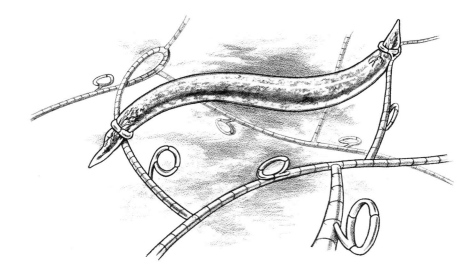

Fig. 3.1. *Arthrobotrys dactyloides*. The soil fungus *Arthrobotrys dactyloides* has snared a nematode in two of its loops. It will kill and digest the worm in a matter of hours.

A. dactyloides is only one of many fungi that depend on live animals to provide at least part of their diet. Animal-eating fungi fall into two large groups: those that eat relatively slow-moving creatures like protozoans and those that specialize in more energetic beasts like nematodes, rotifers, and mites. *Rotifers* are very small, water-living, multicellular animals (see fig. 2.6). Their name comes from a band of hairlike cilia around their mouth that looks like a rotor or wheel when the cilia are moving. They have a thin, transparent, segmented shell that makes them look like a stubby telescope. *Mites* are eight-legged spider relatives, cousins to the larger ticks that sometimes bite dogs and people (see fig. 2.5).

Acaulopage macrospora is a fungus that belongs to the protozoan-eating group. If an amoeba happens to come in contact with a strand (called a *hypha*) of the fungus, it will soon find itself stuck and unable to move. Within an hour or so the amoeba dies, and the fungus grows into the animal and eats it.

The fast animal trappers have developed a variety of techniques for capturing their prey. Most involve the use of various kinds of sticky "traps" produced on side branches of the fungal hyphae. One kind has canoe-shaped spores that look like a cluster of bananas. Another has tentacles with knobby ends that rotifers bite and can't let go of. Some form three-dimensional networks that look like a jungle gym, while others form loops like *A. dactyloides*. One of the strangest varieties resembles a microscopic missile launcher. When an animal brushes against a "trigger cell," a "missile" of fungus tissue is forced out of a flasklike structure and pierces the animal's skin. That missile grows inside the animal, killing it and eventually producing fungal spores that can germinate to form more fungi.

Why do fungi attack these animals? Apparently, because the animals possess certain chemicals that the fungi either can't get or have a hard time getting any other way. In the case of *A. dactyloides*, for example, its ring traps will disappear after it has eaten enough nematodes. It also can live for a long time without nematodes. When they reappear, however, it grows new ring traps and snags these high-protein snacks.

As you can see, the world would have some unexpected dangers if you were only a millimeter tall, but there are many unexplored opportunities as well. Most species of both fungi and nematodes are waiting to be discovered. Perhaps predatory fungi will be found that can be used commercially to protect crops from roundworm damage, or perhaps the fungi's techniques for producing instant adhesive can be used in our larger world.

The mysteries and struggles of this living frontier lie just beneath our feet, waiting to be discovered by a curious traveler, like yourself, who takes the time to explore and study this microworld.

ACTIVITIES

Analyzing Some Experiments with Predatory Fungi

Consider and respond to the following two scenerios.

1. It has been observed for many of the predatory fungi that if their spores germinate into a sporeling and don't trap their normal prey within a limited period of time, the young fungus degenerates and dies. Once such a fungus consumes its prey, it grows and branches extensively.

   What do you think the prey species might have that the fungus needs? Be as specific as possible.

   Why couldn't a given fungus eat any creature that floats by?

2. Nematode-trapping fungi often don't form traps when no worms are present. Within 24 hours of introducing worms to a fungus culture, traps appear.

   What might cause the traps to form?

Follow-up experiments showed that only water that the worms had been raised in needed to be added to the fungus cultures to get them to form traps. What does this tell you about the nature of the "message" passing between worm and fungus?

Observing Fungi

If you still have the microbe jungles you created as part of the activities in chapter 2, have your teacher take a small sample of a fuzzy fungus from rotted fruit or bread and "tease" it apart with a needle on a glass slide. Look at the fungus under magnification.

📖 IN YOUR NOTEBOOK

Draw what you see. Are the fungal threads (hyphae) divided by cross walls (called *septa*), or are they a continuous tube? What reproductive structures are present? Can you see spores?

Watching a Rain of Spores

A mushroom or toadstool is the fruiting body of a soil fungus. Mushrooms beneath trees are often a good indication of the species of fungus that may be forming mycorrhizae with the tree's roots. They also can provide a good demonstration of fungal spores.

Collect a few *fresh* toadstools, perhaps from the school lawn after it has been well watered. Take one and cut off the stem close to where it joins the cap. Discard the stem and pin the cap, gill side (bottom side) up to a piece of corkboard or other soft board. Invert the board so that the mushroom cap can hang gill side down inside a clear glass jar or beaker. Turn off the room lights and shine a tight beam of light through the beaker. Each tiny, glittering speck is a single fungal spore. A field mushroom with a cap 8 cm across may produce 600,000 spores per minute over a period of four days. Fortunately, only a small fraction find a good place to grow.

Making Spore Prints

Gather mushrooms as in the preceding exercise and remove the stems in the same way. Select some paper that your teacher provides and place your mushroom caps, gill side down, on the paper. Cover with a jar or lid to reduce air currents near the caps. On the following day, carefully remove your caps. The image on your paper is a unique pattern created by millions of spores from the cap of the mushroom!

📖 IN YOUR NOTEBOOK

Describe the color and pattern of your prints. Why do you think fungi produce millions of spores instead of just a few? What kind of conditions do you think the spores might need to germinate?

Spray your spore prints with an artist's fixative and tape them in your notebook.

From *Explorations in Backyard Biology.* © 1996. Teacher Ideas Press. (800) 237-6124.

VISITING THE THIRD KINGDOM

Background: What's a Fungus, Anyway?

Fungi once were referred to as members of the third great kingdom of living things because they didn't quite qualify as either plants or animals. Today, they are considered by many experts to be members of one of five kingdoms, with the single-celled Protoctists (protozoans and algae) and Monerans (bacteria and blue-green algae) inhabiting kingdoms of their own.

Fungi might best be described as colorless consumers. This doesn't mean they are drab or uninteresting, however. Lacking chlorophyll or any other pigments to make food of their own, they exist by breaking down organic material—usually the dead remains of all the other kingdoms—and absorbing it into their bodies. The student article focuses on predatory (or, at least, ensnaring) fungi that get their food a little fresher than most of their relatives but still absorb it rather than ingest it like animals. The novelty of this situation may serve to spark interest in a group of creatures that students think they know quite well.

All fungi reproduce by producing spores. As you saw if you created the student microbial jungles described in chapter 2, these spores are often housed in colorful sporangia borne on long stalks. When they fall on suitable material (soil, food, cow manure, or whatever) they germinate to produce pale threads called hyphae. A large mass of hyphae is called a mycelium. Most fungi are recognized by the sexual structures produced by collections of hyphae, such as molds, mushrooms, and morels.

There are at least 100,000 kinds of fungi, and they are very hardy creatures. The cell walls of fungal hyphae are composed of chitin, the same hard material found in insect exoskeletons, and are resistant to drying. Most fungi are found on land and may have helped green plants invade terrestrial environments more than 300 million years ago by helping them get water and rare minerals from the soil.

Although fungi do cause disease in plants and animals, they are most important in living ecologies because of their symbiotic association with plants. Most trees are dependent on fungi called mycorrhizae that surround their roots and aid in water and mineral absorption. Fungi are also the source of many antibiotic chemicals, like penicillin, that fight off bacteria and other pathogens.

Fungi are, in fact, factories for a variety of complex organic compounds including an assortment of alkaloids that may produce everything from strange visions to death in mammals such as ourselves. Lichens, symbiotic liaisons between algae and fungi, produce unique lichen acids, some of which have antibiotic properties, serve as lichen "sunscreens," and help lichens dissolve their rock substrates.

Notes on the Student Activities

Analyzing Experiments with Predatory Fungi

1. Students are apt to list "food" as the thing the fungus most needs. Try to get them to be more specific by listing things in food that are important, like vitamins and minerals. Chances are their normal prey species has a particular mineral or vitamin that is hard to get elsewhere.

2. Students may suggest a number of things, including that it might be necessary for the fungi to touch the worms. Make a list of their suggestions.

Try and get students to see that some chemical that is produced by the worms and that dissolves in water is serving as the stimulus. Point out that both taste and smell in humans are based on water-soluble chemicals that stimulate sense receptors in the nose or on the tongue.

Observing Fungi

Garden of Microbial Delights by Sagan and Margulis, listed in the "References" section for chapter 2 at the back of this book, will provide valuable information for interpreting what students see. Undoubtedly you will learn as much as they will. Biological supply houses like Carolina Biological Supply carry living cultures and slides of *A. dactyloides* discussed in the student article. If time and budget permit, you can send for a culture and provide a demonstration slide to look at under the microscope.

Watching a Rain of Spores

You may want to set this up as a demonstration rather than have individual students do it. A lot will depend on the time and equipment you have available. Figure 3.2 shows you the setup.

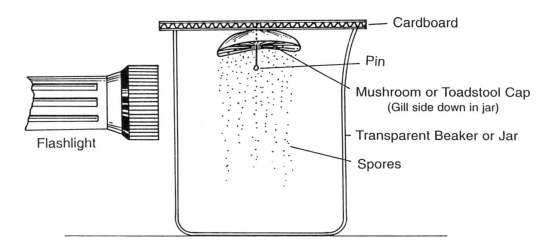

Cardboard

Pin

Mushroom or Toadstool Cap
(Gill side down in jar)

Transparent Beaker or Jar

Spores

Flashlight

Fig. 3.2. "Rain of Spores" apparatus. This simple device will allow you to see some of the vast number of spores produced by a mushroom.

Making Spore Prints

Provide several different colors of paper. Some spores are white; others are brown, black, or other colors. The results can be very visually pleasing!

Have students list what conditions might allow a spore to germinate. Consider things like moisture, temperature, nature of the substrate, nearness to proper food and minerals, etc. Fungi reproduce by the "shotgun technique": Shoot off a big burst and some will reach their target.

Notes on the References

Roderic Cooke's *The Biology of Symbiotic Fungi* is fairly general in its approach but requires some background in biology.

Culturing Bacteria and Fungi, written by Daniel E. James and Jackie E. Kylander and produced by Carolina Biological, is a small paperback useful if you want to grow some living species in the classroom. *A Sourcebook for the Biological Sciences* by Evelyn Morholt, Paul F. Brandwein, and Joseph Alexander is a great general reference for culturing and preparing demonstrations on a wide range of living subjects.

Five Kingdoms: An Illustrated Guide to the Phyla of Life on Earth by Lynn Margulis and Karlene V. Schwartz is a great visual book that surveys the phyla of life on Earth and summarizes the characteristics of each.

My book, *Dinosaurs in the Garden: An Evolutionary Guide to Backyard Biology*, has a whole chapter on mushrooms and predatory fungi, which will give you additional background information on these amazing creatures.

Chapter 4

MONSTERS IN THE MUD PUDDLE

THE POND SCUM THAT CHANGED THE WORLD

What can live at a place in the Atacoma Desert of Chile, where no rainfall has ever been recorded? What creature can spend 107 years as a museum specimen and "be brought back to life" with a drop of water? What can survive immersion for $7\frac{1}{2}$ hours in liquid helium at a temperature of -269° C or grow less than a mile away from ground zero during a nuclear bomb drop? In short, what is perhaps the toughest life-form on the face of the Earth?

If you guessed pond scum, you are absolutely correct. Not only is pond scum tough, but 2 billion years ago it changed our entire planet.

Granted, *pond scum* is not a very precise term. The creatures I speak of are officially called *cyanobacteria.* They used to be called blue-green algae when they were considered close relatives of green, microscopic plants, but the cyanobacteria consist of many species of mostly colonial bacteria with blue-green pigments that give them their distinctive color. These pigments plus sunlight plus a new way of using water are what helped them change the world forever. Here's how.

The Birth of Pond Scum

More than 3 billion years ago primitive bacteria in Earth's oceans were the highest form of life. They were so successful that they grew and multiplied until their food supply was nearly exhausted. Their "food" consisted of complex organic compounds that had accumulated in the oceans over the preceding billion years or so. Solar energy and lightning converted carbon dioxide, methane, ammonia, and other gases in Earth's primitive atmosphere into more complicated carbon compounds. Early bacteria fermented these compounds to get energy, turning them mostly into alcohols and carbon dioxide. But by 3 billion years ago bacterial growth had exceeded the rate of production of these necessary, energy-rich materials.

Somewhere in the vast population of bacteria, a few cells contained colored compounds (pigments) with a peculiar property: They were able to absorb and capture the energy of sunlight and use the energy to make their own carbon compounds. This amazing ability is called *photosynthesis* (literally, to build with light). The requirements for photosynthesis are simple: a source of hydrogen, a source of carbon, sunlight as an energy source, and one or more pigment/catalysts to help bring everything else together.

33

How Pond Scum Survived—and Thrived

The Earth's young atmosphere consisted of 95% carbon dioxide. That, plus significant amounts of hydrogen gas and hydrogen sulfide, provided all the raw materials for the first photosynthesizing bacteria to thrive for another billion years. But the success of these bacteria caused another crisis: The carbon dioxide in the atmosphere decreased, much of the free hydrogen gas bled off into space, and the quantities of hydrogen sulfide from volcanoes, hot springs, and ocean vents were insufficient for a world full of hungry microbes. A new source of hydrogen was needed. Fortunately, most of the bacteria were swimming in a "hydrogen mine" of H_2O—good old water.

The cyanobacteria were the first creatures to use hydrogen from water along with carbon dioxide to make sugars, using sunlight as the energy source and chlorophyll as the catalyst. This created another big problem, however. The by-product was a poisonous gas: oxygen. For tens of millions of years this posed no serious threat. Oxygen first combined with iron in ocean water to form various iron oxides that would eventually create the banded iron formations people mine today for iron ore. But eventually the oceans completely "rusted," and oxygen gas began to accumulate in the atmosphere. The older types of bacteria either became extinct or found spots free of oxygen beneath sediments or in other isolated areas.

During this long "Age of Bacteria," microorganisms created unique structures called *stromatolites.* Stromatolites consist of alternating layers of inorganic sediments, bacteria, and cyanobacteria. Cyanobacteria live at the top of these structures, sulfur and purple bacteria live beneath them, followed by those microbes that can't tolerate any oxygen. Fossil stromatolites are common from sites 2 to 3 billion years old. Today, living stromatolites are only found in places where other creatures can't survive, like the highly salty Shark Bay area of Australia.

Ultimately, organisms solved the "oxygen pollution" crisis by learning to use the oxygen to more efficiently "burn" carbon compounds like sugar to yield more energy. The process of respiration, used by all complex organisms from ants to aardvarks, produces 18 times more energy than fermentation.

Cyanobacteria, the creators of this photosynthesis/oxygen revolution, still thrive today as a crucial part of Earth's living network. Some of their descendants may have merged with other nonphoto-synthesizing bacteria to create the earliest forms of the more complex cells seen in modern plants, animals, fungi, and single-celled organisms. Not only did cyanobacteria change the world, but in a very real sense they *became* the living world we see today.

ACTIVITIES

Pond Scum Safari

Cyanobacteria can be found in many places. Look first near ponds, temporary pools of water that have been around for at least a week, drainage ditches, or other places where water is standing. Take samples in glass jars with sealable tops. In your notebook record the date, time of day, approximate temperature, whether the area is exposed to full sun or is in shade, and any other observations you want to make. How many different colors can you see in the pond scum? Try and match them with a color sketch if you have colored pencils with you.

Cyanobacteria have several pigments, and each absorbs light in a slightly different part of the spectrum. *Chlorophylls* may be green or yellow. *Phycocyanin* pigments are bluish. *Phycoerythrins* are red, and *carotenoids* are yellowish orange. Because a pigment reflects the light it *doesn't* use (absorb), a blue pigment absorbs in the red-yellow end of the spectrum and vice versa. What is the advantage for a plant to have several light-absorbing pigments?

Do you see any clear, roundish balls in the pond scum? Collect some if you do. A species of cyanobacteria called *Nostoc* sometimes forms these floating "butterballs" of filaments with a surrounding layer of mucilage.

Cyanobacteria are also found in places you might be less likely to look, such as the surface of stones submerged in water, just below or on the surface of moist soil, on wet boards or moist bridge timbers, and on the surface of damp cliffs. If you have access to areas like these, take samples and keep them moist until you can get them back to the classroom to look at them. Keep good records in your notebook of the places you try.

Pond Scum Survey

With pond scum samples in hand, and a microscope, dissecting scope, or hand lens available, you are now ready to explore a microscopic world unknown to humans until the seventeenth century when a Dutch lens maker, Antony van Leeuwenhoek, got curious and turned one of his lenses on water with "green clouds floating through it." "I found floating therein," he said, "divers earthy particles, and some green streaks, spirally wound serpent wise, and orderly arranged..."(Dobell 1960, 110). Antony had just entered the worlds of 10^{-3} and 10^{-4} discussed in chapter 2.

First, look for cyanobacteria. Select some of the "green clouds" that look more bluish green than grass green. (If you found some of the "butterballs," pick one of those.) Put a drop of water on a glass slide. With tweezers, pick up a very small amount of green material and place it in the drop of water. If it's in a clump, spread it out a little. Look at it under 10X to 20X magnification with a loop or dissecting microscope. Describe and draw what you see in your notebook.

Cyanobacteria have thin, bluish green filaments divided into narrow compartments like the examples in figure 4.1. Some species have large round or oblong clear cells scattered along the filament. These structures, called *heterocysts,* are where cyanobacteria can change atmospheric nitrogen gas into nitrogen compounds that plants and animals can use. Like other bacteria, cyanobacteria have a simple cell structure with no nucleus or other specialized organelles. They look much like fossils 2 to 3 billion years old found in spots in Africa and Australia.

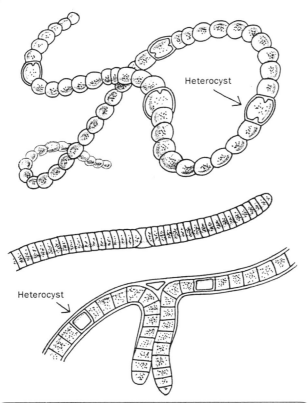

Heterocyst

Heterocyst

Fig. 4.1. Three cyanobacteria. Three common types of cyanobacteria: *Nostoc* (top), *Oscillatoria* (center), and *Scytonema* (bottom). Many cyanobacteria exist in segmented filaments of this type, interrupted in places with thick-walled heterocysts. *Nostoc* forms muscilaginous "butterballs."

Not all cyanobacteria form filaments. Some are single cells or groups of cells in a mucilaginous sheath. The best way to tell cyanobacteria from more advanced green algae is by their distinctive blue-green color and by their smaller size.

You may find several types of filamentous green algae. *Spirogyra* looks like clear tubes with a twisted green strip in each cell resembling a coil or staircase. Other types seem to have green "stars" in each cell or seem to be filled with many green bubbles.

Single cells, somewhat brownish orange in color, often looking like knobby rods or pill boxes, are called *diatoms.* Other similar cells that may be crescent-shaped and narrow at the middle are called *desmids.* These are members of single-celled floating plantlike creatures that provide food for small animals (see fig. 4.2).

Fast-moving, roundish clear animals covered with a hairlike fringe of bristles are called *ciliates.* The hairlike structures are called *cilia* and propel the animal through the water. Slower animals that twist and spiral through the water may be *flagellates.* Flagella are long, whiplike tails that pull the cells along. Some of these creatures have colored pigments and can make their own food like plants.

Amoebae are bloblike creatures that move by flowing in the direction they want to move. Some of their close relatives also look like spiked balls. When a smaller creature bumps into one of them, it gets hooked on the spikes, which are like conveyor belts of moving tissue that carry the animal to the center of the cell, where it is surrounded and eaten.

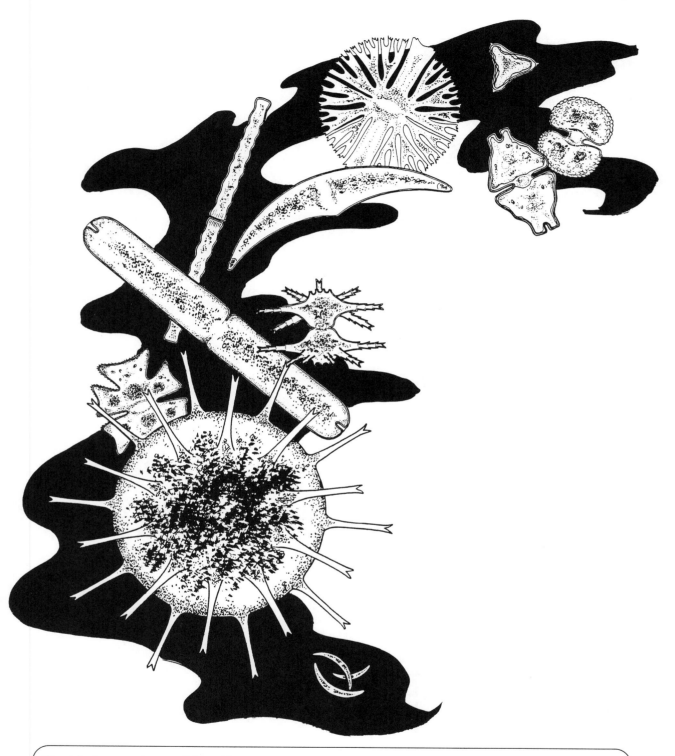

Fig. 4.2. An assortment of desmids. These are a sampling of the single-celled organisms called desmids. Desmids have a two-part structure consisting of two semicells connected by a narrow bridge, called an *ismus.* Reprinted from *Dinosaurs in the Garden,* courtesy Plexus Publishing, Inc., Medford, NJ.

Now and then something quite large may pass by. It might be a thrashing round worm called a *nematode* or a strange creature with a buzz sawlike mouth called a *rotifer* (see fig. 2.6).

Draw some of the creatures you see. Try to estimate their size as you did for the beasts found in your microbial jungle in chapter 2. If your teacher has some identification keys available, try and discover to what group of microorganisms they belong. The world of these small creatures is so large that you may find new and strange kinds almost every time you look. Far from being monsters, however, these are the organisms on which the larger life on our planet depends—not only for food, but to recycle and maintain the very air we breathe.

TURNING MONSTERS INTO MENTORS

Some Background Information

Biologists divide all living things into five kingdoms: Monera, Protoctista, Fungi, Plantae, and Animalia. Bacteria and the cyanobacteria make up the kingdom Monera and display fundamental differences from all the other phyla in physiology and cellular organization. Considering the fact that Monerans were pioneer life-forms on our planet, this is not too surprising. What may be surprising to the average animal kingdom chauvinist is how successful and necessary this vast group of organisms continues to be to the prosperity and survival of the other living kingdoms.

Monerans have prokaryotic cellular organization. The word *prokaryon* literally means "before kernel" or "before nucleus," and reflects the fact that Monerans do not have their genetic information localized in a nucleus. All other living things are eukaryotic in cellular organization. They possess a "eukaryon," or true nucleus. Table 4.1 summarizes the differences between Monerans and other creatures:

Table 4.1. The Differences Between Prokaryotic and Eukaryotic Animals

Prokaryotes (bacteria and cyanobacteria)	Eukaryotes (protoctists, fungi, plants, and animals)
Cell size is small, generally 1 to 10 μm	Cell size is large, generally 10 to 100 μm
Unicellular or colonial forms	Mainly multicellular with tissues, organs
Microscopic	Mostly megascopic
Anaerobic or aerobic metabolism (sometimes can do either)	Aerobic metabolism
Flagella, when present, are flagellin protein	Flagella or cilia made with microtubules
Cell walls are made of particular sugars and peptides	Cell walls are made of cellulose or chitin, but are lacking in animals
No membrane-bounded organelles	Chloroplasts, mitochondria, and other membrane-bounded structures
No nucleus; DNA in cytoplasm	DNA in chromosomes in membrane-bounded nucleus
Reproduce by binary fission; asexual (sometimes parasexual)	Reproduce by mitosis or meiosis (mostly sexual)

The history of life on Earth is largely the story of microorganisms. Figure 4.3 shows some of the major innovations in microorganisms that developed during this time along with the discoveries that support scientific inferences. You may want to reproduce this figure for students and emphasize that if the history of life on Earth were represented by a football field, the length of time humans have been around could be represented by a little more than three-quarters of an inch in the end zone.

The student article provides the opportunity to discuss a little chemistry! Keep the discussion as basic as you like. The overall equations are pretty simple and are shown in figure 4.4. If students come away with the idea that both fermentation and respiration are energy-generating processes in cells and that fermentation is much less efficient, you will have succeeded. With regard to photosynthesis, students should understand that it requires three things: light energy, a catalyst (a chemical mediator that is large enough to serve as a site for reactions), and a source of both carbon and hydrogen. The result is "food" (some sort of carbon compound that can be fermented or further broken down by respiration) and some sort of "waste" product. In early bacterial photosynthesis the waste product might be hydrogen sulfide (rotten egg gas), whereas in green plant photosynthesis the waste product is oxygen, which animals and other creatures find quite useful.

Notes on the Student Activities

Pond Scum Safari

Collecting "pond scum" samples could be treated as either a homework assignment or class activity. All you really need are glass jars and, if people are timid about getting their hands in the water, perhaps a few of the dip nets used to scoop fish out of aquaria. You can seal the jars fairly tightly for transport, but loosen them when you get them back in the classroom to keep the oxygen users alive.

Cyanobacteria will be among the first to appear in temporary water that's been around for a week or two. They will be common in almost any water sample, especially during the warmer months. When lakes have lots of nutrients, sometime as the result of agricultural runoff, cyanobacteria and green algae may "bloom" and discolor a lake. Occasionally blooms produce toxins poisonous to fish and livestock.

Don't neglect cliffs moistened by the spray of a waterfall or damp soil. In areas of the country where there is a pronounced rainy season, cyanobacteria may color patches several square yards in extent. Cyanobacteria also grow within the shells of certain mollusks and may live in, on, or with a variety of other creatures. Some species of *Oscillatoria* even live in the digestive tracts of humans and other animals.

Have students keep careful observations in their naturalist's notebook and encourage them to make sketches of the habitats from which they take samples. Label collecting jars to correspond with numbers or locations recorded in their notebooks.

Pond Scum Survey

The pond scum survey will require either microscopes or dissecting scopes. The format you follow will depend on what kind of access you have to equipment and on your own background in using it. If one or only a few instruments are available you may want to set up demonstrations by making simple wet mounts with slides and cover glasses for the compound microscopes and putting pond water samples in shallow, transparent bowls for dissecting scopes. This way, you can set up proper lighting and make sure there is something to look at. If equipment and class size permit, spend a day getting students oriented to the equipment, then another class session or two making wet mounts and exploring their own catches.

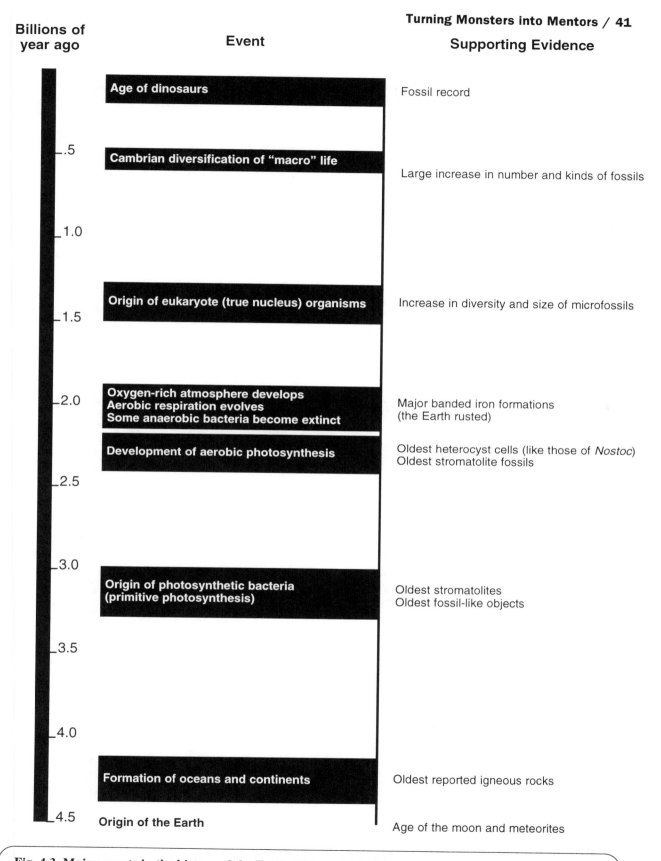

Fig. 4.3. Major events in the history of the Earth. This geological time line shows major events since the origin of the Earth. Human beings have been around such a short time that their stay on the planet doesn't show up at this scale.

Fermentation

$$Sugar \rightarrow Pyruvate \rightarrow Alcohol + CO_2 + 2ATP$$

Respiration

$$Sugar \rightarrow Pyruvate \rightarrow \left(\text{Citric Acid Cycle} \right) \rightarrow CO_2 + H_2O + 36ATP$$

Bacterial Photosynthesis

$$CO_2 + H_2X \xrightarrow{\text{Light}} H_2O + Sugar + X$$

Hydrogen donor   Pigment catalyst

Green Plant Photosynthesis

$$CO_2 + H_2O \xrightarrow{\text{Light}} Sugar + H_2O + O_2$$

Chlorophyll *a*

Fig. 4.4. The basic equations for fermentation, respiration, and photosynthesis. Fermentation gets relatively little energy from sugars. Respiration, using enzymes in the Citric Acid Cycle, does 18 times better. Harnessing the energy of the sun through photosynthesis averted the first food shortage. Using water as the hydrogen donor produced a pollutant—oxygen— that animals now find quite useful.

Plan to have copies of the "How to Know" references and Elsie Klots's *The New Fieldbook of Freshwater Life* on hand to look up some of the creatures you find. In addition to the cyanobacteria, keep your eyes open for members of the following groups:

Chlorophyta: Grass-green algae in a variety of forms, from single cells to colonies to filaments. These algae have chloroplasts and starch-storing bodies call pyrenoids (which stain black with iodine). Individual cells often have two, sometimes more, whiplike flagella.

Diatoms and desmids: Diatoms look like elongated pill boxes, rods, or instrument cases. They may appear yellow-green or yellow-brown in color and glide slowly across the field of view. Under high magnification their shells have incised grooves of intricate design. Desmids often look like two joined cells because many of them are narrow in the center. Some look like "green bananas" or crescents.

Euglenophytes: Microorganisms that are often teardrop shaped, fairly slow moving, and have one long flagellum to pull them around. They have green chloroplasts and often a red, light-sensitive eyespot.

Dinoflagellates: Microorganisms that look like armored balls or branches. They tend to be yellowish in color and may corkscrew through the water as they flip a pair of flagella.

Ciliates: These microanimals are single-celled and covered with hairlike cilia. They move quickly and come in a variety of shapes and sizes. The slipper-shaped *Paramecium* is often shown in textbooks.

Rhizopoda: Include the bloblike *Amoeba* as well as more exotic forms like *Arcella* (a kind of shelled *Amoeba*) and radiolarians—creatures with long spines that look like land mines.

Rotifers: Multicellular animals with forked tails and wheel-like mouths. Their bodies are transparent, so you can see their digestive organs as they move about.

Hydra: Multicellular animals with a tube-shaped body that can contract to a ball or stretch quite thin. Their heads are crowned with long tentacles to catch small ciliates and rotifers. Sometimes they appear green with algal symbionts.

Gastrotrichs: Microorganisms that are long and slender with a knoblike head and forked tail. They have spinelike projections on their body and may appear clear or colored depending on what they've eaten recently. They are multicellular beasts like rotifers.

Have students try to find and draw a cyanophyte first. Remember, they are blue-green in color, usually smaller than green filamentous algae, and have no nuclei or chloroplasts. *Nostoc* looks like a string of beads with large, clear heterocyst cells at random intervals. *Oscillatoria* has thin, unbranched filaments that weave back and forth in the water. If you add a little diluted India ink to a slide preparation, you can often see the mucilaginous sheath around the cells.

After they have found examples of "the pond scum that changed the world" have them draw several other creatures for their notebooks.

Notes on the References

Garden of Microbial Delights by Sagan and Margulis is a good reference featuring many illustrations along with text written by an expert in the field. *Micro-cosmos* by the same authors is a good read for a popular audience but without the visual support of the first book. It looks at the history of life from the perspective of microorganisms.

My book *Dinosaurs in the Garden* has three chapters that may be useful: "Surveying the Kingdoms," "Microscopic Gardens," and "Exploring Inner Space." Clifford Dobell's *Antony van Leeuwenhoek and His "Little Animals"* is a good one if you are interested in the history of early discoveries.

Both the books by James L. Gould and Carol Grant Gould and William J. Schopf are excellent but written in the style of articles in *Scientific American.* Helen Tappan's *The Paleobiology of Plant Protists* is quite large and technical, if you really get into the subject. Most of the rest of the references are for identifying creatures you and your students discover. The variety in even a small sample of pond water is staggering. Enjoy!

Chapter 5

BEFORE INSECTS COULD FLY

GREAT JUMPING SNOW FLEAS!

Did you ever walk across a field of snow on a sunny winter day, perhaps near a stand of trees, and see a shifting pattern of salt-and-pepper specks move out of your way? Sure, it may have been your imagination or just the play of light through the bare branches overhead. On the other hand, it may have been a half million snow fleas out for a stroll.

Snow fleas are not really fleas and they don't bite, but they are small: None is longer than a sharpened pencil lead and most are considerably smaller. They're active all year long but are rarely seen except when their numbers get large and they blunder up through holes in the snow from their soil and leaf litter homes.

A snow flea is a kind of springtail, a group of creatures that move by hopping from place to place. A tail-like structure called a *furcula* is held in place by a hook on the underside of these animals, much like a closed safety pin. When the animal wants to move quickly, the furcula springs loose, tossing the springtail as much as 4 to 6 inches away. This doesn't seem far until you realize it would be like a human being hopping the length of one-and-three-quarter football fields!

Scientists know of at least 2,000 different kinds of springtails, most of which live in the soil or near water. Springtails have six legs, two antennae, and segmented bodies, which make them sound like a lot of insects you've seen. They probably are very close relatives of insects, but because they have enough differences, scientists put them in their own class: the Collembola.

An Englishman who first studied these creatures noticed that they had a short, peg-like tube on their underside. This organ is much like a straw. Springtails use it to suck up water from the soil and ooze droplets of water from it when they want to clean up their bodies—which is quite often. They use their forelegs like a cat uses its paws to rub a drop of moisture over antennae and other body parts. A clean body lets a springtail breathe easier because it absorbs much of its oxygen directly through its skin.

Although people don't see them often, springtails are everywhere. One study of pasture soil revealed nearly 250 million of them per acre. A springtail may call home any place that is cool and humid. They like leaf mold, fungus gardens, moss, decaying logs, tree bark, and ant and termite nests. They live on mountaintops and in the arctic. Planes taking air samples have even scooped them up 2 miles in the sky!

A Day in the Life of a Springtail

What do springtails do all day? They like snacking on things like plant pollen, bacteria, fungi, and algae. Some kinds especially like mushrooms and the floating pond weed called duckweed. A few species are considered pests because they like human crops like tobacco and sugarcane. One kind of springtail that lives with termites hangs out on the heads of soldier termites. These soldiers are fed by worker termites, who tend to be a bit sloppy. The springtails gobble up the leftovers.

Snow fleas and their relatives live in a dangerous world. Spiders, ants, and other small arthropods find some kinds tasty.

One kind of ant specializes in eating springtails (fig. 5.1). These ants have jaws like bear traps that are spread wide when they are searching for a meal. Sensory hairs between the jaws tell them when a springtail is within reach. The jaws snap shut so quickly that their prey often can't hop fast enough to get away.

Overall, though, snow fleas and other springtails have proved to be survivors. Their remains have been discovered in 400 million-year-old fossils that date back to the time when tiny plants and animals first invaded dry land. Their small size and adaptable behavior allowed them to survive harsh environments. They were land pioneers before people left footprints in the snow, before salamanders burrowed in soft swamp mud, even before insects knew how to fly. Next time you see a patch of dirty snow, see if it moves when you get close. It could be some adventurous snow fleas exploring new territory.

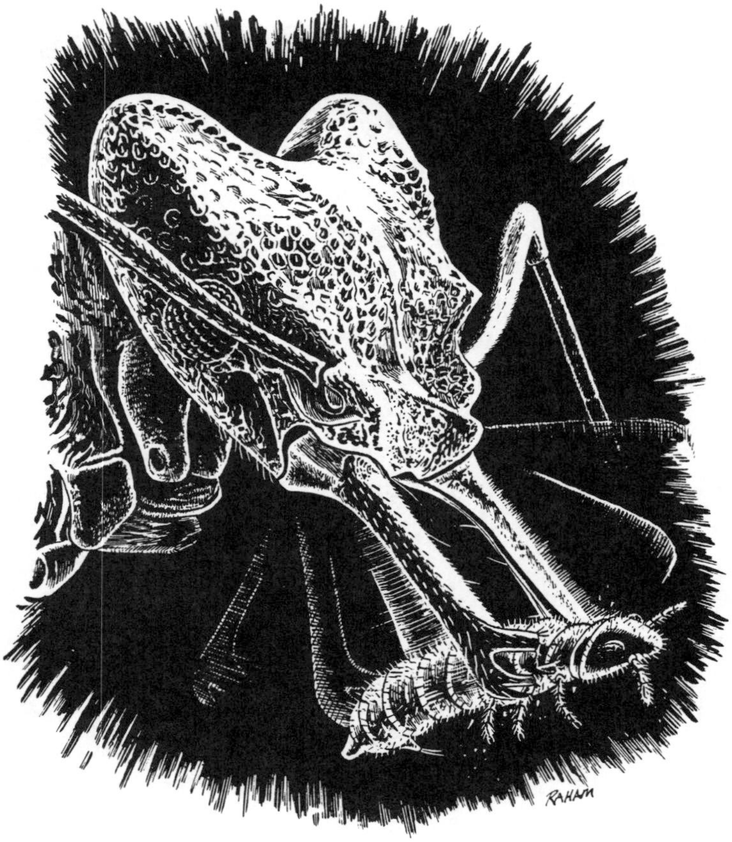

Fig. 5.1. Trap-jawed ant eating a springtail. Some species of ants, like this Australian *Orectognathus versicolor*, have spring-loaded jaws that snap shut in as little as one milli-second when their prey trip sensory hairs between the jaws.

ACTIVITIES

Hunting for Springtails

Break up into several groups at the direction of your teacher. Each group will collect a soil sample from a different location.

📖 IN YOUR NOTEBOOK

Record the following information:

Where was the soil collected and at what time of day?

Was it in a sunny or shady location?

Was it wet, damp, or dry?

Was it gummy like clay, dark and crumbly like garden soil, or mostly sandy in texture?

Can you see anything living in the soil? Look for insects, worms, plants or plant parts, fungi (mushrooms, molds), spiders, pill bugs and sow bugs, millipedes and centipedes, insect larvae and pupae, etc.

When you have recorded everything you can see, place a portion of the soil sample in the Berlese funnel, according to your teacher's directions.

Examining the Catch

Here comes the exciting part: discovering what creatures have been living in the soil samples you've collected. Many, like the snow fleas you've recently learned about, will be smaller than a pencil lead.

The most important clue in figuring out what you've found is to count legs. The second best clue is number of body segments. If you count eight legs, you probably have a spider or a mite. If the body has two parts, your eight-legged beast is a spider. If the body is all in one part, you have a mite.

If you count six legs on a creature, it is a hexapod, a word that literally means "six-legged one." If the animal has three distinct body segments—head, thorax, and abdomen—it is most likely an insect. Most, but not all, insects also have wings. If your hexapod has a number of very similar-looking segments, it is either a springtail, proturan, or a dipluran.

If your beast has no antennae, is white, less than 2 mm long, and has a pointed rear end it is a proturan. Not much is known about their biology even though they're common in soil, but they feed mostly on fungi.

A creature with two antennae and a two-forked tail is a dipluran. These blind animals have biting mouth parts and like dark places.

Animals with a long tail extending from abdominal segment four and a peglike tube on abdominal segment one are springtails. Compare what you have found with pictures your teacher provides to see if you've discovered a snow flea.

Some springtails are brightly colored. As with larger creatures, this coloration may warn predators that they taste bad. What else might make bright colors valuable to these animals?

📖 IN YOUR NOTEBOOK

Survey your collection. Sketch as many of the animals as you can. List the major groups of animals (spiders, mites, insects, proturans, diplurans, and springtails) in descending order, with the most numerous groups first. Do you think the group at the top of the list would have more plant/fungi eaters or predators? Why? Can you tell something about what they eat from their mouth parts?

Compare the number and kinds of creatures found in different soil samples. What kinds of soil have the most variety of plant and animal life?

CREATURES IN THE SOIL AND OTHER DARK PLACES

Some Background Information

Most of the six-legged creatures you see and call "bugs" belong to the class Insecta. They have an external skeleton like other arthropods and a three-part body plan consisting of head, thorax, and abdomen. To grow larger, insects must cast off their old skins now and then and make new, roomier ones. Each successive juvenile phase is called an instar. Sometimes the instars look like small adults, but some insects, like butterflies and moths, go through a metamorphosis that involves a major reorganization from a wormlike larvae to a winged adult. Most, but not all, insects either have wings at some stage in their life cycle or their ancestors did.

The springtails discussed in the student article are one of three classes of six-legged, wingless beasts not considered to be true insects. As mentioned in that text, they are in the class Collembola. Their strawlike collophore and springlike tail set them apart from two other groups that are also small in size and live in similar dark, moist habitats.

Minute white animals called proturans are common in soil. Because they are usually less than 2 mm long, few people see them and scientists don't know a great deal about them. They have no antennae, but their forelegs are used to sample the environment while their last two pair of legs are used for getting around.

Diplurans, also called two-pronged bristle tails because of their forked rear ends, are common in soils and can reach sizes of $\frac{1}{4}$ inch (7 mm or so). These creatures are blind and have antennae and five-segmented legs. Collembolans, proturans, and diplurans all have mouth parts enclosed in their heads whereas insects have mouth parts that are easily seen protruding from the head area (see fig. 5.2).

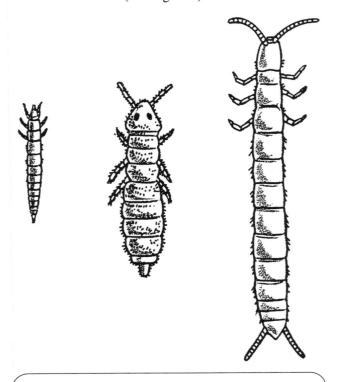

Fig. 5.2. Proturan, collembolan, and dipluran. A proturan (left), collembolan, or springtail (center), and a dipluran (right) drawn to the same scale.

Although students don't need to know all this neat information, they will undoubtedly ask a thousand "what-is-this?" questions during the following activity, and the above information can help you sound more erudite. A good insect key with lots of pictures will also make a handy reference. The Golden Guide paperback *Insects: A Guide to Familiar American Insects* by Herbert S. Zim and Clarence Cottam is inexpensive and easy to use, but doesn't have much information about the three groups discussed above. *How to Know the Insects* by Roger G. Bland and H. E. Jaques is more complete. For eight-legged arthropods like spiders and soil mites, *A Guide to Spiders and Their Kin* by Herbert W. Levi and Lorna R. Levi, another Golden Guide book, is very good.

Don't worry a great deal about getting the right name for every creature, however. If the kids come away with a notion of how many kinds of strange and fabulous creatures live in a fistful of soil and that they all contribute to a thriving, interactive community, you will have accomplished the goals for this exploration.

Notes on the Student Activities

Hunting for Springtails and Examining the Catch

This activity will take at least two sessions on two consecutive days. One day will be for collecting and observing the soil samples, the second for looking at the small creatures forced out of the soil placed in the Berlese funnels. More time could easily be devoted to the project if you set aside soil portions in water and check for the growth of algae and other plants over the course of several days. Soil samples are best stored in zipper-type plastic bags. If you don't have the equipment to set up several funnels, collect one sample large enough for everyone to look at and place a portion of it in one funnel setup.

The Berlese funnel is easy to make. Get a large plastic funnel and cut a piece of screen mesh to fit inside near the bottom of the funnel. Place your soil/leaf litter sample on top of the screen. The narrow end of the funnel should project down into a container of liquid: either plain water or alcohol. (The former will probably be easier to work with.) The funnel can either be suspended from a ringstand, if one is available, or affixed in a large, narrow-necked container. A 100-watt lightbulb should be suspended over the top of the funnel. The heat from this bulb will drive the small creatures down into the liquid. You may need to experiment a little to see how close the bulb needs to be to the top of the soil sample. Figure 5.3 shows the basic setup.

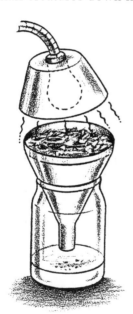

Young instars of mites may have just three pairs of legs, but unlike insects and other hexapods (six-leggers) they still have just a roundish, single-part body plan.

Large mites are called ticks. Some parasitize mammals, including humans. Although the ones you have trapped in water or alcohol from the funnel should be dead, keep an eye out for them when first examining the soil samples. Check with local experts before collecting soil samples if there are "tick seasons" in your area.

As an aid to identifying soil creatures take a look at the quick key based on counting legs in chapter 15. It may be useful here as well.

Bright coloration in springtails could signal sexual maturity or be used in mating behavior.

Vegetarians, at the base of the food chain, are more abundant. Plant eaters tend to have sucking, tubelike mouth parts, while predators have jaws or pinchers of some sort.

Rich, loamy soil, with lots of decaying plant material, will tend to have the greatest variety of living things in it. A microscopic survey would also show lots of bacterial growth and activity.

Fig. 5.3. Berlese funnel. A Berlese funnel can be made with a lightbulb in a gooseneck lamp, a funnel, and a wide-mouth jar containing either water or alcohol. The heat from the lamp forces the soil animals down the funnel into the liquid trap.

Materials needed:

self-sealing plastic bags
small bottles
rubbing alcohol (70% isopropyl)
funnel
ringstand (optional)
paper/pencils

tweezers
hand lenses
shallow trays
collecting bottle
100-watt lightbulb
insect/spider keys

Part II

The Hunters and the Hunted

Chapter 6

THE EYES HAVE IT

WOULD YOU LOOK AT THAT?

"Would you look at that?" "I'll believe it when I see it." "I see that, now." "Watch out!" Language is full of references to our sense of sight, and it's no wonder: As primates, we are very visually oriented creatures, possessing an accurate, 3-D, full-color, light-processing system. How well do human eyes compare with those of other animals in terms of image quality and the range of things we can see? What is the role of the brain in processing visual information? If there were awards for "Best Vision," who would be the nominees?

Light receptors, or "eyes," fall into two categories: those that form images and those that don't. Many primitive creatures have the latter kind—organs that can tell when light is present and roughly what direction it's coming from, but little else. The single-celled *Euglena* has a light-sensitive red eyespot. Earthworms and some other burrowing creatures have light-sensitive cells spread over their body, but no well-defined eyes as such. Arthropods, some mollusks (squid, octopi, some clams), and vertebrates like ourselves possess true, image-forming eyes. These more complex light-gathering organs fall into two basic types: simple and compound eyes.

Simple and Compound Eyes

Simple eyes resemble cameras. Most have lenses that focus light onto a layer of light-sensitive cells collectively called the *retina*. This form of eye developed independently in mollusks, arthropods, and vertebrates. Arthropods (with one or two oddball exceptions) invented the compound eye—an eye composed of many individual, light-gathering units called *ommatidia*. Spiders, people, and eagles provide good examples of simple eyes, while trilobites, bees, and praying mantises display some of the compound models.

Jumping spiders are wandering hunters that, unlike most of their relatives, possess great eyesight. They have eight simple eyes called *ocelli*. One large pair of eyes dominates the front of their head and forms clear images of their prey. The other six eyes serve as motion detectors, letting the spider know when a possible snack is moving nearby (see fig. 6.1). Scientists are pretty certain these spiders see in color, based on the different receptors in their retinas and various behavioral studies. They can also detect ultraviolet and polarized light (see chapter 10's student article, "Spider Talk," and chapter 13's, "Good Bee-Havior"), something our eyes cannot see.

53

From *Explorations in Backyard Biology.* © 1996. Teacher Ideas Press. (800) 237-6124.

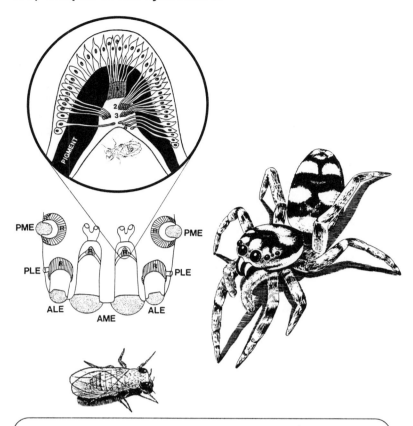

Fig. 6.1. *Salticus scenicus* eye structure. Jumping spiders like this striped *Salticus scenicus,* have eight ocelli: a pair of main eyes (labeled AME) and six lateral eyes (labeled ALE, PLE, and PME). The diagram of a section through the head-trunk region shows the relative size and structure of these eyes. *R* stands for retina, the light-sensitive cells within the eyes. The main eyes form sharp, clear images while the lateral eyes are more motion detectors. A close-up of the retina of a main eye shows how receptor cells are arranged in four layers. Layers 1-3 are sensitive to different colors of light, while layer 4 is believed to respond to polarized light. Illustration appeared in *Backyard Bugwatching,* no. 13, 1991. Reprinted by permission.

Images project onto the retina (containing the rods and cones) and are most sharply in focus at a spot called the *fovea.* Muscles that change the shape of the lens allow their owners to focus on both close and distant objects.

Compound eyes, first seen in 500 million-year-old fossil arthropods called trilobites, provide a different view of the world (see fig. 6.3). They are called compound because each eye is made up of a series of cylinders, packed closely together, each with its own lens. Each element of a compound eye is called an *ommatidium.* A light receptor called a *rhabdome* sits at the end of the ommatidium opposite the lens. Compound eyes can have a few hundred ommatidia or thousands. The more ommatidia, the better the image produced by the eye. The image produced by even the best compound eyes, like those of praying mantises and dragonflies, is probably "grainier" than the continuous image seen in a camera-style eye, but compound eyes are excellent at detecting motion. When we go to a movie where images are flashed on the screen at 24 frames per second, we see continuous motion of our favorite movie stars. A bee in a human movie theater would see a series of still frames, because it can detect up to 265 flashes per second!

Eagles and other birds of prey and human beings are vertebrate animals with excellent, camera-style eyes (see fig. 6.2). The light-receptive cells in vertebrate eyes are called *rods* and *cones* because of their shapes. Rods are good low-light detectors and provide night vision. Cones detect different wavelengths (colors) of light. In both eyes light enters through a lens. The amount of light allowed through the lens is controlled by a colored ring of muscle called the *iris.*

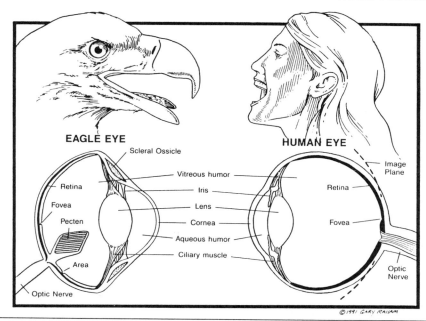

Fig. 6.2. Eagle and human eyes compared. Eagles and their raptor cousins see with the most precision of any vertebrate on Earth. Light entering an eagle's eye is focused all along the curvature of the retina, which is packed with three times as many cone cells as the human eye. In the human eye the image plane is behind the retina except near the fovea. The pecten, a structure unique to birds and most elaborate in daytime hunters, may play a role in motion detection. Illustration appeared in *On the Wing*, vol. 6, Spring/Summer 1991, Rocky Mountain Raptor Program. Reprinted by permission.

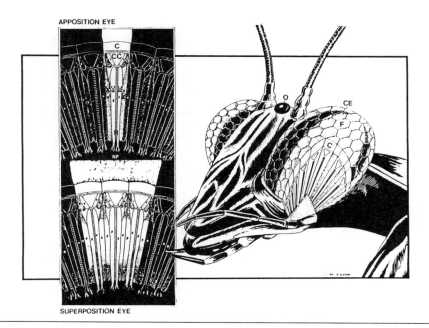

Fig. 6.3. Compound eye structure. A praying mantis head illustrates the general structure of a compound eye (CE). The number of eye facets has been reduced for clarity. There is also another pair of ocelli (o) farther back on the head. A praying mantis has a compound eye adapted for daylight vision (called an apposition eye). Daylight eyes are shielded by pigments to give clear images but need more light to stimulate them. Night-adapted eyes (called superposition eyes) gather light from several ommatidia so that its owner can detect light, but the image quality suffers. Illustration appeared in *Backyard Bugwatching*, no. 13, 1991. Reprinted by permission.

The primary function of eyes is to collect light. The key to what an animal sees is how the brain processes the information it gets from its eyes. In our eyes, for example, the image projected through the lens is turned upside down when it hits the retina. Our brain allows us to see the world "right side up." Special glasses have been given to people to make everything they see upside down. If they wear the glasses long enough, however, the brain compensates and things look normal (until they take the glasses off again!). Arthropod brains also have to process the multiple images coming from individual ommatidia to give their owners an integrated image of what they see.

And the Winner Is . . .

Here are a few "The Eyes Have It Awards" in the animal kingdom:

Ability to See Most Colors: Pigeons and many other birds that have five different light-receptive pigments (instead of our three) and five oil drop filters. Second place goes to the shanny fish and marine stickleback fish.

Greatest Focusing Range (called accommodation): Diving birds like cormorants and mergansers, which have a 10 times greater range than humans.

Ability to See Most Kinds of Light: Goldfish. They can see from the far red end of the spectrum (like TV remote control beams) to the ultraviolet (tanning radiation).

Ability to See Faintest Light: Gigantocypris, a deep-sea crustacean. Second place: Australian net-catching spider.

Sharpest Day Vision: The eagle and some other birds of prey can spot rabbits from 2,000 meters in the sky. They have lots of cones, multiple foveae, and special pits that give them telephoto views near the center of their visual field.

Clearest Night Vision: Toads (8 times better than humans)

Best All-Around: Human?

Perhaps we can legitimately give ourselves this last award. Our day vision is excellent, though it falls short of the eagle. Our night vision is quite good, although some nocturnal specialists can outperform us. And we do have an excellent light processor, which devotes a lot of room to light interpretation: the brain.

ACTIVITY

Images Without Lenses: Making a Cardboard Eye

Eyes (and cameras) typically have four things in common: 1) a light-shielded enclosure (eyes are shielded by pigments from the back side); 2) a lens to focus incoming light; 3) light-sensitive receptors (rods, cones, or similar sensory cells for eyes; film for cameras); and 4) something to regulate the amount of light coming in (irises for eyes, iris diaphragms for cameras). The simplest eyes and the first cameras can and did make do without lenses.

For at least 1,000 years people have known that if you eliminate all light in a room except for that coming from a pinhole in one wall you will get an image of what's outside the room projected on the opposite wall. Such a pinhole device is called a *camera obscura*. The size of the pinhole determines how sharp the image will be. For most practical purposes, the smaller the hole, the sharper the image, although if the hole is *very* tiny the image is replaced by a series of rings. Let's create a simple camera obscura—a kind of cardboard eye.

Materials needed: a sturdy cardboard box, roughly two heads high by three or four heads long; white paper; black electrician's tape; clear tape; a utility knife; scissors; aluminum foil; a sewing needle or pin; a sweater or shirt

Directions:

1. Select a sturdy, cardboard box without holes or seams that let in light when it's closed.

2. Cut a piece of white paper that will fit one end of the box and tape in place (see fig. 6.4). This will be the screen for the image created by the pinhole opposite it. In an eye, this would be the retina.

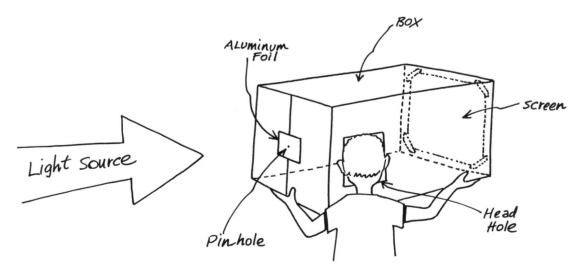

Fig. 6.4. A simple pinhole camera. This simple camera obscura shows how an image can be formed without a lens when light passes through a pinhole. Your eyes need to be adapted to the dark in order to see the image easily.

3. In the center of the opposite end of the box from the screen cut a small hole with the utility knife about an inch square or so. Cut a piece of aluminum foil big enough to cover this opening and tape it all around the edge.

4. With a sewing needle or pin poke a small hole in the center of the foil. Poke with a twisting motion to avoid getting a ragged hole.

5. Cut a hole in the side of the box close to the end with the pinhole. The hole should be big enough that your head fits fairly snugly in it.

6. With your head in the box and the pinhole facing the sun, you should see an image on the white paper. It may take awhile for your eyes to adapt to the dark. You may also have to cover your head with a shirt or sweater to block out light leaking in around your head.

7. If your box has lots of light leaks, tape them over with the black electrician's tape.

You now have a simple eye like the one shown in figure 6.4. Once your eyes have adapted to the dark and you can see the image on the screen, have people walk into your field of view. Can you recognize who they are? Try holes of different sizes to see how size affects the image. Experiment with the length of the box to see when you get the sharpest image.

You also now have a solar observatory. During a solar eclipse, when the moon passes directly between the Earth and the sun, you can point the pinhole at the sun and see the eclipse safely on the screen. *Never look directly at the sun during an eclipse!*

A primitive sea creature called the *Nautilus* actually has a lensless, pinhole-style eye, and it's apparently served him quite well for 400 million years or so. Lenses bend incoming light and focus it at a point but aren't necessary to form an image.

📖 IN YOUR NOTEBOOK

Light is a type of energy and is part of the electromagnetic spectrum (em spectrum, for short). The visible spectrum (the colors in a rainbow) is a small part of the em spectrum. The energies in the em spectrum show many of the characteristics of waves. They have crests and troughs like ocean waves. The distance between crests is called the wavelength. Although the spectrum of energies is continuous from very long wavelengths to very short ones, we give names to the different kinds. In this notebook activity you will make one drawing that shows all the electromagnetic energies to scale and another that shows the parts of the visible spectrum we call color. In other words, you will be measuring the spectrum, visible and invisible.

Continued on next page.

IN YOUR NOTEBOOK (continued)

Look at the rainbow of colors produced by a prism. Each color that you see has a slightly different wavelength. The glass that makes up the prism bends light as it passes through. Because short wavelengths (the blue end of the spectrum) are bent more than long ones, prisms are able to separate the individual colors of the visible spectrum.

Wavelengths of light are measured in nanometers (billionths of a meter). The drawing in chapter 2 for the world of 10^{-6} shows the wavelength of a light beam in comparison to the size of a bacterium. Visible light has wavelengths from roughly 400 to 700 nanometers. Let's draw the visible spectrum to scale.

Materials needed: English and metric rulers; notebooks; colored pencils; prism; pencil or pen

1. In your notebook draw a narrow rectangle 10 x 1 inches wide. Off to the side somewhere, draw a line 1 inch long. This inch will represent 30 nm (nanometers) on our 10-inch-long spectrum. Write 1" = 30 nm near the 1-inch line.

2. At the bottom of your 1-x-10-inch box, write 400 nm. Measure 1 inch from the bottom toward the top and make a mark. This mark should be labeled 430 nm. Continue measuring off 1-inch portions and label them by adding 30 nm each time. The top of the rectangle should be 700 nm.

3. Draw a horizontal line across your rectangle at 670 nm. Color everything above it red.

4. Draw a similar line at 580 nm. The space between it and 670 nm should be orange.

5. Make a mark at 565 nm (halfway between 550 nm and 580 nm). The space between there and 670 nm should be yellow.

Continued on next page.

IN YOUR NOTEBOOK (continued)

6. In a similar fashion, color the space between 490 nm and 565 nm green; the space between 475 nm and 490 nm blue; the space between 420 nm (you'll have to estimate it) and 475 nm indigo (blue-violet); and the space to the bottom violet. You now have a scale model representation of the color spectrum. Notice that the first letters of each color spell out the name ROY G BIV, a good way to remember the order.

7. Now, on a different page, using a metric ruler, draw a rectangle 2.5 cm x 25.4 cm (this should be the same size as your visible spectrum rectangle). This new rectangle will represent the entire em spectrum, which goes from long radio waves at the bottom to gamma rays at the top.

8. Measure 6.9 cm (69 mm) up from the bottom and draw a horizontal line. The distance from there to the bottom represents the portion of the em spectrum called long radio waves. These waves have wavelengths ranging from about the diameter of the Earth to the height of Mount Everest.

9. From the 6.9-cm mark, measure up 1.1 cm. This narrow band represents radio broadcast frequencies whose wavelengths are about as long as a football field.

10. From the 1.1-cm mark, measure up 4.8 cm. This band represents shortwave radio with wave crests around a meter apart.

11. From the 4.8-cm mark, measure up 2.2 cm. This band represents infrared wavelengths from about .1 mm to 1 μm (micrometer). Infrared energy is heat energy. Rattlesnakes have special pit organs that allow them to "see" the heat energy of their prey at night.

12. From the 2.2-cm mark, measure up .6 cm (6 mm). This is the rainbow of energies we can see—the visible spectrum.

Continued on next page.

IN YOUR NOTEBOOK (continued)

13.   The next band is 1 cm wide. It represents ultraviolet light. Insects, birds, and a few other animals can see part of this portion of the spectrum. These are also the energies that tan your skin.

14.   The next band, 2.8 cm wide, represents X-rays. Wavelengths here run from about the width of a coil of DNA to the diameter of some atoms. X-rays can damage DNA and cause mutations.

15.   The next 3-cm band represents cosmic rays and the last 3-cm band represents the range for gamma rays. At this end of the em spectrum wavelengths are equal to or less than the size of atomic nuclei. These energies are very destructive to living tissue.

From *Explorations in Backyard Biology.* © 1996. Teacher Ideas Press. (800) 237-6124.

SURVEYING ANIMAL EYES

Notes on the Student Article

In conjunction with students reading this article, you may want to have them collect pictures of all the different animal eyes and light receptors they can find. After they read the article they can sort the pictures into nonimage-forming eyes, simple eyes, and compound eyes. They may find it difficult to find pictures of nonimage-forming eyes. Look for pictures of starfish, flatworms, or single-celled organisms to serve as examples. All vertebrate eyes are simple camera-style eyes, regardless of color or shape, as are the eyes of octopi and squid. All insect eyes with a honeycomb pattern on their surface are compound. Ones that appear shiny black are simple. As in the praying mantis example, many insects have both types. Crustaceans like crayfish and shrimp have compound eyes as well.

Jumping spiders are fascinating. Students can explore jumping spider vision and how it relates to behavior more fully in the article "Spider Talk," in chapter 10. The inset to the spider eye picture (fig. 6.1) shows the four kinds of receptors in the spider eye retina. One layer is sensitive to light in the 360-nm range (ultraviolet), another layer is sensitive to blue-green light from 480 to 500 nm, a third to yellow-orange light of 580-nm wavelength, and the last layer is believed to respond to polarized light (see chapter 13, "Good Bee-Havior").

The eagle eye, shown in comparison to the human eye in figure 6.2, has several interesting features. The pecten, a structure loaded with blood vessels for nourishing the eagle's eye, also may cast a shadow on the retina, which is thought to aid motion detection. Although the shape of the eagle's eye permits more of its field of view to be in focus at one time than that of the human eye, their field of vision doesn't overlap as much, giving them poorer depth perception. They compensate by cocking their head to get two views in quick succession—a kind of distance estimation by parallax (closer objects seem to move more than distant objects with each glance). We, on the other hand, have to take several glances to be sure of detail, but have instant depth perception.

The inset in the illustration of the compound eye (see fig. 6.3) demonstrates the arthropod's solution to night vision: Reduce the light-insulating pigment between adjacent ommatidia so that the light reaching them can be "summed" to trigger a receptor. The trade-off is that image clarity suffers. Dragonflies and other daytime species want each ommatidium well shielded to maximize image resolution.

One additional note on eyes: You can nearly always tell predators from prey by the field of view they enjoy. Prey species tend to have eyes positioned at the sides of their head to maximize their visual fields. Distance perception is more critical for predators, so their eyes face forward with an overlapped field of view. Tigers don't usually have to be worried about something sneaking up behind them.

Several of the references for this article are a bit on the technical side. One exception is *Supersense: Perception in the Animal World,* by John Downer, who surveys the animal kingdom with respect to different sensory modalities. My articles "Through Raptor's Eyes" and "Through Arthropod Eyes" were written with a general audience in mind but may be harder to find. Write to me in care of the publisher if you'd like copies.

Notes on the Student Activities

Images Without Lenses: Making a Cardboard Eye

This activity is best done on a bright, sunlit day. Getting eyes adapted to the dark, so that students can see the image, is most important. If possible, have them put their head in the box before going out into the bright light. Make sure the sweater or shirt wrapped around their head doesn't flop over the pinhole. If someone gets dizzy with their head in the box, have him or her get a breath of fresh air!

If using the camera obscura for watching an eclipse, make sure no one looks directly at the sun. Partial eclipses result in the sun appearing as a crescent when projected onto paper. Once, while observing an eclipse near several aspen trees with insect damage to their leaves, crescent shapes were cast all over the pavement, an unusual and rather eery sight. A simple solar viewer can be made just by poking a pinhole in a piece of cardboard and letting the image project onto a piece of white paper. As hole sizes increase, the image of the sun gets fuzzier. Bring along a magnifying glass and you can demonstrate how a curved lens concentrates sunlight at a focal point. Students can put their fingers in the beam projected through the hole and find it to be no hotter than normal sunlight. But at the focal point directed by the magnifying glass, you can char a hole in a piece of paper. Eyes with lenses, like our own, concentrate light in such a way at the fovea on the retina.

In Your Notebook (Drawing the Em and Visible Spectra)

This activity presents a great opportunity to have the kids do some measuring, both in the English and metric systems. They can also refer to this information when they get to chapter 13, "Good Bee-Havior." Also have them refer back to the illustrations and information in "Let's Get Small" (see chapter 2) if they're having trouble visualizing the size of different electromagnetic waves. Figure 6.5 shows what their efforts might look like.

There are several points worth making with regard to the issue of why animals are only sensitive to a narrow range on the em spectrum. Wavelengths shorter than ultraviolet tend to be destructive to living tissue, as Madame Curie discovered the hard way working with X-rays. Most gamma rays and cosmic rays are filtered out by Earth's atmosphere. If phenomena are not encountered often enough to affect an organism's survival, natural selection can't operate to create sensory detectors for them. Longer wavelengths than those of visible light are either detected by other organs (like the pit organ of rattlesnakes) or are of such long length that they can't readily be used to gather useful information by organisms in our size range.

Sunlight, however, is vitally important to nearly every living thing. Plants make use of it by tapping its energy with the help of chlorophyll. Animals sense its presence with the pigment rhodopsin, an essential component in the seemingly infinite variety of animal eyes.

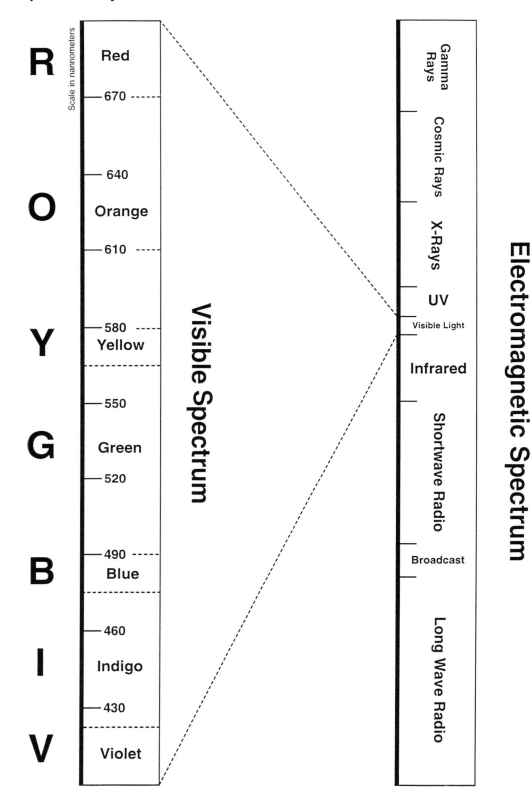

Fig. 6.5. Electromagnetic and visible spectra. The student's spectra drawings should look something like this. Point out that the visible light we can see represents only a small fraction of the electromagnetic spectrum.

Chapter 7

POND DRAGONS

A DRAGON'S MISTAKE

I discovered a mistaken dragon one hot, summer day while sitting at a stoplight, drumming my fingers on the steering wheel and waiting for the light to turn green. The air shimmered over the shiny surface of the hood of my car. Suddenly, a colorful dragonfly swooped down and touched the car hood with her abdomen. I looked around at nearby traffic and discovered that other car hoods were suffering similar "attacks." In some cases dragonflies seemed to be swooping in pairs. I began to wonder if I'd stumbled onto the set of a low-budget sci-fi thriller.

Truth was, the dragonfly had simply goofed. For 300 million years or so her kind had successfully recognized the surface of water by its shiny appearance. Water is where this dragonfly and her sisters needed to lay their eggs. Sometimes dragonflies get fooled by pools of oil or natural seepage of organic material like those of California's La Brea Tar Pits. Those fooled by tar pits may end up as fossils. Those fooled by car hoods may just get a bruised abdomen.

Most dragonflies make the right choices, however. They are agile, adaptable insects with a nearly inexhaustible food source: flies and mosquitoes. What's more, they have virtually no economic importance to human beings (aside from being a food delicacy in parts of Asia), so people tend to leave them alone. But they are fascinating creatures, both as flying adults and ambushing, aquatic larvae.

The Life Cycle of a Dragonfly

Go to a quiet pond or temporary pool of water near midday and you can easily see the males patrolling their territory, wandering slowly back and forth in a limited area. Eventually they will perch on one to three favorite locations and wait for either a potential meal or another male to pass by. If a fly ventures too close, the dragonfly will track its movement with the huge eyes that cover its head, then dart after its chosen victim and catch it in a basketlike enclosure made with its forelegs. The legs deliver the meal to the dragonfly's formidable jaws.

If another male dragonfly happens by, they will compete for territory. In one common species, the white-tailed dragonfly, the dominant male will raise its abdomen 70 degrees, displaying its white tip. If the other dragonfly is intimidated it will lower its abdomen. When there's plenty of room to spread out, one dragonfly may easily chase off the other. When populations are heavy and two or three males are close together, the dominant male will tend to mate with more females.

65

From *Explorations in Backyard Biology.* © 1996. Teacher Ideas Press. (800) 237-6124.

When a female swoops down to investigate the shiny surface she suspects is water, admiring males quickly approach. A male will fly up, grab her by the thorax with his legs, and "load" his sperm pouch near his penis in the second abdominal segment with sperm produced at his tail end. Then, using a pair of tail hooks, the male holds firmly to the female by the neck or upper thorax. She arches her tail around to the male's upper abdomen so her eggs can be fertilized. The result is that the two animals form a loop, which you may either see in midair or perched on a nearby plant.

Once fertilized, the female flies off again to water and dips her abdomen in to wash off the eggs. Some species insert their eggs into aquatic plants beneath water level. Males often follow their mates to chase away other males and thus ensure that their sperm fertilizes the eggs. Adults, with their job done, usually die within a few weeks.

Most of a dragonfly's life is spent as an immature larva, hunting other insects, tadpoles, and even minnows. Dragonfly larvae are stoutly built and hold a deceptive "mask" over their jaws. This mask is actually a set of pinchers on the end of an extendable arm, which flashes out in a hundredth of a second to nab prey. Their appetite is astounding. One researcher raised larvae and found that one of his charges ate 3,037 mosquito larvae, 164 mosquito pupae, and 17 larval damselflies and dragonflies in one year.

Young dragonflies have their own enemies as well, including fish and giant water bugs. They have a unique "jet propulsion" method of escape which involves contracting their abdominal muscles and forcing water out of their rear end. Under less stressful conditions, these contractions assist breathing by forcing oxygen-laden water over the gills in their hindgut.

In warm locations, a dragonfly larva may mature in a season, but in temperate regions it takes two or three years to grow to full size. Then, usually early in the morning, it climbs out on a plant stem just above the waterline and sucks in quantities of air. This expands the body, and the hard larval skin splits. A soft, pale adult crawls out. Within an hour, its skin has hardened, its wings have dried, and it's ready for adult adventures—and those occasional adult mistakes.

Three hundred million years ago, when dragonflies were a new experiment in animal lifestyles, some sported wingspans of more than 30 inches. Today, their descendants, although smaller, are nearly unchanged in form. More than 5,000 species prosper worldwide. We can all admire the beauty as well as the hardiness of these agile and adaptable creatures, whether walking the shore of a quiet pond or just trying to keep our patience in a traffic jam.

From *Explorations in Backyard Biology.* © 1996. Teacher Ideas Press. (800) 237-6124.

ACTIVITIES

Observing Adult Dragonflies or Damselflies

Fortunately, it's fairly easy to observe adult behavior in these insects, both because they will let observers get quite close and because they are most active during midday, just like most of us. A pencil, your naturalist's notebook, and perhaps a little sunscreen is all you'll need, although a pair of binoculars might come in handy.

First, decide whether you're watching dragonflies or damselflies. Dragonflies are stouter, have large "wraparound" eyes, and hold their wings straight out from their body. Damselflies perch more and hold their wings straight up over their back.

Most of the dragonflies that "hang out" near the water for an extended period of time are males. Look for three kinds of behavior: perching, chasing, and patrolling. Males typically stake out territory and select one to three spots from which to survey their domain. Record the perches for the males observed.

Males leave their perches from time to time to patrol the area. Time the length of patrols to see if there is any pattern to this behavior. Do they return to the same perch most of the time or do they spread their time equally between different "home bases"?

When another male enters the area, a chase may ensue. Look for one of three kinds. In the first type, the owner of the territory may simply chase the interloper away. In a second type, the two dragonflies face each other, fly up together a yard or two in the air, then fly back and forth across the territory until one leaves. In a third type, the first male may fly under the second, then rise up and bang into him with an audible clatter. Both then fly up and off to the side of the area.

During male-male encounters also look for two displays: the tail-up motion of the dominant animal and the tail-down submissive gesture. What kind of markings do the dragonflies have on their bodies or wings that other members of their species might be responding to?

Damselfly males also show perching and chasing behavior. Display behavior of the territory-holder includes raising his wings as he raises his abdomen. This is often sufficient to chase another male away.

Look also for the mating and egg-laying behavior described in the student article. Observing the "flying ring" formation of mating dragonflies and damselflies is fascinating. If you are fortunate enough to see egg laying, observe whether the females simply wash the eggs off in the water or insert them in a water plant. Describe the behavior of the attending males.

Cut disks or rectangles of cardboard and cover them with aluminum foil. Are females attracted to these "artificial ponds"? Experiment with different styles and sizes. Which is most effective at fooling females? If a female touches the foil with her abdomen, look for eggs with a hand lens and sketch any found.

From *Explorations in Backyard Biology.* © 1996. Teacher Ideas Press. (800) 237-6124.

📖 IN YOUR NOTEBOOK:
SURVEYING A POND OR RIVER COMMUNITY

Materials needed: pipettes; forceps; field notebook, small ruler, pencil, or pen; white, enamel-coated pan (the white surface makes it easier to see captured critters and the enameling avoids rusting problems or metal contamination of the animals); a simple dip net (this could be a kitchen sieve tied to a long handle); hand screen (two short handles with window screen fastened between them; one person holds the screen downstream while a person upstream turns rocks and disturbs the bottom to dislodge animals); jars of various sizes (small jars with tight lids can hold individual specimens, especially of carnivorous creatures; larger jars can hold unsorted samples); heavy, sealable plastic bags; vials of 70 percent alcohol (to preserve specimens if desired); cotton or sphagnum moss (mayfly, caddis fly, stone fly, and dobsonfly larvae that need lots of oxygen are easier to keep alive transported in moist cotton or moss; when you arrive at school, transfer them to large, screen-topped jars or aquaria with green plants)

Carefully record the sites of collection, noting location, time of day, weather conditions, and the specifics of the sites (whether from the stream bottom, under a rock, etc.). Number each collection in a consistent way. Make sure the number in your notebook matches the number on the label of the specimen.

Back in the classroom, identify and sketch as many organisms as you can. Figure 7.1 should help get you started. The kinds of creatures you find are an indicator of the health of the water system sampled. Healthy ecologies will contain a mix of pollution-sensitive and pollution-tolerant organisms. Unhealthy ecologies will only contain the latter. Here's a checklist:

Pollution-sensitive creatures: mayfly, caddis fly, stone fly, and dobsonfly larvae

Moderately sensitive creatures: crayfish, damselfly and dragonfly larvae, clams, shrimp, and scuds

Pollution-tolerant organisms: mosquito, midge and blackfly larvae, aquatic worms and leeches, water boatmen, backswimmers

From *Explorations in Backyard Biology.* © 1996. Teacher Ideas Press. (800) 237-6124.

A Brief Comparison of Some Common Freshwater Insects

		Look for:	Where Found?	Role in Food Web
MAYFLIES	Adult	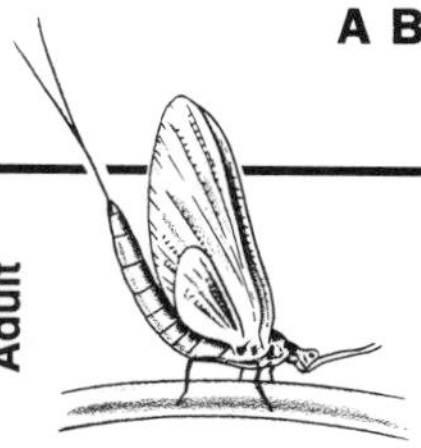 2 or 3 long tail filaments No mouth parts 2 pair of wings, one small, held upright over body	Over streams, often early in the morning (especially males).	Adults don't eat!
MAYFLIES	Nymph	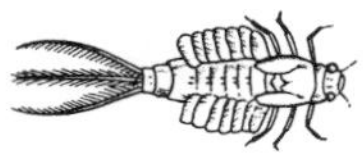 3 (possibly 2) tail filaments emerge from near tip of abdomen Feathery gills on abdomen	Burrowers found in mud. Clingers found on stones. Sprawlers found in bottom mud.	Eat algae, sometimes higher plants. Food for fish, birds, and other insects.
STONE FLIES	Adult	 Long, segmented antennae Wings flat over body 2 cerci on abdomen, small mouth parts	In shade near water. Some species are active in winter.	Either don't eat at all or eat limited amounts of algae and pollen.
STONE FLIES	Nymph	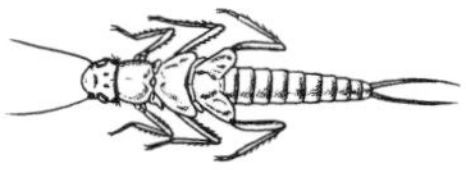 2-pronged tail filament, farther apart, and shorter than mayfly Feathery gills on thorax Large wing pads on thorax	Under rocks or in plant debris.	Eat algae and plant debris. Some eat mayfly and fly larvae. Live 1-3 years and make good trout food.
CADDIS FLIES	Adult	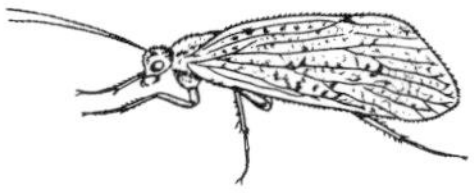 Moth-like, dull colored (brownish) Hairy wings, roof-like over body Long antennae pointing forward	Nocturnal. Hide in vegetation or under ledges by day.	Sometimes eat sweet plant secretions.
CADDIS FLIES	Nymph	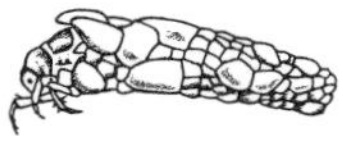 Ornate cases or "houses" Pair of hooks on end of abdomen Front of animal hard and dark, abdomen soft and light, legs directed forward	All aquatic on stones, plants, or river bottom.	They eat everything: algae, plant debris, worms, crustaceans, and insects.
DOBSONFLIES	Adult	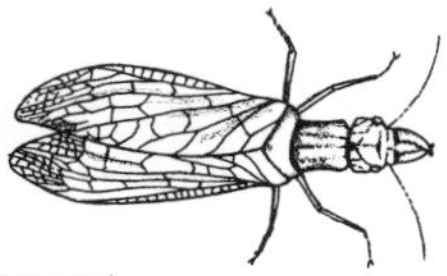 Large jaws (they bite!) 2 pair of membranous wings, flat over body Long, many-segmented antennae	Found near water. Sluggish and nocturnal.	Carnivorous
DOBSONFLIES	Larva	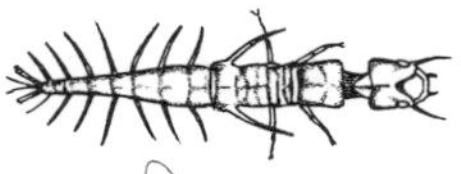 Large jaws Gill tufts on abdomen	On the bottom or in mud under stones.	Carnivorous and cannabalistic. They are eaten by fish and other creatures and live 2-3 years.
DRAGONFLIES	Adult	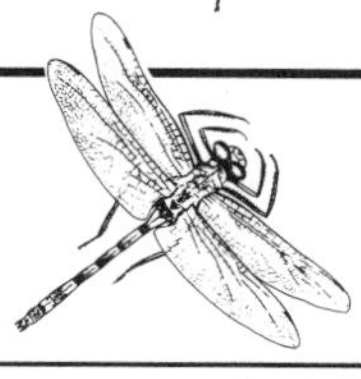 Large eyes that cover head area 2 pair of large, membranous wings held straight out like a plane Long, very narrow body	Found during the day on plants near the water. Males stake out territories.	Carnivorous, daytime hunters.
DRAGONFLIES	Nymph	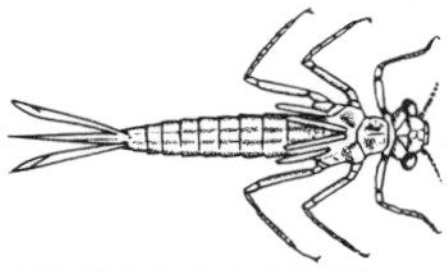 Large eyes Hinged jaws that cover face like a mask 3 tail filaments	Aquatic predators found near the bottom, in plant debris or by stones.	Carnivorous

Fig. 7.1. Common freshwater insects. This chart summarizes the major physical features, habitat, and ecology of some common freshwater insects.

From *Explorations in Backyard Biology.* © 1996. Teacher Ideas Press. (800) 237-6124.

Experiments with Dragonfly Larvae

Larva Speed Contest

If you find some dragonfly larvae, hold a race.

The jet propulsion technique of dragonfly larvae is easy to demonstrate when they are disturbed. In fact, if you pick one up and hold it the wrong way, you may get squirted in the eye. Speed is measured by finding the distance moved in a given amount of time (the number of centimeters, inches, or feet moved per second, for example). Larvae of green darner dragonflies have been clocked at 20 inches per second. Lay out a measured course for your larva and time it with a stopwatch. Determine who has the speediest larva.

Larva Camouflage Test

Depending on their surroundings, dragonfly and damselfly larvae can change color to some extent, mostly in a range from green to brown; however, some can vary from striped or blotched to solid, too. Create different colored backdrops for the containers housing your larvae and observe any change in color from one day to the next.

Prey Stalking

Dragonfly and damselfly larvae are highly visual like their adult counterparts. Observe normal feeding behavior by allowing the larvae to stalk some of the other creatures captured during your collecting trip. Then isolate a larva and offer it crushed food of the same type. It will ignore it. Now put a thin glass barrier between the larva and a living prey species. If hungry, it will track and strike at the moving food item.

DRAGONS IN THE WATER

Some Background Information

Dragonflies have always intrigued people. The Japanese associated them with victory in battle. The Hopi Indians of the American Southwest and, presumably, their Anasazi ancestors viewed them as religious symbols of life. Medieval English "witches" threatened to sew up the lips of lying children with their needlelike bodies. Tennyson praised their beauty in a well-known poem:

Today I saw the dragon-fly
Come from the wells where he did lie.
An inner impulse rent the veil
Of his old husk: from head to tail
Came out clear plates of sapphire mail.
He dried his wings: like gauze they grew;
Thro' crofts and pastures wet with dew
A living flash of light he flew.

It's hard not to be impressed by this ancient insect order, the Odonata, which includes both dragonflies and damselflies. They were some of the first flying insects and possess a primitive wing design in which flight muscles are attached directly to the wing bases. In contrast, most flying insects move their wings by contracting abdominal muscles, which indirectly flap the wings. Nevertheless, the Odonata are not shabby flyers. They can routinely fly at 30 mph while snatching mosquitos on the wing and go perhaps twice as fast under some conditions. In addition, they can hover and turn quickly within a body length. Researchers at the University of Colorado are trying to find out how to make modern planes approach their efficiency of design (see the Nowak article, listed in the "References" section at the back of this book).

Recognizing Dragonflies and Their Kin

Distinguish Odonata from other insects by looking for large-eyed creatures with very short antennae; two pairs of richly veined wings, narrow at the base; legs directed forward; and long, slender abdomens. Dragonflies tend to be larger than damselflies; their eyes are much larger, often meeting down the midline of the head; and they hold their wings straight out like an old biplane. Damselflies are more often found perched on vegetation with their wings primly folded vertically over their abdomens.

The larvae of dragonflies (see fig. 7.2), as mentioned in the student article, are stout (somewhat cigar-shaped) with large eyes similar to the adult, and can move by jet propulsion. Damselfly larvae are similar in overall configuration, but they have three long tail filaments that serve as gills, and they move by waving these back and forth, somewhat like a fish's tail.

Recognizing Other Pond Creatures

A variety of insect groups secondarily returned to an aquatic existence after their ancestors had invaded land habitats long before. If you survey an aquatic community you will want to be able to recognize some of the major types. Some of your students who are fish enthusiasts may recognize these creatures by their common names or even have lures resembling them. *The New Field Book of Freshwater Life* by Elsie Klots is a good general reference.

Mayflies (see fig. 7.3) are insects whose adult life is so short that their order is called the Ephemeroptera. Adults have no mouth parts and can't eat. Their larvae transform, adults mate,

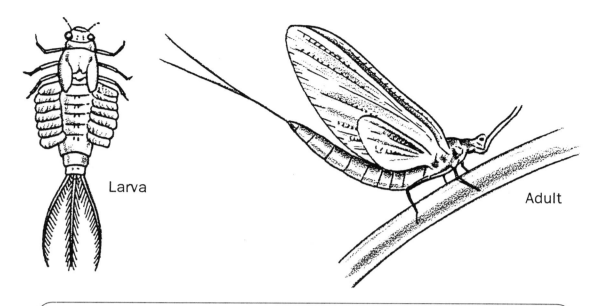

Larva

Adult

Fig. 7.2. Dragonflies. Adult and larval dragonflies.

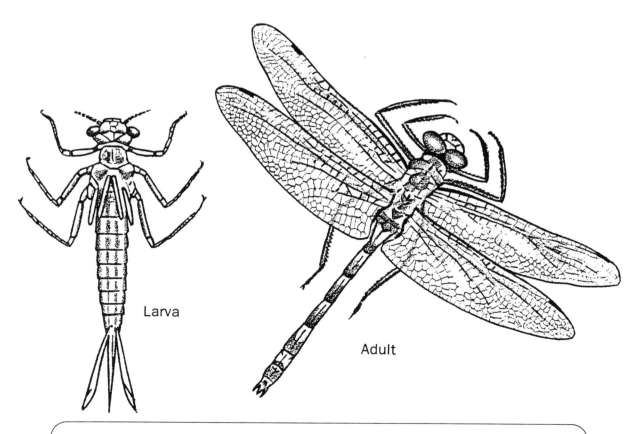

Larva

Adult

Fig. 7.3. Mayflies. Adult and larval mayflies.

lay eggs, and die within a matter of hours or days, sometimes in such great numbers that their bodies and cast skins have to be shoveled from streets near waterways. Adults have two pairs of wings—one pair quite small—that they hold upright over their body. They have two or three very long tail filaments.

Mayfly larvae may live several years in streams or other waterways in temperate climates. Some species are burrowers whose tail filaments protrude from the muddy banks of rivers; other species cling to stones in fast streams. A third group roam amid the debris of muddy streambeds. Most eat algae or other plants and are eaten, in turn, by fish, birds, and other insects. The larvae are long and thin with three (sometimes two) tail filaments, and they have feathery gills on their abdomens.

Stone fly adults like shade near the water where they emerge. Some species even transform to adults on warm winter days when competition is light. They have long, segmented antennae; hold their wings flat over their body; and have two projections called cerci at the rear end of their abdomens. They have small mouth parts for nibbling on algae or pollen grains (see fig. 7.4).

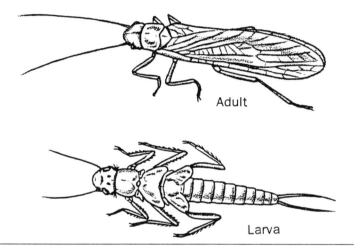

Adult

Larva

Fig. 7.4. Stone flies. Adult and larval stone flies. See text for explanation.

Stone fly larvae have two tail filaments, shorter and farther apart than those of mayflies. They have large wing pads on their thorax that look a bit like armor mail and feathery gills located on the thorax. You'll find them under rocks or in plant debris. They eat plant material as well as mayfly and fly larvae. They live several years and fall victim to trout and other fish.

Caddis fly adults are rather dull, brownish-colored creatures, somewhat mothlike in appearance. They hold their hairy wings rooflike over their body. They have long, forward-pointing antennae. Caddis flies are nocturnal and can be attracted by a light source. They hide in vegetation or under ledges by day. Adults sometimes suck sweet liquids produced by plants (see fig. 7.5).

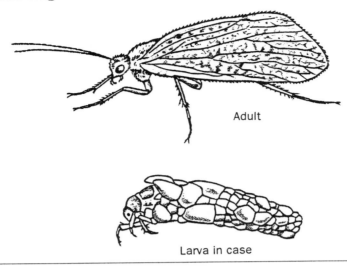

Adult

Larva in case

Fig. 7.5. Caddis flies. Adult and larval caddis flies.

Immature caddis flies build homes for themselves out of sand grains or other materials available in streambeds. You can often see them clinging to stones or roaming river bottoms looking for algae, plant debris, worms, crustaceans, or insects. The larvae have a pair of hooks on their rear end to hang onto their homes. The front of the animal is hard and dark, the rear end soft and pale. Legs project forward.

Dobsonflies (see fig. 7.6) have large jaws, are carnivorous, and can bite. Fortunately they tend to be sluggish and are nocturnal. They have two pairs of membranous wings, which they hold flat over their body, and sport two long, many-segmented antennae. Their larvae also have big jaws and have gill tufts on their abdomens. Found on bottom mud or under stones, they eat other insects as well as their own kind from time to time. They live several years and often become fish food themselves.

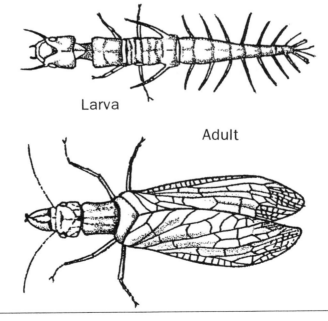

Larva

Adult

Fig. 7.6. Dobsonflies. Adult and larval dobsonflies.

Notes on the Student Activities

Observing Adult Dragonflies or Damselflies

A Guide to Observing Insect Lives by Donald W. Stokes will prove most useful here. All of his field guides are quite good.

Surveying a Pond or River Community

This activity could encompass both a class field trip to collect specimens and class time to examine the "catch" in detail. Alternately, the teacher could do the collecting and bring samples to class, but the students would miss seeing these fascinating creatures in their natural habitats. Better yet, students could create much of their own collecting equipment before the day of the field trip and review the kinds of critters they could expect to see.

Experiments with Dragonfly Larvae

Howard Ensign Evans's discussion of dragonflies in *Life on a Little Known Planet* provides background for some of the work done with larvae. You'll probably think of many variations of your own, depending on your catch from year to year. Every expedition is guaranteed to be a unique learning experience.

Chapter 8

STORIES IN STONE
THE FIRST PREDATORS

MYSTERY OF THE PREDATOR FOUND IN PIECES

What do a jellyfish, an odd-looking shrimp, a squashed sea cucumber, and a shelled creature with jointed legs have in common? Answer: nothing and everything. Are you confused? So were the paleontologists (scientists who study fossil life) who discovered and described some well-preserved creatures from an ancient sea floor community that used to exist where the Canadian Rockies rise today.

In the Beginning . . .

The beginnings of this riddle began at the very dawn of complex life on our planet. A thriving community of marine life lived on, in, or near mud and other sediments at the base of a gigantic reef. The water lay warm and shallow there, and hundreds of small animals the size of common worms and clams called the area home. One day a disaster struck. A huge shelf of sediments broke away and slid like a river of mud into a deep, cold, ocean trench where even bacteria found it hard to survive. The mud slide quickly crushed and buried all the creatures in the community, creating a tomb that was almost sealed forever.

The Discovery

"Forever" turned out to be 540 million years. In 1909, Charles Walcott, then a senior scientist with the Smithsonian Institution in Washington, D.C., stumbled onto an important rock. Actually, it may have been his wife's horse that did the stumbling—some of the details are a little unclear—but the rock was a piece of shale that once was mud beneath the ancient reef, and it contained a perfectly preserved fossil animal. The shale deposit lay near the small town of Burgess, British Columbia. Walcott would come back to this spot over the next several summers and discover a wealth of both familiar and strange soft-bodied animals not usually preserved in the fossil record.

One of these creatures Walcott called *Sidneyia* (fig. 8.1), after his son, Sidney, who helped him on his fossil hunts. *Sidneyia* was a segmented creature that Walcott thought was an early arthropod (a relative of modern insects, crustaceans, and spiders). Walcott found several examples of a segmented limb that he called Appendage F (see fig. 8.2) because he thought they were used for food gathering. These limbs were so big he thought that only *Sidneyia* was large enough to carry them, so he guessed they were parts of the same creature.

He also found a flattened animal with an indistinct body that seemed to have a

76

Fig. 8.1. *Sidneyia*. *Sidneyia*, one of the larger creatures of the Burgess Shale, preyed on shelled animals like trilobites and the hyolithids shown in the foreground. (Shelly remains were found in the stomachs of some specimens.) Researchers at first thought that *Sidneyia* was the only predator big enough to have limbs as large as Appendage F.

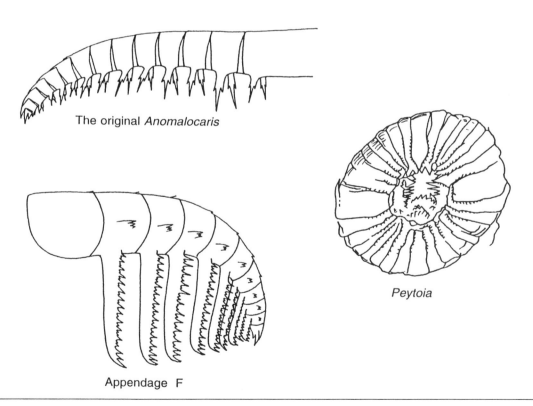

The original *Anomalocaris*

Peytoia

Appendage F

Fig. 8.2. Appendage F. The original *Anomalocaris* and Appendage F are redrawn from D. E. G. Briggs *Palaeontology* 22, text figures 1 and 20 (with permission of the Palaeontological Association London). *Peytoia* was redrawn from D. E. G. Briggs article "The Largest Cambrian Animal" *Philosophical Transactions of the Royal Society of London* 309 (1985): 569-609.

roughly circular mouth surrounded by a ring of plates. He named this beast *Laggania* and thought it was a type of sea cucumber.

Peytoia was the name given to a strange fossil that consisted of a ring of 32 lobes around a central opening. Walcott eventually called this animal a jellyfish, although it was different than any jellyfish alive today.

Several years before, in 1892, a Canadian paleontologist had found a segmented creature with spines, but no head, about 2 miles from Walcott's quarry site. He called it *Anomalocaris,* which means "odd shrimp." Walcott found more of these and also thought they were shrimplike crustaceans.

Walcott described his odd collection of animals in a 1911 paper and stored his fossils in the Smithsonian Institution. At the time, they were considered interesting but not overly remarkable except for how well they were preserved. Fortunately, three scientists, Simon Morris, H. G. Whittington, and Derek Briggs, took a closer look and discovered just how unusual the Burgess Shale animals were.

The Results

In 1978 Morris used a dental microdrill to try and see more of the structure of *Laggania* from Walcott's collection. He found a specimen of *Peytoia* where Walcott had described an indistinct mouth. He thought at the time that the two animals might have accidentally been buried together.

In 1979 Briggs realized, after studying hundreds of examples of *Anomalocaris*, that this wasn't a whole animal, but only a leg or some other appendage. In fact, it looked not too unlike the Appendage F fossils. Perhaps these were two different legs on the same creature. But, if so, why had nobody found a 3-foot body to go with the 7-inch legs?

H. G. Whittington had a large, indistinct fossil in his Burgess Shale collection, not unlike *Laggania*, that had always intrigued him, but he didn't know what to do with it. In 1981 he decided to "dissect" the fossil further, much as Morris had done with his specimen, even though there was some danger in damaging it. To his surprise he discovered that two *Anomalocaris* "legs" were actually feeding arms near the mouth of his fossil animal and the mouth was *Peytoia,* Walcott's strange "jellyfish" (see fig. 8.3).

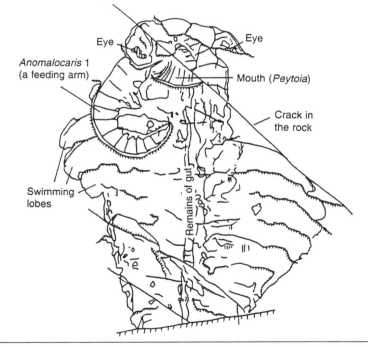

Fig. 8.3. A mashed monster: *Anomalocaris*. The real *Anomalocaris* was revealed by Harry Whittington during a more complete dissection of a large, but indistinct, fossil. The old *Anomalocaris* was one of two feeding arms (the other was found on the mirror image half of the fossil slab). The "jellyfish," *Peytoia*, was really the mouth of *Anomalocaris*. Appendage F is one of two feeding arms in a related species. Note the remains of a digestive tract in the middle of the animal. Redrawn from D. E. G. Briggs article "The Largest Cambrian Animal," *Philosophical Transactions of the Royal Society of London* 309 (1985): 569-609.

Suddenly, a lot of things began to make sense. Instead of four strange animals there was only one, and this animal, by scientific convention, had to be called *Anomalocaris*, after the first fossil found in 1892. The "new" *Anomalocaris* once existed as at least two species: one that had Appendage F feeding arms and one that had the "old" *Anomalocaris* feeding arms. All had a wicked, circular mouth with rows of teeth, two stalked eyes, and broad lobes on either side of a conical body. The entire animal was about 2 feet long—very long compared to other animals of the time— and apparently a predator of trilobites and other hard-shelled creatures in the ancient seas (see fig. 8.4).

In recent years, *Anomalocaris* fossils have been found in China, Australia, Greenland, Utah, and other places with rocks of the right age exposed. These creatures survived and thrived in prehistoric days, but today nothing alive is remotely similar to these strange predators. Other odd beasts have come from the Burgess Shale, including a five-eyed animal called *Opabinia* with a claw on the end of a segmented arm where a snout would usually be. Paleontologists are learning about the origins of all the major groups of animals alive today by studying the creatures of the Burgess Shale.

They're also learning about body plans that failed, like those of *Anomalocaris* and *Opabinia*. They expect more mysteries, too, before they're finished, but they don't mind. After all, there are few things as satisfying as solving a good mystery.

Fig. 8.4. Modern *Anomalocaris* reconstruction. This rendering of *Anomalocaris* shows her swooping down on a trilobite attempting a rapid retreat. A priapulid worm is in the right foreground. Two mollusks called *Hyolithes* lie in sediments in the left foreground.

ACTIVITIES

Making Future Fossils

Fossils come in a variety of forms depending on the conditions at the time they were preserved as well as what happened during the long years they lay in the ground. The fossils of the Burgess Shale are thin films of carbon (the remains of their original bodies) preserved by a layer of calcium aluminocilicate from the clay sands that buried them. Wood and bones are often mineralized *(petrified)* when water carrying phosphates and/or silicates leaches through the strata in which they're buried. Insects and other small arthropods may be trapped in pine resin, which later hardens to amber, a gemstone.

Sometimes the original organism rots away, leaving a cavity where it once was. This cavity is a mold of the outside of the creature. If this mold is later filled with another mineral, a natural cast of the original animal may be formed. Footprints of dinosaurs, birds, and other animals are sometimes preserved and represent a special type of mold that can tell a lot about the size and mobility of its owner.

What objects from our own world would make good candidates for future fossilization? How much could you tell about their form and function by looking at a mold or cast-type fossil? Let's find out. Divide into several groups. Each will create its own "Future Fossil," which other groups will try to interpret.

Materials needed: modeling clay; plaster of paris; spray oil like WD-40 or hair spray; water; disposable or washable containers for mixing plaster; toothpicks; a small, firm object that can be pressed into clay without deforming or breaking

Directions:

1. Find a small, firm object that can be pressed into clay without breaking or bending too much but that is distinctive enough to have some surface detail. Keep its identity secret from the other groups.

2. Press the object firmly into a fairly thick piece of modeling clay lying on a flat surface, then remove the object carefully so that the clay mold you have just created is not damaged.

3. Spray the clay mold with some hair spray or oil.

4. Mix up some plaster of paris according to the label directions and fill the empty clay mold with the plaster.

5. You may want to use a pair of toothpicks to help remove the hardened cast from your mold. A portion of toothpick left in a partially set cast could be used as a "handle" to pull it out.

6. Let the plaster set until hard and then remove your cast.

7. Exchange your cast and the clay mold with that of another group.

IN YOUR NOTEBOOK

Make a sketch of the cast object. Can you identify what it was? Which is easier to interpret, the cast or the mold? Circle which of the following you can determine from either the cast or the mold: size, weight, color, internal structure, external structure, whether it was once alive or dead, how it was used.

Repeat the procedure with other groups, if time permits. How many objects could you correctly identify?

Fossils in Your Backyard

Visit a local museum or library and find out what fossils can be found in your area. Contact local rock clubs or geology clubs and find out when and where they have field trips and what their membership dues are. Look for advertisements for rock and gem shows and attend. You can count on finding several vendors with fossils to sell and information to share.

Famous Paleontologists

Do a research report on famous fossil hunters, past or present. Several have written autobiographies, and their stories are fascinating. Here are some names to look for.

Thomas Jefferson was an excellent amateur paleontologist. He found the claw of an extinct giant sloth, among other things. His interest in natural history contributed to his sending Lewis and Clark to explore the American West.

Joseph Leidy, Othniel Marsh, and *Edward Cope* were some of the earliest dinosaur hunters in the western United States. Cope and Marsh competed so much for the biggest and best finds that tons of dinosaur bones were excavated during the latter half of the nineteenth century. Some still lay unstudied in major museums.

Charles Sternberg hunted with Cope during the 1870s and nearly got in the way of Chief Sitting Bull traveling north after the Battle of the Little Big Horn in Montana.

Robert Bakker, a controversial bone hunter at the University of Colorado in Boulder, pioneered the idea that some dinosaurs, at least, were warm-blooded, agile predators.

Jack Horner discovered Maiasaurs of all ages in Montana trapped during an ancient volcanic eruption. His work showed that Maiasaurs cared for their young, much like communal birds, and developed at a rate similar to warm-blooded mammals today. Both Horner and Bakker were advisors for the movie *Jurassic Park.*

SOLVING ANCIENT MYSTERIES

Notes on the Student Article

Biology and geology intersect at the science of paleontology. The story of the Burgess Shale fossils allows you to explore the high-interest area of past life-forms with some fascinating, nondinosaur creatures, as well as point out one of the major features of scientific inquiry: to ask questions of nature that can be answered by experiment and by new discoveries. Too often science becomes a list of facts to be memorized. Emphasize that scientific hypotheses may change as new facts come to light and old assumptions are reexamined. Fossil hunting can be especially fun, too, because the next rock you turn over could contain a creature never before seen by another human being.

In chapter 4, "Monsters in the Mud Puddle," we looked at some of the early events in the history of life on Earth on a time scale measured in billions of years. The Burgess Shale creatures represent the real beginning of the fossil record in terms of fairly large, complex organisms that can be easily seen and recognized. They occupy the spot on figure 4.3 marked "Cambrian diversification of 'macro' life" at the .5 billion-year mark near the top of the chart. You may want to introduce a simplified, conventional geological time scale, like the one shown in figure 8.5, to show students where the Burgess animals appeared relative to dinosaurs, for example. This time scale is measured in millions rather than billions of years, and still, most of the beasts we are familiar with appear only in a thin sliver near the top, which is expanded to the right of the main chart.

Stephen Jay Gould's book *Wonderful Life* is, perhaps, the best popular reference for reading about the Burgess Shale fauna. "Terror of the Trilobites," by Derek E. G. Briggs and Harry B. Whittington, and the *National Geographic* article on the Cambrian explosion by Rick Gore are also good. The latter article, as you might suspect, has great pictures. The journal articles by Briggs and McMenamin are more technical. If you are really into this aspect of paleontology, *The Fossils of the Burgess Shale* by Derek E. G. Briggs, Douglas H. Erwin, and Frederick J. Collier is the book you should have. Figure 8.6 shows my reconstruction of the Burgess Shale community based on the work of these researchers.

EVENTS

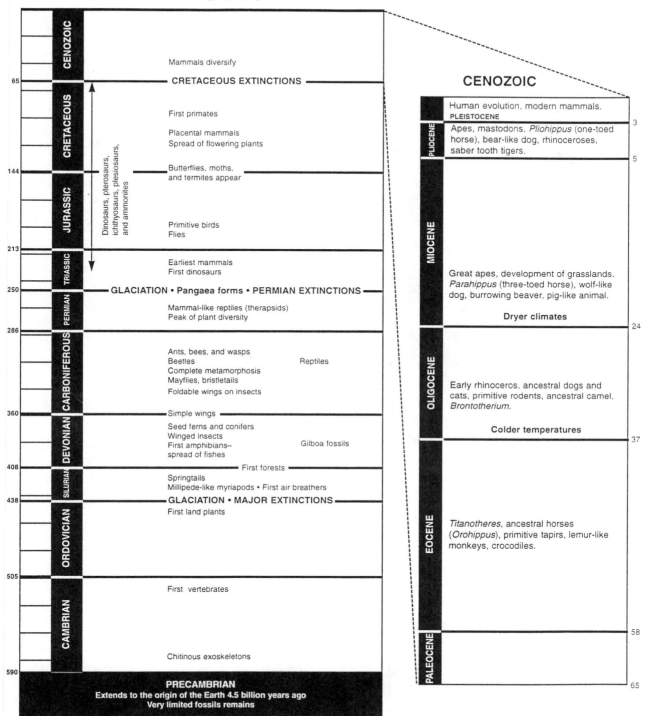

Fig. 8.5. Geological time scale. The geological time scale, marked by a sequence of fossil groupings going back 600 million years or so, represents about one-ninth of our planet's history. The Burgess Shale organisms lived about 540 million years ago. Reprinted from *Dinosaurs in the Garden,* courtesy Plexus Publishing, Inc., Medford, NJ.

Fig. 8.6. Animals of the Burgess Shale. This reconstruction of the seafloor community that would later become home to the Burgess Shale fossils shows some of the species from several major groups of animals. The five-eyed, tentacle-snouted form near the center called *Opabinia* has no known living relatives. It is shown grabbing *Hyolithes*, one of the few mollusks found at the site. A priapulid worm rears out of its burrow. Its living relatives look much the same today. The stalked *Dinomischus*, like *Opabinia*, belonged to a group now extinct. In the foreground, a many-legged arthropod with large "horns" scuttles over a rock while the scaled and spiked *Wiwaxia*, a possible mollusk, plows through the sediments. The treelike forms are sponges. Reprinted from *Dinosaurs in the Garden*, courtesy Plexus Publishing, Inc., Medford, NJ.

Notes on the Student Activities

Making Future Fossils

This simple exercise in making molds and casts will help clarify the way many common fossils are formed. *Fossils for Amateurs: A Handbook for Collectors* by Russell P. MacFall and Jay C. Wollin describes well some of the variety of ways living things can be preserved over long periods of time. The *Eyewitness Handbook of Fossils* (Walker and Ward) has great photos of different kinds of fossils. Here is a brief rundown:

1. Ice Age mammoths and other creatures of the Pleistocene were sometimes quick-*frozen* in permafrost. In some cases, the meat is still fit to eat!

2. In dry climates, organic remains may become naturally *mummified* as water slowly evaporates.

3. Very dense bones, like teeth, and hard shells may be preserved for millions of years in basically their *original state.* Shells do lose a little of their color and luster after 20 million years, however!

4. Organisms may be *petrified.* This can happen in one of three ways: (a) dissolved minerals may fill up pores and channels in tissue (like trees or coral), leaving original organic material around them; (b) dissolved minerals may fill up pores and channels and another mineral may replace the original carbon of the organism, resulting in the preservation of detail with microscopic clarity; or (c) an organism can be trapped in lava or mud that hardens into a mold—minerals fill the mold, creating something that looks like the outside of the organism, but the inside can be agate, quartz, or some other rock.

5. Heat, pressure, and bacterial action can convert a living thing to a thin film of carbon. Insects, leaves, and soft-bodied critters are often *carbonized* in this way.

6. If an organism is buried in material that hardens around it, then rots away, a *mold* is formed. If the mold fills with more sediment or minerals, a *cast* of the original animal forms. Internal detail is not preserved. Insects trapped in *amber* represent a special category of molds because a thin film of carbon lines the chamber and often preserves an amazing amount of detail.

7. *Trace fossils* form from things animals leave behind: footprints, tunnel borings, trails, and excrement, usually. The latter are called coprolites.

8. *Pseudo fossils* look like fossils, but aren't. Banded flints can sometimes be mistaken for corals, mollusks, worms, or trilobites. Wave action on ancient beaches can be preserved and may resemble shells. Minerals may form in dendritic patterns that resemble ferns or other plants.

Select small objects that are hard enough to push into the clay but that have some interesting surface detail. Pens, small bottles, safety pins, key chains, or anything else that will leave a clear impression and can be extracted again without too much trouble are good choices.

You can use self-hardening clay, which will create a firmer mold, or plastic modeling compounds. With the latter, students will have to be more careful removing finished casts if they want to use the mold more than once. The spray oil will help in removing the hardened casts.

By adding a little food coloring to the plaster of paris you can show how casts take on the color of the mineral that forms them.

"In Your Notebook" Questions: Casts are usually easier to recognize than molds. Molds and casts can give you an idea of the size of the original object (although they may be distorted by pressure and folding), information about external features, and hints about function. Weight, color, and internal structure can only be guessed at. Determining whether the object once lived depends on its resemblance to modern living forms.

Fossils in Your Backyard

Librarians or museum personnel may know of local rock clubs. Members are usually quite happy to expound on their areas of expertise and may often be willing to donate samples to local teachers. They may also be willing to visit classrooms. Museums can usually give you a lead on fossils local to your area. Rock clubs often organize summer field trips to nearby sites.

Famous Paleontologists

Check your local library for resource materials. Url Lanham's *The Bone Hunters* is a good investment. Charles Sternberg's account of his own adventures (*The Life of a Fossil Hunter*) is also a good read. *Digging Dinosaurs* by John Horner provides a look at a modern dinosaur hunter and ties in with popular movies like *Jurassic Park*. There have also been a few fictional treatments of fossil hunters, based loosely on some of the experiences of nineteenth-century explorers.

Chapter 9

ROBBERS, COPYCATS, AND OPPORTUNISTS

FLYWAY ROBBERY

The robber stood on high ground and waited, now and then swiveling his head from side to side, scanning the scrubby, sunlit land in front of him. Soon, his patience was rewarded. A gold-and-brown shape lanced across his field of view, and the robber launched himself on an intercept course. His victim had little chance. The robber's bristly, strong hind legs scooped up his prey, his knifelike mouth part pierced its side. The animal struggled briefly, banging the robber's thick mustache of hair and bristles, but its efforts proved hopeless. The robber carried off his treasure to eat it slowly on his lofty perch, then dropped its empty shell and began carefully scanning the horizon again, looking for another meal.

Robbers

The hungry thief described above is commonly called a robber fly or assassin fly. His victim this time was a honeybee, but it could easily have been any insect of the proper size, including other flies—even one of its own kind. Robber flies are true flies belonging to the order Diptera: They have one pair of wings, a set of balancing organs called halteres, a large thorax, and a complex life cycle with several distinct stages. Unlike houseflies, fruit flies, and other flies you may be more familiar with, robber flies have mouth parts specially adapted for stabbing other insects rather than sucking the juices of flowers or animal wounds. You can see the anatomy of this assassin in figure 9.1.

Robber flies are common all over the world. In temperate climates, like most places in the United States, look for these fascinating insects on sunny days near the edges of woodlands and fields, perhaps near bodies of water. Many species also like the semiarid country of the American West. Look for insects darting out from the tips of twigs or edges of leaves and returning to their starting point. Robber flies, though they have large, impressive eyes, need to get a close look at objects before they know for sure that they're good to eat. They can be fooled by thistledown or a small pebble thrown into their territory.

An observer may be fooled by a robber fly's appearance, because it's not uncommon to see species that resemble bees or wasps, but the robber fly's prey-catching behavior, as described above, gives him away. Robber flies watch over a territory about 5 yards in circumference but catch most prey within a yard of their outpost. About 15 percent of their flights are successful.

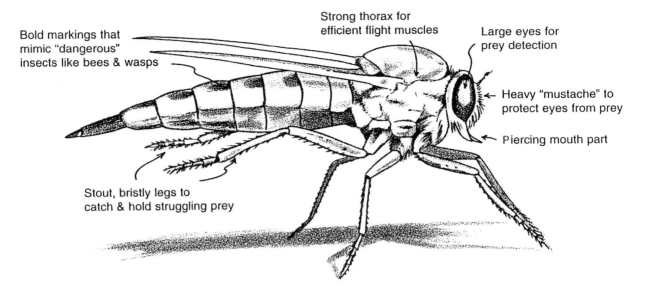

Bold markings that mimic "dangerous" insects like bees & wasps

Strong thorax for efficient flight muscles

Large eyes for prey detection

Heavy "mustache" to protect eyes from prey

Piercing mouth part

Stout, bristly legs to catch & hold struggling prey

Fig. 9.1. Anatomy of an assassin. The anatomy of a typical robber fly features a strongly muscled thorax for flight muscles; large, compound eyes; stout hind legs for catching prey; and a swordlike mouth part. Robber flies are often marked to look like bees or wasps.

Copycats

Robber flies may also be confused with other flies that look like bees and wasps. Bee flies and Hover flies look very convincing as bees, which apparently also fools birds and other predators into thinking they have a dangerous stinger. Like bees, and unlike robber flies, these flies suck the nectar of flowers. Flies as a group are second only to bees, wasps, and ants as nectar eaters and flower pollinators. Bee flies do eat other insects but only in their immature or larval forms. These larvae infest bee burrows and nests and eat their young. Others specialize in parasitizing spiders. Inchwormlike larvae can crawl along spider webs and burrow into spiders, slowly eating them from the inside out.

Opportunists

Like the jumping spiders described in chapter 5, male robber flies have to be careful when they court their mates, or they may get mistaken for supper. One solution is to approach a female when she's already eating, which is a common tactic for robber flies. Related species of predatory flies may bring lunch with them. The female picks the male with the best offerings and lets him mate. Various robber fly species apparently use wing and leg movements, hovering behavior, and high-pitched buzzing sounds to woo their mates, but the details for many species are incomplete. After mating, females lay their eggs in soil or sometimes on plants. Larvae overwinter in the soil, eventually changing into a resting, or pupal, stage and hatch out as adults when the weather warms.

One of the biggest mysteries regarding various species of flies is why so many of them resemble bees and wasps. In some cases, this may protect them from common predators. In others, the resemblance may let the fly get close to its intended victim without alarming it, but sometimes there seems to be no obvious connection between appearance and lifestyle. Chances are this is because this successful, but often annoying, group of animals (from a human's point of view) has been incompletely studied. There are many opportunities for new discovery for biologists who become interested in working with this large and diverse group of insects. Of course, many people have the attitude of poet Ogden Nash, who wrote:

God in His wisdom
Made the fly
And then forgot
To tell us why.

ACTIVITIES

Observing Robber Flies

If you have the opportunity to take a field trip near the edge of woods, fields, or water, keep an eye out for robber flies. They are large-bodied, bristly flies with long legs that perch on leaves or twigs. Although they may look beelike, their behavior is not.

Materials needed: notebook; pencil; hand lens

Directions:

1. Observe side-to-side head movements. Robber flies are always looking for a potential meal.

2. The fly will dart out toward some other insect or object drifting in the air, then return to its perch, with or without a victim. Try tossing a small twig across its field of view. How does it react?

3. If you see a robber fly catch another insect, observe how she handles it. She may fly up briefly so that she can get a better grip with her hind legs as she feeds.

4. If you've watched a fly for some time in the same location, go over to its perch and look for the remains of its victims on the ground. Record the number and kinds of insects eaten, if you can. Does your fly seem to have a food preference?

5. If you are lucky enough to see two flies mate, record the sequence of things both animals do. Listen for distinct buzzing. Look for wing or leg movements or the display of some prominent feature by the male.

📖 IN YOUR NOTEBOOK

Make specific notes concerning each of the steps you followed above, but also make general notes describing everything you actually see.

Drosophila: *The Scientist's Favorite Fly*

Drosophila melanogaster, the common fruit fly, has been one of the scientist's favorite tools for studying animal genetics since the 1940s. As a result, scientists have developed easy ways to grow them in the lab, providing a great opportunity to observe the life cycle of a typical fly.

Materials needed: fruit fly cultures; pencils and notebooks; magnifying lenses or dissecting scopes

Look at the fruit fly culture provided. You should be able to see the three major life stages of this insect: adult, larva, and pupa. The adults are easy to see crawling or flying about the container. Typical, "wild"-type flies have bright red eyes. Some variations, or mutants, have white eyes. Males tend to be smaller than females, and the rear end of their abdomen is rounded and darker. Pregnant females will have noticeably larger abdomens.

Adults lay eggs in the growth medium, which hatch into larvae. Larvae are white, wormlike creatures whose dark mouth hooks moving back and forth are usually the first things you notice when you look closely at the growth medium, which the larvae are eating. If the growth medium is tinted with food coloring, the white larvae will be easier to spot. Larvae go through three skin sheddings, called molts, so that they can increase in size. The newly hatched larva is called the first instar, the larva after its first molt is called the second instar, and so on.

The third instar eats its fill, then goes into a "resting" stage called the pupa. It is only resting in the sense that it is not moving. The resting stage is actually a stage of transformation where new genetic information is unlocked to produce the features of the adult fly. Look for darkish amber lozenge-shaped structures on the sides of the bottles above the growth medium. In pupae nearly ready to "hatch" into adults you can often see red eyes, two dark patches that will become the wings, and legs folded down the length of the animal.

📖 IN YOUR NOTEBOOK

Draw each of the stages of the fly life cycle. You may not see the eggs unless your teacher has prepared a demonstration, but you can sketch a larva, a pupa, and an adult. In the adult, label eyes, thorax, abdomen, wings, legs, and halteres.

In the larva, look for the dark mouth hooks at the front of the animal. Trailing back from these are a pair of sacklike salivary glands. If the mouth hooks are pulled out of the animal, the salivary glands come with them; scientists use the giant chromosomes of the cells of these glands to study insect genetics. You may also see a nerve chord running the length of the animal near the top surface and a winding digestive tract in the middle to rear end of the animal.

Try and find an older pupa and label eyes, wing pads, mouth parts, and legs.

Dance of the Housefly

If you want some entertainment on a warm summer day, take the time to watch a housefly dance. The movements they make when they land on a surface follow a regular pattern that could well be called "The Let's-Do-Lunch Shuffle." The following experiment will give you a chance to observe this dance and check out a fly's mealtime preferences.

Materials needed: houseflies; three small cups or containers; water; sugar; cotton-tipped swabs or tissue; an eyedropper; notebook; and pencil

The housefly has a long, coiled mouth part called a proboscis, which it lowers when it feeds on something. In this activity, pay special attention to what the proboscis is doing while the fly is walking.

1. Put equal amounts of water in three containers. In the first, dissolve one teaspoon of sugar; in the second, two teaspoons of sugar; and in the third, four teaspoons of sugar. Use different colored containers or label them so you can tell them apart.

2. Put a drop of the weakest sugar solution in the path of your wandering fly. Let her have a short taste, then wipe up the drop with a tissue or cotton-tipped swab. Describe the fly's behavior. How would this behavior help the fly find a lost food source?

3. Repeat the procedure with the other two sugar solutions. How does the behavior differ?

📖 IN YOUR NOTEBOOK

Describe in your notebook the kinds of movements you noticed the fly make as it walked over the surface. Also record your observations from the sugar experiment.

Flies' taste receptors are located in their feet. How does this fact help explain why flies move as they do when walking over a surface?

LET THE FLIES TEACH

Declare a truce! Hang up the fly swatters for a few days and let the flies give a few lessons on adaptability, maneuverability, and effective resource exploitation. Translation: They do some neat things. Sure, flies help spoil food and spread disease, but they also are the initial step in waste recycling. Without them we'd be up to our necks in . . . unpleasant stuff.

About one out of four of all the insects you meet in temperate climates are flies. They are second only to the beetle in number of species. They belong to the order Diptera, which means "two-winged." What would have been a second pair of wings in more primitive insects, like dragonflies, has evolved into a pair of balancing organs called halteres. The origins of halteres were demonstrated nicely by a mutant form of *Drosophila,* whose halteres reverted back to a winglike structure.

Three suborders of flies, listed from primitive to complex, display the diversity of flies: the Thread-horned flies (Nematocera), the Short-horned flies (Brachycera), and the Higher flies (Cyclorrhapha). The Thread-horned flies include gnats, midges, crane flies, and mosquitoes. They tend to be delicate, long of body and antenna, and their larvae are often aquatic. The Short-horned flies include our friend the robber fly, bee flies, horseflies, and other heavy-bodied, sometimes showy flies. Higher flies are a large group that includes houseflies, fruit flies, blowflies, deerflies, and the colorful bluebottle flies.

Flies owe their success in life to three things: their mouth parts, their flying ability, and the diversity of their larval stages. Although mainly suited for liquid feeding, fly mouth parts have been modified for sucking, lapping, and piercing (as in robber flies). The flies' two pairs of wings, flapped by powerful thorax muscles, combined with the gyroscopic functions of the halteres, give them amazing maneuverability, which anyone who has seen them land upside down on ceilings can testify to. Lastly, their larvae feed in entirely different ways and habitats than adults, so they don't compete for resources. Larvae survive in a wide range of moist microhabitats, from rotting fruit to cow dung, and pupae are tough and impermeable, able to ride out shifts in temperature and moisture.

Notes on the Student Activities

Observing Robber Flies

Depending on the number and kind of field trips you can take, you might want to combine the observation of robber flies with activities suggested in other chapters, such as "Pond Dragons" (chapter 7) or "The Milkweed Universe" (chapter 15). This activity could also form the nucleus of a science project or outside activity for a budding naturalist. Donald W. Stokes's *A Guide to Observing Insect Lives* has a chapter on both robber flies and syrphid flies, which are beelike nectar feeders.

Drosophila: The Scientist's Favorite Fly

This is a good way of observing the life cycle of flies without a lot of mess and bother. Most likely you encountered this fly during your own school experience. Living cultures and supplies may be ordered from several supply houses. I'm most familiar with Carolina Biological Supply (main offices: 2700 York Rd., Burlington, NC 27215). Individual cultures are about $5. A student kit (which would probably serve a whole class, if you allow enough time to subculture your flies) will provide you with everything else you need for about $30 (1995 prices).

If your budget is really tight, or you want to be more enterprising and study local creatures, here is an old recipe for making fly cultures from Cream of Wheat cereal:

1. Measure out 3¼ cups water, 4 ounces of molasses, and 3½ ounces of Cream of Wheat.

2. Add the molasses to two-thirds of the water; bring to a boil.

3. Mix the Cream of Wheat with the remaining third of cold water and add this to the boiling mixture. Continue to stir, and cook for 5 minutes after boiling begins.

4. Pour the medium into sterilized bottles and tilt the bottles as they cool (to increase the surface area of the growth medium). Stopper the bottles with cotton while still hot to prevent contamination by mold. When the cultures are cool, remove the stopper, add a strip or two of paper towels to serve as perches for the flies, and place the unstoppered bottle near a source of fruit flies for an hour or so.

It is hoped that the flies will have laid some eggs there, or you may even be able to trap a few when you restopper the bottle. If you have trouble with mold, you can paint the surface of the culture with 95% alcohol or a solution of 1 part carbolic acid and 8 parts water (with the adult flies removed).

Drawing the different stages of the life cycle will make students look carefully at these little creatures. Provide 10X magnifying glasses, if possible, or have a dissecting scope available for a demonstration. Figure 9.2 is a sketch of the life cycle for your reference.

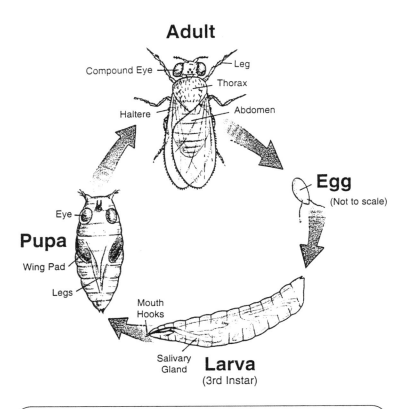

Fig. 9.2. *Drosophila* life cycle. The *Drosophila* life cycle is typical of insects with complete metamorphosis. The egg hatches into a larva, which molts several times before forming a pupa. The pupa usually survives in soil while its tissues reorganize into the adult form. Adults mate and lay eggs to complete the cycle.

Dance of the Housefly

Here's where those pesky flies in the classroom come in handy. You may want to lure some flies ahead of time with a bowl of sugar water placed on a stiff cardboard surface or, better yet, a piece of plexiglass. Trap the flies with a transparent plastic cake cover, then startle them long enough to remove the bowl (this may take two people and some practice). Assuming the cake cover is expendable, you can poke an eyedropper-sized hole in the top near an edge with a hot screwdriver. Drip some sugar solution through the hole. When the fly has had a taste, slide the plexiglass so that it is outside the rim of the cover and wipe away the sample. Observe the fly's behavior, then slide the plexiglass back to its original position for the next drop. If you use plexiglass you could also position it between supports so that you could see the fly's feet and proboscis from beneath.

Observe with the students that flies tend to walk in jerky, short, straight lines with their probosci extended periodically like little pile drivers. When a food source is removed, the fly gets agitated and tends to move in ever-widening circles. This maximizes the fly's chances of finding the lost food, although the fly hasn't reasoned this out. It is trial-and-error behavior that has been hard-wired into the fly's brain over millions of years of evolution. Students should come away from the lesson understanding that the circle dances get more frenetic the sweeter the food source. When a fly's foot touches a food source it will orient toward that foot and extend its proboscis.

Notes on the References

Many good references on insects abound. *The Encyclopedia of Insects*, published by Facts on File and edited by Christopher O'Toole, is well illustrated and seems to bridge the gap between too simplistic and too technical discussions. *The Natural History of Flies* by Harold Oldroyd gets down more to the scientific nitty-gritty of fly memorabilia, but it is still quite readable.

The chapter on flies in *Life on a Little Known Planet* by Howard Ensign Evans is very entertaining as is the small paperback *To Know a Fly* by Vincent Dethier. The latter book also gives a glimpse of what it would be like to be an entomologist specializing in flies. Sue Hubbell's recent book, *Broadsides from the Other Orders*, has three entertaining chapters on the Diptera: Midges & Gnats, The Blackflies, and Syrphid Flies.

A Guide to Observing Insect Lives was mentioned earlier—a good book to have on your shelf for background on insect behavior you might see in the field. *How to Know the Immature Insects* by H. F. Chu is a field guide to larval and pupal stages of insects you might encounter. (Most regular insect keys rely on adult appearance.)

Part III

Animal Communication

SPIDERS SAY THE DARNDEST THINGS

SPIDER TALK

Spiders don't talk, you say? Of course not. They do, however, have ways to send messages to each other. If you know what to look for, you can "listen in."

Some of the easiest spiders to find and study are "jumping spiders." You have probably seen them but may not have known what they are called. Jumping spiders hunt by day, and you can often find them on the side of your house or under larger rocks in the garden. When you get close to them, they will turn quickly toward you. If you get too close, they may hop away. Some can jump about 25 times their body length.

Jumping spiders move with quick, jerky motions, but you can usually catch them pretty easily with a bottle, as long as they are on a flat area where they can't scoot into a crack. Capture spiders carefully. Although jumping spiders rarely bite people and their venom is not harmful, some people may be more sensitive to their bites than others. When you catch one, take a close look. They are rather short, fat spiders with one pair of legs that are heavier and longer than the rest. A common black-and-white one called *Phidippus* (fie DIP us) has a large first pair of legs with tufts of white hair and scales on top. Look at its face, and you will see two large eyes looking back at you. Look even closer, and you may see six more eyes. There are two pairs of smaller ones just to the outside of the large pair. There is another pair near the middle of the head (see fig. 10.1). Now you know why *Phidippus* can see you so well! *Phidippus* also has bright green mouth parts tipped with red fangs that it uses to kill bugs for its lunch.

You can learn how *Phidippus* or another jumping spider "talks" if you make one your pet. Keep it in a clear bottle or a clear plastic box. If you don't need the box for other things, you can have an adult cut a small hole in the top with a hot knife and tape a piece of screen over it to let air in. You can feed your spider many kinds of live bugs about its own size or smaller. (Hint: You can put the box and spider in the refrigerator for 5 or 10 minutes to slow the spider down when you put the bugs in.) Watch the spider stalk the bug and then jump on it quickly when it gets close enough.

Find a small mirror that you can place near the spider. What does the spider do? Most likely it will raise up its large pair of legs and stand on tiptoes. It thinks it's seeing another spider, and it's "saying" something like, "I'm large and dangerous—you had better watch out." If you leave the mirror near the spider's box, it will often sit and "posture" in front of it.

This article originally appeared in *Highlights for Children*. Used by permission of Highlights for Children, Inc. Columbus, Ohio. Copyrighted material.

A

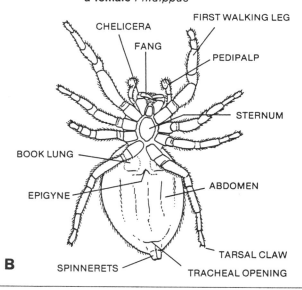

**Ventral (belly) side of
a female** *Phidippus*

CHELICERA

FANG

FIRST WALKING LEG

PEDIPALP

STERNUM

BOOK LUNG

EPIGYNE

ABDOMEN

B

SPINNERETS

TARSAL CLAW

TRACHEAL OPENING

Fig. 10.1. (*A*) *Phidippus.* (*B*) The anatomy of *Phidippus* is similar to other spiders except for the large principal eyes and the extra-long first pair of walking legs, both characteristics of jumping spiders. Pedipalps are large, often "showy" appendages that shouldn't be confused with legs. Reprinted from *Dinosaurs in the Garden,* courtesy Plexus Publishing, Inc., Medford, NJ.

If you put two jumping spiders together, one of several things may happen. If they are different kinds, they both will raise their legs and try to threaten each other. The smaller one will eventually turn and run. The larger one will stalk it and attack if there is no place to escape. If they are the same kind of jumping spiders and of the same sex, you may see very similar behavior. But if you have a male and a female of the same kind, you may get to see a courtship dance.

Males start off courtship by raising their long legs. But instead of raising their legs in response, the females sit quietly and hunch close to the ground. If the female remains quiet, the male may then move back and forth in front of her, gradually getting closer. If you made a tracing of his path, it would be a zigzagging line with shorter and shorter zigzags as he got closer to the female. The male may also wave his legs or his palps. The palps are leglike extensions near the mouth that help him to catch prey. They also help him smell and taste. They are a lot like your hands and nose and tongue all rolled into one.

Males may also "talk" to females by showing colorful spots on their bodies. These become visible when they raise their legs or abdomens. One kind of *Phidippus* has a red spot on his forehead that "says" he is a male. If the male gets close enough, he will touch and stroke the female with his palps. The message here is "It's OK, I'm a friend." If the male doesn't talk plainly and correctly at this point, he's in trouble. He could get eaten. If all is well, however, the female remains quiet and the male will crawl on top and use his palps to fertilize her eggs. The male then climbs down and leaves quickly.

If you keep your spider long enough, it will probably spin a small nest in the corner of its container. It will use this as a home base from which it will make hunting trips when you provide insects. A female may lay her eggs there and, if you're lucky, you may see spiderlings emerge in a few weeks. They are born already knowing what you have learned only a little about: spider talk.

ACTIVITIES

Making a "Spider Arena"

Watching spider behavior will be easier with an enclosed space that you can control.

Materials needed: a piece of heavy acetate approximately 8 x 24 inches; clear tape; heavy cardboard, wood or masonite base about 12 inches square; a piece of picture Plexiglass 12 inches square; white paper ruled at least 9 inches square; a small mirror; modeling clay; metric ruler

Directions:

1. With pencil or pen, rule your paper clearly in square centimeters. Tape this paper to the center of the piece of cardboard, wood, or masonite base. The ruled paper will allow you to estimate the distance between spiders or between spider and prey. Graph paper may also be used as long as you know how big each square is.

2. Bend the acetate in the shape of a cylinder and tape the edges securely together with clear tape. Center the acetate cylinder over the ruled paper.

3. With a little modeling clay create a base to hold the mirror. This can be placed inside or outside the cylinder or handheld, depending on how your spider cooperates.

4. When the spiders are in place, position the glass on top of the acetate cylinder.

You are now the proud creator of a spider arena. It should look something like that shown in figure 10.2.

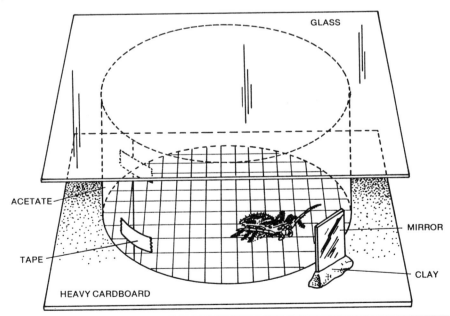

Fig. 10.2. A spider arena. Reprinted from *Dinosaurs in the Garden,* courtesy Plexus Publishing, Inc., Medford, NJ.

From *Explorations in Backyard Biology.* © 1996. Teacher Ideas Press. (800) 237-6124.

Observing Spider Behavior

Materials needed: your naturalist's notebook; 3-x-5 inch cards or paper; regular and colored pencils; jumping spider(s); spider arena; mirror

Directions:

♦ Place a jumping spider in your arena. Gradually move the mirror closer to the spider until she reacts to it.

♦ Answer the following questions in your notebook:

1. Does the spider turn to face the mirror?

2. How close did the mirror have to be for this to happen?

3. Does the spider raise a pair of its legs? If so, which pair?

4. How are the parts of the spider's body positioned? For example, is the abdomen in line with the cephalothorax (head-trunk) or cocked to one side?

5. What happens if you move the mirror farther away?

6. What happens if you move it closer?

Leaving the mirror in one position, describe what the spider does during a 10-minute period. Using the centimeter grid of the floor of the arena as a guide, record how far and in what directions the spider moves.

Try and discover what part of the spider's reflection it is responding to. Look at the spider "eye to eye." What do you see? Two large eyes, two raised legs, perhaps white or colored markings on the head or front of the abdomen, and/or colored fangs? On a 3-x-5-inch card or piece of paper make a simple drawing, in color, of your spider's appearance. It will have to be fairly small, nearly spider size. For *Phidippus* the picture might look like that shown in figure 10.3.

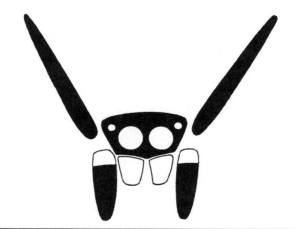

Fig. 10.3. A *Phidippus* model. A spider's-eye view of another spider: Raised legs, eyes, colored patches on pedipalps, head, or abdomen, and fangs are all things another spider might respond to.

Mount your drawing on a piece of modeling clay, as you did with the mirror. Show the drawing to the spider. Does she respond like she did to the mirror image? If so, try the following experiment. Make new drawings just like the first, but leave out one element at a time. For example, make one drawing without the eyes and test your spider with it. Does she still respond? Test her at least five separate times and record her response in each case.

In the next drawing remove the fangs and test in a similar manner. Repeat until all features are removed.

Did the spider respond better to one feature than another? If so, which one? Did she respond to that feature as well as to the complete drawing or to her image in the mirror? Did some combination of features work better at getting a response than any single feature alone? Why do you think it is important for jumping spiders to be able to recognize their own kind in nature?

Spiders and Their Prey

In this experiment you will be observing how a spider stalks its prey. The spider must first recognize that a snack is nearby, then it must stalk the animal, attack and kill it, and finally eat it. You may need to watch the behavior once to get an idea of the process, then carefully look for details the next time through.

Materials needed: In addition to the materials listed previously, you'll need a small insect about the spider's size and a stopwatch.

Directions:

♦ Read through all the directions before starting, because once you put spider and prey together, things may happen quickly.

♦ Place the spider at one edge of the arena and the prey on the opposite edge. Place the cover on top of the acetate cylinder.

♦ In your notebook answer the following questions:

1. How far were spider and prey apart when you put them in the arena?

2. How far apart were they when the spider turned toward the prey?

3. Describe the spider's behavior as it approached the prey.

4. How close was it when it made a leap to catch the prey?

5. Describe the spider's feeding behavior as best you can.

Spider-to-Spider Interactions

Materials needed: spider arena; two spiders; your naturalist's notebook

Directions:

♦ If you have collected several individuals of the same species, try observing the behavior of pairs of spiders. Jumping spider females are larger than their male counterparts and usually have an abdomen that's as large or larger than their cephalothorax (see fig. 10.4). Be aware that two spiders of the same sex placed together are apt to "fight to the death" unless there is room for one to escape. Opposite-sex pairing may result in a similar outcome unless males dance the proper dance, but if you can observe this behavior it's quite fascinating.

Fig. 10.4. Spiders paired off in the arena. A female *Phidippus* (left) observes the display of a male in a spider arena. Reprinted from *Dinosaurs in the Garden,* courtesy Plexus Publishing, Inc., Medford, NJ.

In your notebook make two columns. Write Spider #1 at the top of one colunm and Spider #2 at the top of the other. If you know they are different sexes, label one heading Female and one Male.

Describe what happens in the order it occurs in the proper column. If the spider in the left column does something before the one in the right column, the description for the left spider's behavior should be higher on the page than the description for the right spider's behavior. If the spiders do something at the same time, record what happens in the proper columns side by side.

LOOKING AT SPIDER BEHAVIOR

A Spider Review

Spiders are everywhere! And whether you appreciate that or not, it's very good that they're abundant because they keep insects from taking over. At least 30,000 spiders possess scientific names and descriptions, but many more crawl and spin their webs as yet undiscovered.

Spiders, like insects, are arthropods sporting segmented, external skeletons, but they walk on eight legs instead of the insect's six. Spiders have two-part body designs instead of the insect's three-part model. The spider's combined head and trunk, called the cephalothorax, joins with the abdomen via a thin stalk called the pedicel. Spiders possess no wings or antennae, but manipulate prey with unique mouth parts called pedipalps. Males also use them in place of a penis for sperm transfer.

Spiders might also be described as the creatures who exploited silk for nearly everything: prey capture, nest building, parachutes, drag lines, sperm cups, and more! Spider's silk, pound for pound, is stronger than steel. It's been used for crosshairs in gun sites and may have a future in clothing and other human applications. Spider silk flows through tiny spigots at the rear of the abdomen called spinnerets. One spider may spin several different silks depending on the task at hand.

As a rule, spiders are not keen-sighted. Web spinners in particular rely on their ability to sense vibrations and interpret whether they are being courted or are just having guests for dinner. The spider stars of this chapter, however, peer through some of the best eyes in the animal kingdom for their size. Jumping spiders are wandering hunters perhaps as visually oriented as our own species.

A Jumping Family

The Salticidae family of spiders, to which jumping spiders belong, contains more species (at least 4,000) than any other spider family. Most species are tropical, but there are undoubtedly many kinds where you live, because jumping spiders have been found from intertidal areas to 6,000 meters above sea level on Mount Everest. Only Antarctica seems inhospitable to these endearing little predators.

"Endearing? Hah!" I can hear many of you say, but it's true. Jumping spiders, with their large pair of eyes in front, bushy facial hairs, and inquisitive look, will surely remind you of lemurs or tarsiers after awhile—especially while their iridescent fangs are neatly tucked beneath them. Small, gray, and white-striped varieties, often referred to as zebra spiders (*Salticus scenicus*), are common in most areas, and can be handled with no fear of biting because their fangs are too small to break the skin. A husband-and-wife team of researchers, the Peckhams, even trained jumping spiders to jump onto their hands for food and to jump from finger to finger in ever-increasing distances up to 8 inches.

Larger species in the genus *Phidippus*, black with white markings on the abdomen, could possibly bite if provoked, but are easily captured in bottles or petri dishes and can be handled with few problems by a willing teacher. Note that all spiders have venom, with a few species carrying seriously toxic kinds, so take care in handling unknown varieties.

Because the behavior of *Phidippus sp.* was described in the student article, and because they are easy to see, you may want to set up a demonstration of behavior with one of these, then let students work directly with the zebra jumpers, *Salticus scenicus*, if some are available (see fig. 10.5). Alternately, you may wish to do all the spider handling and simply let students manipulate what the spiders see and make observations of behavior. As mentioned in the student article, you can slow down spiders for handling by placing them in a refrigerator for a minute or two or cooling their container in an ice bath.

Notes on the Student Activities

Making a Spider Arena

You or your students can create the spider arena out of materials close at hand. Fashion the base out of any smooth cardboard or use a sheet of artist's illustration board and cut to a convenient size—perhaps 10 x 12 inches or so. The glass for the top can be scavenged from an old picture frame. For the enclosure buy clear (not frosted) acetate from a hobby shop or artist's supply store. It should be heavy enough to support the weight of the picture glass. Ask to see the different thicknesses of acetate and select one that feels stiff enough to do the job. A piece 25 inches long can be bent into a cylinder about 8 inches in diameter, which would fit the 10-x-12-inch base nicely. (Just divide your circumference— the length of the acetate sheet—by pi— 3.14—to figure the diameter of the finished cylinder.) The cylinder only needs to be 3 or 4 inches high so, depending on the width of the acetate, you could get several cylinders out of one 25-inch length. Tape the edges of the cylinder together with clear tape. Rule the grid pattern on the base and your arena is complete.

Fig. 10.5. *Salticus scenicus* **or the jumping spider.** A small jumping spider, *Salticus scenicus*, is called the zebra jumper because of its black-and-white color pattern. This one is posing on a sprig of juniper (see also fig. 6.1). Reprinted from *Dinosaurs in the Garden*, courtesy Plexus Publishing, Inc., Medford, NJ.

Observing Spider Behavior

One of the most important skills in science is to make careful, critical observations. Students will need help on deciding what to look for. You may wish to create a checklist of things to watch for and discuss this list with students before they begin to observe the spiders. Also, have students plan and create a chart for themselves in their notebooks to fill in when they actually make observations. If this is done a day prior to the observations, you can make copies of the agreed-upon form to hand out to all students.

Spiders will face the mirror and typically raise their first (long) pair of legs in a threat display. Often the abdomen will be cocked at an angle to the head-trunk. Details may vary between species. Once the mirror is out of visual range (about 30 to 40 centimeters), the spider may lose interest. If the mirror is moved closer, the spider will either flee or attack—probably the former, as its image will appear larger in the mirror.

The technique used in drawing the simplified spider image is similar to what behavioral scientists do when trying to discover what stimuli initiate certain behaviors. You may want to experiment with this before having the kids try, to see how small and how detailed the drawings need to be to get a response. You could also try photocopying figure 10.3 several times at a reduction and white out different elements on the different copies. For most species the raised leg shapes will be critical, but other factors may be important, too. You could be charting new scientific territory!

Spiders and Their Prey

Typically, *Phidippus* begin stalking prey at 30 to 40 centimeters once they move into visual range. The final leap will span 1 to 5 centimeters. The prey is impaled with the fangs, felt with the pedipalps, and held by the jaws (chelicerae). Venom squirts from fangs into the victim to paralyze it. Digestive enzymes are forced from the spider's mouth into the prey. This liquifies the prey so the spider can pump a liquid meal into its own stomach. Details are impressive when seen through a dissecting microscope or hand lens.

Spider-to-Spider Interactions

Courtship details are as described in the student article. Details of what happens when another spider becomes prey are described above.

John Crompton, in *The Spider* describes the Peckhams' work with zebra jumpers. This research team put half a dozen zebra jumpers of each sex in a large box. With most spiders this would be a free-for-all with heavy casualties, but apparently the jumpers sorted things out because by morning the sexes had paired and created six web tents spaced about the enclosure. If you can create such a spider nursery, students could make daily observations until spiderlings hatch.

Notes on the References

The Golden Book *Spiders and Their Kin* by Herbert W. Levi and Lorna R. Levi will be the easiest book for students to use. It is a good general key with lots of pictures, like the other books in that series. *How to Know the Spiders* by B. J. Kaston is the best book for spider identification but will require more teacher assistance. *The Spider* by John Crompton is a fairly easy read with lots of anecdotal information on a variety of spider groups. Crompton also talks about some of the work of the Peckhams.

The World of Spiders by W. S. Bristowe describes interesting behavioral studies with spiders dating from the 1950s. Rod and Ken Preston-Mafham's *Spiders of the World*, on the other hand, is a fairly recent (1984) Facts on File book with lots of good color photos.

Rainer F. Foelix's *Biology of Spiders*, translated from the German, is the best all-around reference on spider biology. It's fairly technical, but good if you get interested in the subject.

I've included the original references on the 1889 work by the Peckhams, but the journals may be hard to locate unless you're near a good college library.

Chapter 10 in my *Dinosaurs in the Garden* goes into more detail on both the feeding and courting behavior of *Phidippus* and provides a general background on spider anatomy, collection, and evolution.

Chapter 11

SNEAKY CREATURES

WHAT YOU SEE IS WHAT I'M NOT

Although animals may not give long, windy speeches, they do send a lot of messages. What they can't say in words they express with colors, designs, motion, odors, light, and sound. When a female moth releases her perfumes she's saying, "Yoo-hoo, I'm over here" to a male moth of the same species. However, a female moth would be in big trouble if a bat could smell her perfume, too, and therefore know that a snack was fluttering nearby. Thus, some of the messages animals send are meant to confuse their enemies or mislead potential prey. It turns out there are many ways to say "What you see is what I'm not."

"I'm not really here" is a common misleading message used by animals who look like their surroundings. The caterpillars of geometrid moths, for example, often look just like the twigs they nibble on the branches of trees (see fig. 11.1). When threatened, they stop the looping traveling technique that gave them their common name of inchworm and remain still, with their rear legs firmly grabbing a branch and their front end sticking up like a very uninteresting twig. There are also adult moths and tree frogs that look like lichen-covered tree trunks, spiders that look like flower parts so they don't scare off their lunch, and leaf-hopping insects that look like leaves.

Other animal messages are even more cleverly misleading. The larva of the tortoise shell beetle has a long, forked tail on which it piles old, shed skins and excrement (see chapter 14, "Of Beetles and Bindweed"). The beetle larva holds this dark mass over its body like an umbrella, saying "I'm just a piece of junk" to birds that might be passing overhead.

Female fireflies blink their lights in a certain pattern to attract males of their species. Some species of fireflies, however, make a living by copying the signals of other species so they can eat the males that show up. "Watch my blinks," they might be saying. "I'm a mate."

In a somewhat similar fashion certain bolas spiders say "I smell like your mate. Come see." These spiders sit in their webs and give off chemicals that smell just like the scents that female moths use to tell males where they are located. When the unlucky male arrives, the spider flicks out a silk line with a sticky glob on the end that tangles up the moth and allows the spider to inject her poison.

A kind of assassin bug lives in the nest of certain termites. Usually, soldier termites fight off their enemies by squirting gummy liquids that stop their attacks. The assassin bug, however, has some goo of his own produced by his antennae. He uses this material to paste pieces of the nest to his body so that he looks like and smells like "home." The termites may walk all over the assassin bug before he eats one of them, saying, "Don't worry, I'm just part of the nest."

109

Fig. 11.1. An inchworm. This "inchworm," really the larva of a moth, looks just like a twig when it's resting.

stalked by jumping spiders. These spiders, unlike web-weaving spiders, have very good eyesight and stalk their prey like cats (see chapters 6 and 10). When jumping spiders meet one another, they raise their legs in a kind of "threat-greeting." "This is my territory," they might be saying. "Unless you're a female of my species, get lost." Snowberry flies and some tephritid flies have striped markings on their wings. When the wings are raised and flapped a few times they look very much like the leg-waving behavior of jumping spiders. Thus, jumping spiders think they are meeting a potential rival or a mate. By the time the spider raises his own legs in response to the message "I'm another spider, be careful," the fly is saying "Bye, bye."

Next time you're out in the garden, try intercepting a few animal messages. Just make sure you watch carefully—and don't believe everything you see.

Many brightly colored animals are advertising "I'm not good to eat" or "Watch out! I'm dangerous." The black-and-orange monarch butterfly feeds on milkweed plants, which contain chemicals poisonous to most creatures (see chapter 15, "The Milkweed Universe"). If a young bird eats one monarch he will throw up and quickly learn the message of this butterfly's colors. The viceroy butterfly doesn't feed on milkweed and, thus, could be eaten by birds because he is so easily seen, but, because he looks very similar to the monarch, predators avoid him, too. The viceroy is saying "I look like something that gave you a stomach ache." What do you think the gopher snake in figure 11.2 is saying?

A few species of flies fool their predators in an unusual way. Flies are often

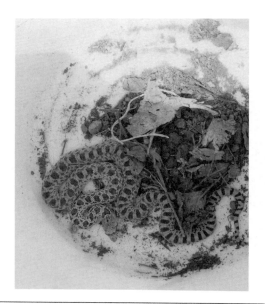

Fig. 11.2. A gopher snake. This nonpoisonous gopher snake hisses loudly when disturbed and may even flatten its head and shake its tail. What message is it trying to send?

ACTIVITY

Alien Lifestyles

Imagine a world very similar to Earth but filled with a whole new set of plants and animals. Because there are only so many ways to making a living—that is, to grow, eat, avoid enemies, mate, and reproduce—we can expect that these strange animals would interact much like creatures on our planet.

For example, let's consider a beast called a Slobber. He, or she, is not too unlike a sloth, a mammal that hangs from jungle tree limbs by a long, strong tail. The Slobber is blind and catches his insect meals by, well . . . slobbering. With large, down-turned ears and sensory whiskers, the Slobber is good at hearing and sensing the movements of insects as they visit nearby flowers. Using the flower's scent as a guide, the Slobber dangles long strands of sticky mucus that wrap around the insects. When the Slobber reels these sticky threads back to his mouth, dinner is served.

One of the Slobber's natural enemies is a slender, dark-haired predator called the Hiri-Hiri. The Hiri-Hiri lies on branches and dangles its long tail like a jungle vine. When some animal, like a Slobber, ventures too close, the Hiri-Hiri strangles him with his strong tail.

📖 IN YOUR NOTEBOOK

Try drawing a picture of the Slobber and the Hiri-Hiri. Your teacher may show you pictures of a sloth and other jungle creatures to give you an idea of animal forms, but you are free to imagine all the details of these creatures for yourself.

Answer these questions in your notebook:

1. Based on the description of the Slobber, in what ways might it send the message "I'm not really here"?

2. Assume the Hiri-Hiri has scent glands that can send chemical messages to the Slobber. What might these messages be?

3. How is the Hiri-Hiri's method of getting a meal similar to that of the assassin bug?

4. If the Slobber had bold yellow and orange colors that made it stand out, what message might you guess it was sending to the Hiri-Hiri?

Continued on next page.

IN YOUR NOTEBOOK (continued)

The Slobber and the Hiri-Hiri were invented by a scientist/writer named Dougal Dixon who also creates animated films. They appeared in his book *After Man*: *A Zoology of the Future*. Using principles of ecology and evolution, Dixon imagined how animals and plants might evolve from existing ones in the next 50 million years if human beings became extinct. If you look up this book, you can compare your drawings with the ones there. Your teacher may also show you my versions of the Slobber and Hiri-Hiri. Do they look anything like yours?

THE SLOBBER AND THE HIRI-HIRI

Imagining Other Times and Other Ecologies

In 1981 Dougal Dixon wrote a delightful book called *After Man: A Zoology of the Future*. He asked and answered the question What might the natural world look like in 50 million years if human beings became extinct today? He constructed this future world by extrapolating geological changes like continental drift and postulating how these changes would, in turn, affect climate and habitats. Then, starting with the animals and plants of the modern world, he showed how the mechanisms of natural selection and genetic drift might act on them to produce his future zoology. The detailed introduction to the book shows how these forces acted in the past to produce the world we're familiar with today.

Two of his future creatures are the Slobber and the Hiri-Hiri. Figures 11.3 and 11.4 show my interpretations for these beasts. Both of these animals live in a tropical forest that arose as the continent of Australia continued its slow drift north and even tually collided with mainland Asia. The collision, 40 million years in our future, raised a chain of mountains that helped keep Australia relatively isolated from many mainland species. Thus, the Slobber and the Hiri-Hiri are descended from marsupial mammals and nurse their young in an abdominal pouch like a kangaroo.

Fig. 11.3. The slobber. Author's version of a Slobber.

Fig. 11.4. The Hiri-Hiri. Author's version of a Hiri-Hiri.

The Slobber is a kind of sloth that hangs upside down from trees and creepers. It is blind and gets its name from its technique of catching flower-visiting insects by trapping them in long strands of sticky mucus that dangle from its mouth. The Slobber possesses large, down-turned ears and sensory whiskers that tell it when to drop its mucus. It aims at a flower's scent. Parasitic algae invade its spiral-tufted fur, making it look like just another creeper as long as the Slobber keeps still.

The Hiri-Hiri is a predator descended from the Tasmanian devil, a marsupial bearlike creature. It lies in wait on low branches, dangling its tail like a vine. When an animal comes too close, the Hiri-Hiri grabs and strangles it with its strong tail.

Notes on the Student Activity

Have fun with this project! Join in on the drawings! The idea is to show that interactive strategies of animals and plants are a function of their biology and the way that biology deals with the physical environment. Workable strategies have been repeated over millions of years with millions of species. If the devil is in the details, as someone once said, so is the fascination, because similar themes display endless, unique variations. Don't forget to address the questions in the student activity section to which the students responded:

1. Make a list of student responses, without being critical at this point so that ideas flow freely. Try and keep students focused on the idea that they are looking for ways the Slobber might camouflage himself. Possibilities: The Slobber might look like a tree limb or a vine. It might have blotchy coloration to break up its outline. If it specialized in the insects that visited a single species of flower, it might look like those flowers in some way, like certain spiders today that possess their host flower's bright colors.

2. The messages should attract the Slobber in some way. It might be the same message the bolas spiders give to moths: "I smell like your mate. Come see." The Hiri-Hiri might smell like the Slobber's favorite flowers, attracting it to a good feeding ground.

3. Like the assassin bug, the Hiri-Hiri looks like part of the tree he's resting in.

4. The bright colors, as with the example of the monarch and the viceroy butterflies, usually serve as a warning to predators. One of the Hiri-Hiri's potential prey is probably a bad-tasting yellow and orange something. (It might even be a yellow-orange Slobber with poisonous spit.)

Notes on the References

Two other books of Dougal Dixon's continue with the theme of *After Man*. *The New Dinosaurs: An Alternative Evolution* explores an alternate future for the dinosaurs, very successful creatures that dominated Earth's biota for 160 million years before all became extinct (except for birds and their kin) 65 million years ago. *Man After Man: An Anthropology of the Future* looks at what impact time and nature might have on *Homo sapiens*.

Chapter 12

WHAT THE BIRDS SAY

ENCOUNTER AT THE BIRD FEEDER

Eugene Scheifflin loved Shakespeare. Most people who love a particular writer would be content to read that writer's works, but Scheifflin wanted to do more. To honor his favorite playwright he decided to import all the birds mentioned in his plays to America. In 1890 and 1891 Scheifflin released 100 starlings into Central Park in New York City. Today, millions of these hardy, adaptable birds squawk and fly about the country as a most unusual living salute to a great artist (see fig. 12.1). Chances are, some of them visit your bird feeder. If you watch them long enough, they'll tell you a lot about how birds communicate, sometimes without making a sound.

The Starling: Not Just Another Bird

At first glance, starlings may look like a lot of other blackbirds. Their appearance also varies significantly with age, sex, and time of year. Newly hatched birds are mouse-brown with dark bills until the fall molt, when new feathers are tipped with white, giving them a speckled appearance. Males have the smallest "spots," and they disappear first during winter so that by breeding time in the spring they are nearly gone. Adult females, first-year males, and

Fig. 12.1. The common starling (*Sturnis vulgaris*) in its fall plumage. In the fall, the wing tips of starling feathers are white, giving the birds a speckled appearance. At other seasons, their bodies are mostly black with some green and purple iridescence on the neck and back. Reprinted from *Dinosaurs in the Garden*, courtesy Plexus Publishing, Inc., Medford, NJ.

116

first-year females appear progressively more spotted. As breeding time nears, a starling's legs get redder and the bill changes from dark brown to yellow. A male's bill becomes brighter yellow than the female's and is steel blue at the base, in contrast to the female's pink bill base. A male's eyes tend to be all dark, whereas a female's eyes sport a pale ring around the edge (see fig. 12.2). Mature males strut about in a basic uniform of black feathers that shimmer with green and blue iridescence around the neck.

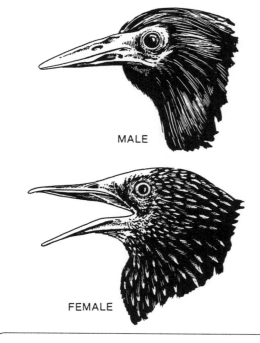

MALE

FEMALE

Fig. 12.2. Sexual differences in starlings. You can often tell males from females by looking at the eyes. Females have a pale ring at the margins of the eye, but males do not. As breeding time approaches a male's bill turns bright yellow and is steel blue at the base. Female bills are paler yellow with a pink base. Reprinted from *Dinosaurs in the Garden,* courtesy Plexus Publishing, Inc., Medford, NJ.

Let's Communicate

Although you will see individual starlings from time to time, they are social birds that sometimes flock in huge numbers. In this regard they are not unlike red-winged blackbirds and grackles, which may mob your bird feeder at the same time. Social animals need ways to communicate with each other so they can coexist with minimal friction. With a little patience you can discover their signals as you watch their antics at the feeder.

Look for individuals that puff out their feathers and fix a glaring stare on another bird (see fig. 12.3). Such an individual may also tilt his or her head and bill upward and raise the feathers on the crown of its head. The bird that receives these signals from another may crouch submissively or begin wiping its beak on the wire or branch on which it's sitting. This latter behavior during feeding may signal that a bird is finished eating and need no longer be considered a competitor.

Two birds may get more actively aggressive during a "fly up" (see fig. 12.4). They will fly up to a height of a yard or two, stabbing with their bills and kicking with their feet. Finally, they will land amid squawks, chattering, and a rapidly repeated chacker-chacker sound.

One bird may charge another with its beak open. Usually, the second bird retreats. A new arrival may settle to the ground, rapidly flicking the tips of its extended wings (see fig. 12.5). During feeding, this behavior is aggressive. It may also be used as a means of calling other starlings' attention to the fact that a predator is near. In the latter situation, a group of starlings can "mob" a much larger predator and drive him away.

On power lines or branches near the feeder you may see sidling behavior (see fig. 12.6). The aggressor bird sidles close to another bird, forcing it to move along until it reaches some obstacle—or falls off the end of the branch.

Fig. 12.3. Staring. The bird on the left stands upright, raises its crown feathers, and stares the other bird into apprehension. The apprehensive bird holds its head higher with a slightly open bill. Reprinted from *Dinosaurs in the Garden,* courtesy Plexus Publishing, Inc., Medford, NJ.

Fig. 12.4. Fly ups. Birds fly up and call at each other while stabbing with beaks and kicking each other. Reprinted from *Dinosaurs in the Garden,* courtesy Plexus Publishing, Inc., Medford, NJ.

Fig. 12.5. Wing flick. The tips of the bird's wings are extended and rapidly flicked. This behavior may be associated with a "squeal call" or "mobbing calls" that recruit other birds to attack a common enemy. Reprinted from *Dinosaurs in the Garden,* courtesy Plexus Publishing, Inc., Medford, NJ.

Fig. 12.6. Sidling. One bird, often a male, moves sideways along a branch, forcing another bird off. Reprinted from *Dinosaurs in the Garden,* courtesy Plexus Publishing, Inc., Medford, NJ.

The flocking behavior of starlings is one of the things that often gets these birds in trouble with humans. They produce large, noisy collections of birds that leave messy white deposits. They may rise up like one organism and swoop into a field like a cloud of locusts to devour some farmer's seeds and fruits. Starlings are not terribly fussy about where they roost either. You can find them in cattail, reed, and alder stands; in pine, cedar, maple, and mixed deciduous stands; and under bridges, on buildings, and in bell towers. Some roosts may hold a quarter million birds!

Creatures of Habit

Roosting sites may be used over a long period of time, too. In England, one study showed that 70 percent of roosting sites were used more than 5 years and 12 percent were used for more than 50 years. Some sites have been in use for more than 100 years. At first thought, this would seem to be a disadvantage to the birds. Predators would know right where to look for a meal, and lots of birds would be feeding in a small territory. However, studies have shown some clear advantages to such predictable behavior.

1. More birds means more eyes. At least a few birds will notice a predator and sound the alarm.

2. In a large flock, the chance of any one bird being taken is small.

3. Older birds get the safest spots near the center of the flock, but younger birds benefit from being shown the best feeding sites.

4. The birds often act together to "mob" predators, something impossible for single birds to do.

Eugene Scheifflin's tribute to Shakespeare more than 100 years ago turned out to be an unwitting experiment in animal behavior and distribution. Not everyone was happy with the results. Some native birds were displaced from their habitats, and starlings probably destroy as many crops as they save by eating insects. But a person has to admire the adaptability and resourcefulness of this creature that eats everything and takes opportunity where she finds it. Perhaps the starling reminds us a bit of ourselves.

ACTIVITIES

Ask a Starling to Lunch

The way to ask a starling to lunch is to make him think the buffet is already set and he's missing out. To do that, you need to make some starling decoys.

Materials needed: heavy paper (cover weight) or cardboard; black and yellow markers; coat hangers or other stiff wire about a foot long; scissors or a utility knife; tracing paper and a #2 or softer pencil; wire cutters; your naturalist's notebook

Directions:

1. Trace the outline of the bird in figure 12.7 with a soft lead pencil on some tracing paper. Flip the tracing paper over onto a piece of cover-weight paper or cardboard and retrace the outline of the bird. (Tape the tracing paper in place, if necessary, to keep it from moving.) When you lift up your tracing paper you will have a reverse outline of the bird on the cardboard.

2. Cut out the bird shape.

3. Color both sides of the body black and the bill yellow.

4. Cut a piece of wire about a foot long. Poke it through the decoy so that it either appears to be a feeding bird or an "alert" bird (see fig. 12.8).

5. Twist the wire to create two legs you can stick into the ground. Feeding decoys should be positioned so that the beaks are nearly touching the ground as if they were feeding. "Alert" decoys should be positioned with their heads up as if they were looking for potential predators or competitors.

Using one set of feeding decoys first, record the number of starlings that land amid your "flock" in a given period of time, say, 20 minutes. Run several trials. Repeat the procedure for the alert decoys using the same number of trials and the same time interval. Which decoys attracted the most animals and why? If you have time, try modifying the decoys to see if you can make them either more or less attractive to starlings.

Making Starling Movie Stars

Materials needed: a video camcorder; your naturalist's notebooks; a bird blind or feeder set up near a window

Directions:

Best results require an established feeding or roosting site, patience, and perhaps a blind to hide behind if the birds are upset by your presence. Record 10 or 15 minutes of feeding activity with the video camcorder. Note in your naturalist's notebook the time of day, temperature and weather conditions, and the number of different species you can recognize.

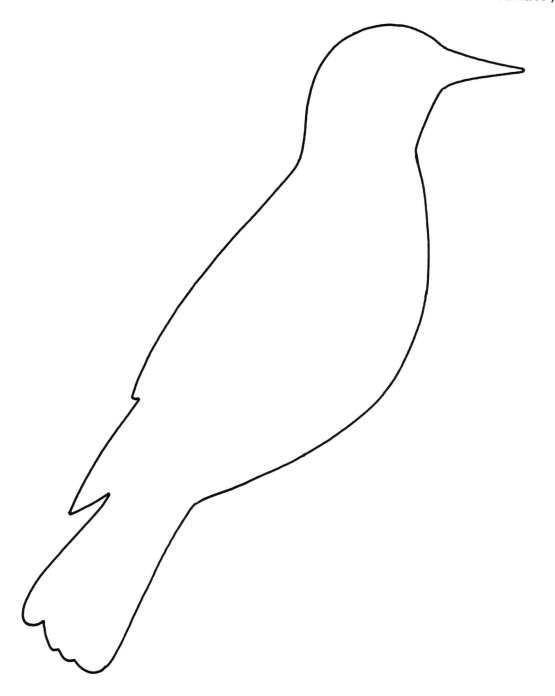

Fig. 12.7. Outline of a typical starling. Use this outline to create the decoys described in the text.

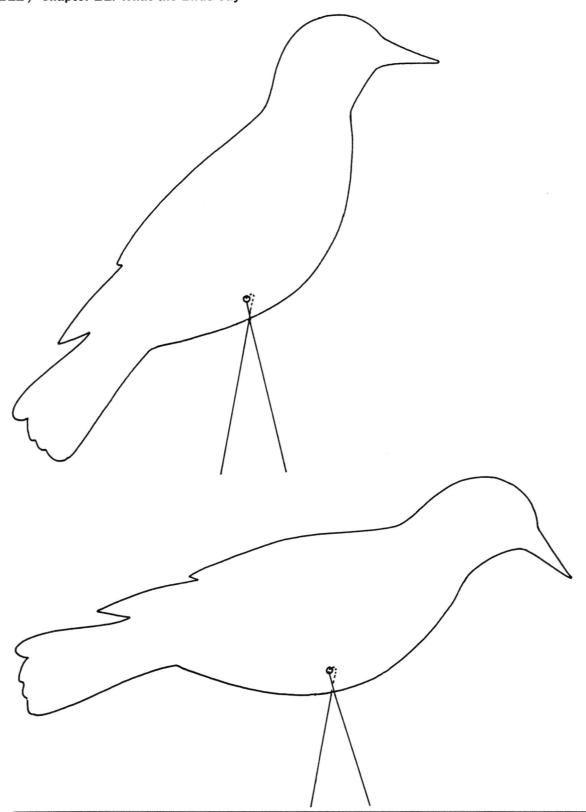

Fig. 12.8. "Alert" and "feeding" starling decoys. This drawing shows how to position wire legs to make "alert" and "feeding" starling decoys.

In the classroom, play the video for the class. List all species seen. Record the following interactions between birds, especially starlings, noting sex and age if you can determine it:

1. *Staring.* Upright stance, crown feathers raised, bill tilted upward. The more apprehensive bird may have its bill slightly open.

2. *Wing flick.* Tips of the wing are extended and rapidly flicked. May be associated with certain calls.

3. *Sidling.* Bird moves sideways along branch or wire, forcing the other bird off.

4. *Fluffing.* Feathers are fluffed out while facing another bird.

5. *Bill wipe.* A bird rapidly and repeatedly wipes its bill on either side of a branch in a submissive display.

6. *Crouch.* The body is lowered and feathers "sleeked" in a submissive gesture.

7. *Fly ups.* Birds fly up, calling at each other while stabbing with their beaks and kicking.

Watching Human Body Language

Collect magazine or newspaper clippings showing people interacting. How important do you think body language is in communicating information and feelings? For each picture you collect, record your impression of what information the people in each interaction are transmitting with their body language. Look for the following:

Facial expressions—smiles, frowns, grimaces, etc.

Eye contact or lack of it

The distance between two people and whether they are leaning toward or away from each other

The way in which they are touching each other

Posture

Gestures—sweeping movements of the arms, pointing, etc.

Appearance

In class, compare your impressions with those of others who see the pictures for the first time.

EXPLORING BODY LANGUAGE IN BIRDS AND STUDENTS

Notes on the Student Article

Christopher Feare's *The Starling* is the major reference on starlings, which you may want to look up if you become fascinated with starling behavior. In my book, *Dinosaurs in the Garden*, in the chapter of the same name, I discuss starling behavior in relation to dinosaur behavior because birds are now considered to be possible direct descendants of dinosaurs. This may provide an additional hook to get some students interested in bird behavior.

Of course it may be that starlings are not as common in your part of the country as mine, or they may not show up at the bird feeders available to you. You may substitute other birds for observation, although doing so may require more research on your part. Donald and Lillian Stokes have published three volumes on bird behavior that provide good material on a variety of birds. Following are a few other "flying dinosaurs" to look out for.

Red-winged blackbirds are abundant across the country and nearly as adaptable as starlings. Males sport bright red shoulder epaulets, which they use in territorial displays in their marshland habitats. Females are dark brown and heavily streaked. Juvenile males look similar to females but have the red shoulder patch.

Male *grackles* have long, keel-shaped tails; glossy black feathers with green, purplish, or bronze iridescence, especially in the neck area; and a light yellow eye. Females are similar with a little less iridescence. They're easily found in farmlands, groves, suburbs, and parks, usually near water.

Brown-headed cowbirds travel with other blackbirds, partially to stick close to their next "host." Female cowbirds lay their eggs in other bird nests and leave the parenting to them. Males are black with a brown head, and females are gray with a pale throat.

Male *brewer's blackbirds* are easy to confuse with grackles (and sometimes mature starlings). Their tails are shorter than grackles, however. Females are grayish brown with a dark eye; males have yellow eyes.

Yellow-headed blackbirds are very pretty and distinctive, but not that common around feeders unless you're near a marshy area. The bright yellow head and white wing patches mark the males. Females are brown with dull yellow on the face and breast and a white throat.

The *common crow* is larger than both starlings and blackbirds. Crows are glossy black, with black bill, legs, and feet and rounded wings and tail. They are common in forests, open areas, farmlands, and suburbs. Crows are very intelligent, have a complex language and social structure, and would make great subjects for behavioral study.

Blue jays, of course, are very distinctive with their pointed crest, black "necklace," and bright blue and white markings. They are aggressive and omnivorous feeders as are their Western cousins the *gray jays,* also called camp robbers.

John Carey's article "Lifestyles of the Rich and Famous" discusses some current research on blackbird behavior, especially the red-winged blackbird. "The Birds Communal Connection," by Patrick J. Weatherhead, talks about flocking behavior in blackbirds.

Notes on the Student Activities

Ask a Starling to Lunch

If each student or pair of students makes a decoy, you should have ample lures. This activity requires that you pick a time when starlings are out and about, of course. You'll have to do a little reconnaissance of your neighborhood. Substitute color and shape of your decoys if other birds are more prevalent. All the blackbirds mentioned above show flocking behavior.

Making Starling Movie Stars

You may want to take your own movies and bring them in or assign the project to a motivated group of students and have them bring in the film. Once in the classroom, you have the luxury of stopping the action and playing back sequences of interest.

Watching Human Body Language

Students may be surprised to learn that 55 percent of human communication is via body language, 38 percent through voice, and only 7 percent through the actual words used, at least according to research discussed in the book *Eye to Eye* by Dr. Peter Marsh. Body language is so important that we even use it unconsciously when speaking on the phone, knowing that the person on the other end can't see what we're doing. Some body language seems almost universal across cultures, like the friendly smile, while other gestures are unique to different cultures. The Greek Moutza gesture, extending five fingers and an open palm toward someone, is considered a gross insult. It's believed to have originated more than 1,500 years ago in Byzantine times when people humiliated criminals and other prisoners by pressing handfuls of dung in their face.

> *Facial Expressions:* Facial expressions can be used to show friendliness or interest in what someone else is saying. A blank expression can be interpreted as lack of interest or even hostility. Weak facial expressions that are badly timed or fade quickly can imply insincerity.

> *Eye Contact:* As a rule, lots of eye contact is good in interactions, with definite looks away now and then. People look more at someone when listening, less when speaking. Looking back to a person after you've spoken gives them the OK to respond. Avoiding eye contact implies nervousness and lack of confidence. Staring conveys hostility and intrusiveness.

> *Distance:* The proximity of two people can indicate how emotionally close they are. The socially acceptable distance between people during a conversation also varies from culture to culture. If someone invades your "personal space comfort zone," you tend to step back.

> *Touch:* A brief touch on the hand, arm, or shoulder can convey warmth and emotional support to someone or can be used to draw his or her attention to an important point. Uninvited touching in other areas may be too intimate. Too many touches to control direction and attention may make you seem too domineering.

> *Voice:* Moderate volume, resonant tone, and varied pitch and pace make for a good impression. A high-volume, booming voice makes you sound like a high-pressure salesperson. Low volume, a thin tone, with a monotonous delivery implies submissiveness or depression.

> *Posture:* A forward lean with straight spine and open arms shows attentiveness. In relaxed postures, people lean back with their limbs akimbo. Slumped shoulders, bowed head, folded arms, deflated chest, and turning away from someone conveys depression and/or lack of interest.

> *Gesture:* Gestures can emphasize or clarify a point. Some, like nodding, convey meanings of their own. In general, distal gestures (those like hand wringing and fidgeting that are directed toward one's own body) imply anxiety and nervousness. Proximal gestures (expansive gestures directed away from one's own body) imply enthusiasm and self confidence.

> *Appearance:* Looking attractive and dressing appropriate to the social situation are advantages in almost any situation.

You may want to take instant photos of the class and let them discuss their own body language or bring up some issues again during oral reports and speeches.

Chapter 13

GOOD BEE-HAVIOR

A ROBOT WITH THE RIGHT BEE-HAVIOR

At first, the real honeybees did not notice the robot bee in their hive. But once the robot began to beat its metal wings, a few nearby bees turned to face it. The metal bee danced. The real bees left the hive and went directly to a pan of sugar water that scientists had placed nearby. The robot was speaking "honeybee language."

This tiny robot bee is helping to solve an old mystery: How do bees tell their hive mates where to find the flowers with the richest and tastiest nectar? For years, careful observers could see that bees communicate, but it took a long time for someone to learn how they do it.

The Waggle Dance

After finding a rich source of food, an explorer bee returns to the hive and dances in a special way on the wall of the hive. In the 1940s a German scientist named Karl von Frisch studied the honeybees' dancing and concluded that the movements were a kind of language.

When a honeybee finds food for her hive, she has some of the same problems that people have when they give directions to an unfamiliar place. (The bees that explore for food are always female, and so are the bees that collect it.) The bee must tell her sisters which way to fly and how far they will have to go. Von Frisch also suspected that she told something about the quality and quantity of the nectar. But how does the explorer bee talk to her nest mates in a dark hive?

The mystery has to do with a dance that the explorer bee does on the hive wall called a "waggle dance." The bee moves in the pattern of a double loop, like a figure eight. She waggles her backside between one loop and the next.

Other bees come over to check things out. The returning bee is somehow "recruiting" them to gather the food she has found. Then, the recruited bees go out and find the new food without any more help.

A Dance Language

Von Frisch tried to understand the bees' dances. He watched honeybees in a special hive with a glass wall. He found out where the bees went after each dance. Then he tried to figure out which part of the dance told the other bees which way to go and which part told how far to go.

Von Frisch discovered that the direction the bee faced when it waggled told the other bees which way to fly to find the flowers. If the explorer waggled while she faced straight up the honeycomb, the others flew toward the sun to find the flowers. If

From *Explorations in Backyard Biology.* © 1996. Teacher Ideas Press. (800) 237-6124.

the dancer waggled when she faced straight down the comb, the others flew away from the sun. If the bee waggled while facing sideways to the right, the others went to the right of the sun, and so on (see fig. 13.1).

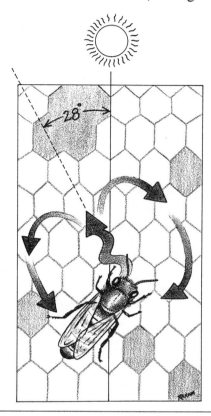

Fig. 13.1. The honeybee's dance language.
Worker bees signal the direction to a rich food source by the direction they're moving during the "waggle" portion of their dance. In this case, the worker is telling nest mates to travel so that the sun is 28° off their right "shoulder."

Von Frisch also noticed that the speed of the dance matched how far away the food was. The faster a worker "looped and waggled," the closer the flowers.

Many scientists thought von Frisch was right. Others had doubts. They were not sure how an explorer bee could get the attention of the other bees in the dark.

Scientists tried to test von Frisch's ideas by building robot bees that could dance in the honeybee's language, but the real honeybees paid no attention to the robots.

Two researchers, Wolfgang Kirchner and Axel Michelson, tried something different. They knew that other researchers had discovered that honeybees can make some sounds with their wings at a lower pitch than their familiar buzzing sound.

Most scientists thought that bees could not hear and that these sounds were not important. But Michelson and Kirchner discovered that honeybees can hear. Like some other insects, honeybees have hearing organs on their antennae.

These "ears" might explain how honeybees can get important information from an explorer bee's dance in the dark. The honeybees might not be able to see which way she faces when she waggles, but they can probably tell by listening.

Metal Bee

Kirchner and Michelson wanted to find out if the dancing bee beats her wings to say, "Listen. I can tell you where to find lunch."

They made a robot body out of brass and gave it metal "wings" that vibrated at the same speed as honeybee wings. A motor controlled the robot's figure eights and waggles. A thin plastic tube delivered a sample of sugar water for other bees to taste. (Real explorer bees give out samples of nectar.) (See fig. 13.2.) This new robot worked. It got the honeybees' attention, and it told them how to find a pan of sugar water lying in a field.

Now scientists are listening in to learn what other kinds of bees have to say. Of the four species of honeybees studied so far, all have some variation of the dance language. Three species that live in dark hives get their nest mates' attention with sound. The fourth species, a dwarf bee, dances silently in the daylight. Do some bees use sound to communicate other kinds of information? Someday we may find out.

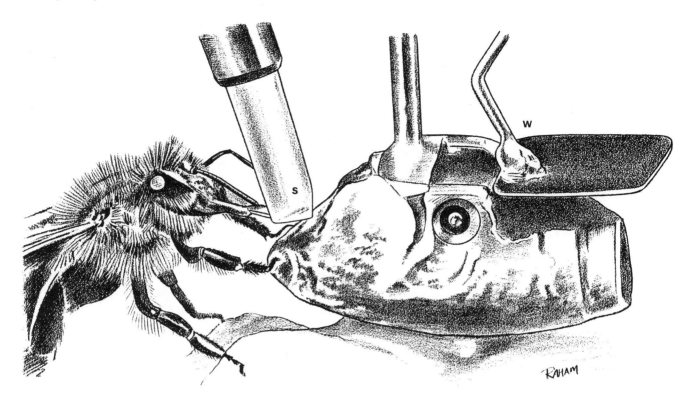

Fig. 13.2. A robot bee. A worker bee sips sugar water from a syringe (S) near the front end of "Robo-bee." An electromagnet vibrates the artificial wing (W) to make the "listen up" sounds.

ACTIVITIES

Talk Like a Bee

Your teacher will select someone to be the "forager bee." He or she will give the forager some candy samples to hand out to hive bees later and tell the forager at which of eight stations the rest of the candy is hidden. The stations will be arranged in two concentric circles around a spot marked "hive" (see fig. 13.3). A light bulb will mark the position of the sun. A "waggle dance indicator" will be pinned to a vertical surface near the hive. When the forager finds out where the candy is hidden, she (or he) must tell a hive bee where it is in bee language.

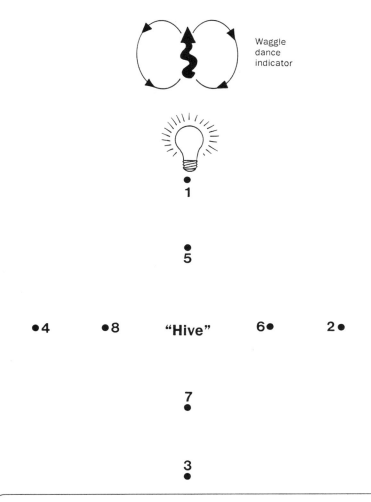

Waggle dance indicator

Fig. 13.3. The waggle dance indicator and chart. Cut out the waggle dance indicator, pin it to a vertical board, and use it as a bee would to point in the direction of the food treat. "Hive" indicates the hive location and the lightbulb represents the sun. The food can be at any of stations 1-8.

For example: If the candy is located at station 6 in the diagram, the forager should turn the waggle dance indicator 90^0 to the right (to three o'clock on an imaginary clock face) because station 6 is 90^0 to the right of the lightbulb. Then the forager should do a fast figure-eight dance (because 6 is close to the hive), buzzing during the waggle portion. When a hive bee comes over and stamps his or her foot, the dancer has to stop and hand out a piece of candy. The hive bee gets to keep the rest of the candy (or gets 10 points) if he or she gets the right station on the first try. The hive bee gets half the candy (5 points) for getting it on the second try and nothing after that.

Repeat the activity several times, then change the position of the "sun" and try again. Remember that *direction* is indicated by the direction of the waggle dance direction arrow, and *distance* is indicated by the speed of the dance. Also remember that the hive bee has to be *recruited* by your buzz and that the hive bee has to stamp to get a food sample.

Flower Power

In your naturalist's notebook carefully draw the flower provided by your teacher. When you're finished, your teacher will provide a picture of the same kind of flower as seen by a bee. How do they differ? Of what use might the markings you see be to a bee? These markings are called nectar guides. Does that information make you change your mind about your answer to the question? How might you test if a bee is really using these marks to find the nectar-bearing parts of flowers?

The Planet Inferno

Imagine a planet called Inferno. It is a young planet whose inner core is still hot, so there is considerable volcanic activity, hot springs, geysers, and similar features. Animal life at least as complex as insects has evolved there. Inferno is so far from its sun that "daytime" is nearly as dark as night, and Inferno has no moons.

What kind of sense receptors might Inferno's animal life have? Why? Heat is energy in the infrared part of the spectrum, a type of energy humans can't see. Would Infernoans find some sort of infrared vision useful? Why or why not? Do you know any Earth creatures that see in the infrared? Answer these questions in your naturalist's notebook.

Imagine an Inferno predator called a lancer. Lancers can fly and have a long snout that can pierce the bodies of laplusters, who eat algaelike plants that live in the hot springs. Draw a picture of a lancer and a lapluster, labeling their sense organs.

TO SPEAK AND SEE LIKE A BEE

Notes on the Student Article

Unraveling the mysteries of bee language has been a fascinating process and serves to illustrate at least two aspects of science in general: 1) Scientific knowledge builds over time, sometimes quickly, sometimes slowly, depending on the skills, interests, and luck of researchers working in a particular area; and 2) the scientific process is self-correcting and self-refining as technical advances allow new experiments to be performed and as new insights allow people to ask better questions.

When Axel Michelsen, of Odense University in Denmark, and Wolfgang Kirchner, from the University of Wurtzburg in Germany, asked themselves several years ago whether dancing foragers vibrated the comb when they danced, they had lasers to help answer the question. Minute changes in laser-generated light reflected from the comb would imply the comb was vibrating. They discovered the dancing bees caused no such changes, but the bees they recruited did. This allowed them to ask what the recruited bees' vibrations were doing and led them to discover that this was the stimulus for the release of food samples by the foragers.

Michelsen and Kirchner decided that if the dancers weren't vibrating the comb, they might be producing sound with their wings. The pitch of any such sound would be affected by wing length. Thus, they clipped the wings of some bees. The bees could fly and dance normally, but they were unable to recruit any nest mates when they returned to the hive. Apparently, their "listen up" signal could no longer be heard.

The researchers proved that bees could hear by running them in a *Y*-shaped maze. They played sounds at one end of the *Y* and rewarded bees that turned toward the sounds with sugar water. When the sounds were low frequency (below 500 hertz), the bees learned quickly. (The wing-generated sounds of dancers are between 250 and 300 hertz, precisely in the hearing range of their nest mates.) Further experiments showed that bees detected these sounds with a sense organ in their antennae.

Gravity turned out to be important in the directional part of the waggle dance. When the hive was tipped on its side so that the comb was horizontal, the dancers couldn't waggle in the right direction, and their nest mates couldn't find the nectar in the field.

James Gould of Princeton showed that odor, once thought more important than dancing in locating a food source, was actually relatively unimportant. He used a bright light to create a "false sun" in the hive. Recruited bees interpreted the forager's dance in terms of the false sun and showed up at the wrong spot outside the hive. If odor had been critical, many of them should have shown up at the right place regardless of the dance.

"The Sensory Basis of the Honeybee's Dance Language" by Wolfgang Kirchner and William Towne talks about these experiments in detail and lists several other references. In addition to this *Scientific American* article, the Scientific American Library has published an entire book on the honeybee, appropriately titled *The Honey Bee*.

To See Like a Bee

The discussion of bee language provides a great opportunity to encourage students to imagine what the world would look and sound like to a familiar yet alien creature like the honeybee. We all tend to forget that our view of the world is dependent on what our senses allow us to perceive. The discussion in chapter 6 provided the basis for understanding the physical difference between cameralike eyes like our own and motion-sensitive compound eyes like those of the bee. Now let's look at what a bee can see with those eyes.

Karl von Frisch showed as early as 1914 that bees can see color. Because bees readily travel between their hives and a food source, von Frisch was able to train them to come to various sweet baits. By changing the colors of the baits he showed that bees could see certain colors.

Human eyes contain sensory cells sensitive to three regions of the spectrum: the yellow, the green, and the blue. This sensitivity allows us to see "all the colors of the rainbow," from red to violet. You may remember that ROY G BIV spells out these colors: red, orange, yellow, green, blue, indigo, and violet. Bees also have three types of sensory cells, but they are sensitive to ultraviolet, blue, and green. Ultraviolet is invisible to humans. Red is the same as black to a bee.

Bend the human-perceived rainbow to form a color wheel and red and violet combine to form the color purple. Colors opposite each other on the color wheel are complementary. The bee color wheel joins yellow-orange and ultraviolet to create a "bee purple" that we can only imagine (see fig. 13.4). One result is that when we look at a yellow globeflower, which reflects almost no ultraviolet, chances are it looks yellow to a bee, also, but when we look at yellow marsh marigolds, which reflect heavily in the ultraviolet, the bee sees bee purple.

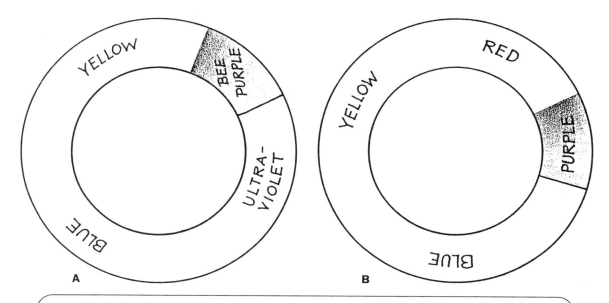

Fig. 13.4. The bee and human color wheels. For bees (*A*), yellow and ultraviolet create "bee purple," which we can't see. For us (*B*), red and blue combine to form purple.

The importance of all this to the bee only becomes obvious when we photograph bee-attractive flowers with special UV-passing filters that allow us to see what the bee sees. Flowers become transformed with stripes, dots, and other markings normally invisible to us. Like glowing road signs, these markings direct the bee's attention to pollen or nectar-bearing plant organs. Bees and flowers both benefit from this situation. Bees can find food easily, and flowers can spread their pollen to other members of their species.

Humans and bees also differ in their ability to see shapes. Because the lenses of our cameralike eyes project complete images on the retina, we see shapes well. The centers of flowers look round, and many petals have a roughly triangular shape. Bees can't distinguish circles from triangles, but they are good at seeing motion and broken shapes (see fig. 13.5). The secret to these different visual skills lies in the structure of the compound eye.

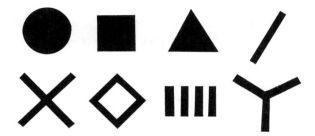

Fig. 13.5. Bee shape discrimination. Because of the nature of the compound eye, bees can distinguish the shapes in the top row from those in the bottom row but cannot tell the shapes in the same row apart.

Each facet in the bee's eye is a lens that projects light to a receptor at the base of a cone-shaped ommatidium (see fig. 6.3). A bee's eyes break up what it sees into thousands of point sources, much like a photograph printed in a newspaper is made up of tiny, individual dots. The more ommatidia an insect has, the more detail it can see. Dragonflies, whose eyes have up to 30,000 ommatidia each, can snatch mosquitos out of the air while flying at 30 miles per hour.

The multiple images gathered by compound eyes allow their owners to see motion easily. A honeybee can distinguish up to 265 flashes every second. Our own eyes can only see 20 flashes per second before the light source looks like a single beam of light. So, we see a field of flowers as a colorful combination of shapes—circles, triangles, and wedges—whereas honeybees see colorful bursts of flickering light whose regular patterns provide the bee brain the clues it needs to find food and avoid enemies.

Honeybees and their insect relatives can see something else we cannot: polarized light. Sunlight becomes polarized when it strikes small particles in the air and scatters. Light waves then vibrate in a specific direction at each point in the sky. As the sun moves through the sky, the overall polarization pattern changes. Even if the sun is covered by clouds, animals who can see this pattern can tell where the sun is and know in which direction they're traveling as long as they have a small patch of blue sky.

Try and imagine, if you can, an even more exotic sense: the ability to perceive magnetic fields. Bees are one of a number of organisms sensitive to the Earth's magnetic field, apparently as a result of microscopic grains of magnetite (the same ore compass needles were made from on ancient sailing ships) that tweak nearby nerve endings as they shift in response to the animal's change in direction.

Notes on the Student Activities

Talk Like a Bee

Materials needed: a lightbulb or some other "designated sun"; hard candy or other reward easy to handle and parcel out to the forager; a cardboard platform that says "hive" and on which you've drawn a diagram of the bee figure-eight waggle dance; eight stations arranged in two concentric rings (you might use plastic margarine containers that you could turn upside down like variations on the shell game); a waggle dance direction dial drawn on heavy paper; a thumbtack to tack the dial to a vertical board; foam core or some other stiff, porous board you can stand near the "hive."

Vary the procedure and rewards to fit your class. If you feel in an acting mood, you could be the forager and have students compete to be the first to give you the number of the right food cache. The point is get them to understand how bee language works and give them some idea how scientists uncovered its secrets.

Flower Power

Figure 13.6 shows some flowers with nectar guides. Sunflowers or orchids might be the easiest to find, depending on your locale. If necessary, you could have your students draw their pictures from photographs or flower catalogs. Reproduce the sketches of the nectar guides closest to the flowers they draw.

Many sunflowers have nectar guides at the center of the flower. Researchers took flowers apart and reversed the petals so that the nectar guides were on the outer tips. When bees landed on these flowers they followed the marks out to the end of the petals, away from the nectar.

The Planet Inferno

Infrared vision receptors would allow Inferno's inhabitants to see in the parts of the spectrum brightest on their planet. It's unlikely that eyes would evolve having sensory cells that respond to wavelengths of light rarely encountered. Rattlesnakes, members of the pit viper family of snakes, have a deep pit on both sides of their head between the eye and nostril that is sensitive to heat (infrared radiation). This organ allows them to hunt rodents and other small, warm-blooded mammals at night and in dark tunnels.

Let the kids have fun with the drawing assignment. The lancers might have big eyes like a dragonfly or an array of heat-sensitive pits. Laplusters might have some method of camouflage that would make them look like the pulsing heat signature of a hot springs, or they might be insulated in some way so that their heat signature is masked. Lancers are likely to be sleek and aerodynamic; laplusters could be large and slow, etc.

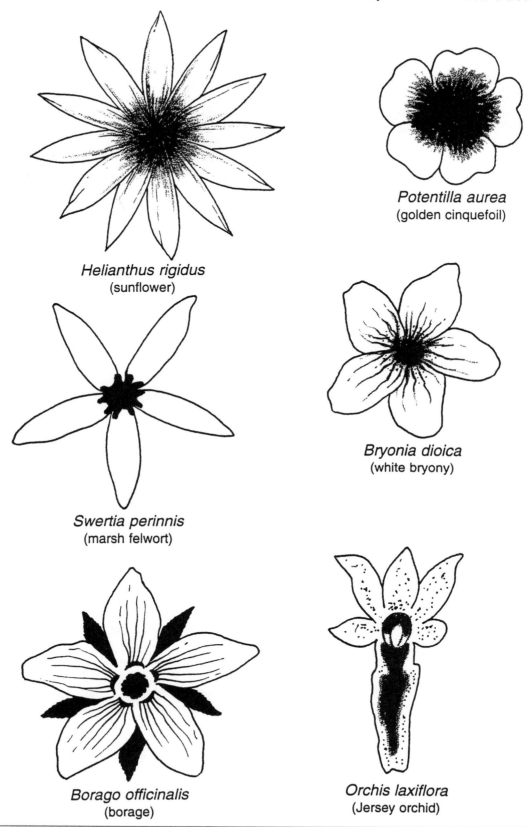

Helianthus rigidus
(sunflower)

Potentilla aurea
(golden cinquefoil)

Swertia perinnis
(marsh felwort)

Bryonia dioica
(white bryony)

Borago officinalis
(borage)

Orchis laxiflora
(Jersey orchid)

Fig. 13.6. Nectar guides in flowers. These are the nectar guide patterns for six types of flowers. Find a kind of flower (real or photograph) similar to one or more of the examples that your students can draw.

Part IV

Your Backyard in Balance

Chapter 14

OF BEETLES AND BINDWEED

THE GOLD BUG WITH THE STRANGE UMBRELLA

Sometimes bindweed looks beautiful. Its white or purplish white flowers, though not as large or showy as its morning glory relatives, make attractive splotches of color in the lawn and coil artfully up the chain-link fence all summer (see fig. 14.1). Bindweed only makes me mad when it chokes the juniper bushes, strangles the beans, and ties up my rosebush like the hostage in an adventure story. It's times like that when gardeners look for revenge.

One day, while shading my eyes against the sun at the local ball field, I glanced toward the bindweed-carpeted ground and saw glints of gold. Looking closer, the gold flecks turned out to be tiny leaf beetles, commonly called golden tortoise beetles because of their shape and color. Their scientific name is *Metriona bicolor* (see fig. 14.2). Each beetle stood near a latticework of holes in the bindweed leaves. Bindweed, it turned out, was their preferred meal—the beetle equivalent of a good cheeseburger.

Fig. 14.1. Bindweed (*Convolvulus arvensis*). Bindweed is the host plant for the golden tortoise beetle and a relative of the morning glory. Illustration appeared in *Backyard Bugwatching*, no. 10, 1990. Reprinted by permission.

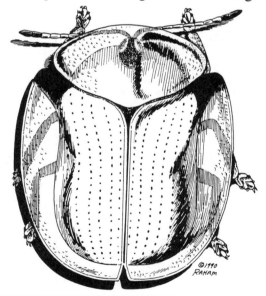

Fig. 14.2. Adult golden tortoise beetle (*Metriona bicolor*). The adult golden tortoise beetle can change color quickly from a metallic gold to dull orange. The mechanisms for color variations are not completely understood. Actual size: 5 mm. Illustration appeared in *Backyard Bugwatching*, no. 10, 1990. Reprinted by permission.

139

I imagined breeding large numbers of these golden avengers to kill the nasty bindweed and benefit gardeners everywhere. I captured several and took them home, housing them in glass dishes. I fed them bindweed leaves and sat down to watch them eat. As usual in such cases, my desire for revenge cooled and turned to curiosity as some of the secrets of the beetle-bindweed relationship became evident.

Female beetles lay their eggs on bindweed leaves, then defecate on them. Scientists believe this provides some protection for the eggs until they hatch five to eight days later. Young, newly hatched larvae are pale yellow, oval-shaped, and fringed with TV antennaelike projections called scoli. An anal fork, half as long as their body, projects from the rear end (see fig. 14.3).

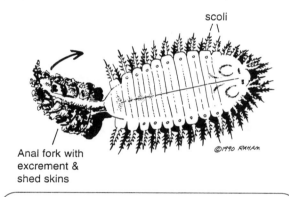

scoli

Anal fork with excrement & shed skins

©1990 RHHAM

Fig. 14.3. Tortoise beetle (*M. bicolor*) larva. The larva uses its anal fork to hold excrement and shed skins over its body like an umbrella. Illustration appeared in *Backyard Bugwatching*, no. 10, 1990. Reprinted by permission.

Like most larvae, they eat continuously, and you can watch plant material pass through their translucent amber bodies. Bindweed that is unused as food has yet another function. The larvae collect excrement and shed larval skins on the anal fork until a large mass has built up. The dark mass, held over the animal's body like an umbrella, serves as camouflage from the air and is often shoved into the face of an ant who thinks the leaf beetle might make an easy meal. After 21 to 25 days of feeding, the larvae find a sheltered spot to rest and become dark-colored pupae. Over the next six to nine days their bodies reorganize. When complete, they break from the pupal shell as adults.

New adults display wing cases that are light brownish orange. Within three hours they turn deep brownish orange and have six black spots. Adults must age from 14 to 27 days to show their metallic gold colors. By this time they are sexually mature.

The Mystery of the Color-Changing Beetle

As adults, these leaf beetles can change colors quickly, in 120 to 1,033 seconds according to one researcher. Such rapid color changes are unique among insects. To see the change, place a metallic gold adult between your thumb and forefinger and squeeze gently. Set the beetle down again and record how many minutes it takes the animal to switch to brownish orange with black spots.

Color variations play some role in protecting leaf beetles, but the exact means are still a little unclear. Gold adults may be hard for birds to see on sun-dappled leaves or when they reflect the shifting colors of their surroundings. The bright metallic color may also mimic drops of rain or dew on leaves. The orange-and-black spot phase may cause birds to confuse leaf beetles with some lady beetles, which often taste bad to birds. Some researchers suspect that the round shape of this beetle's shell may cause some inexperienced birds to drop their prey more often.

The golden tortoise beetle, for reasons unknown, often turns gold when mating. Copulation may last from 15 to 583 minutes. Males may mate with many females, if the opportunity arises. Adults typically live from 25 to 112 days.

How do these beetles change color? Some scientists believe the color changes involve a thin film of water in the outer layer of the wing cases. As the thickness of this film of water varies, it may reflect different wavelengths of light back to the viewer, somewhat like the thinning film of a soap bubble shows a rainbow of colors before it pops. Whatever the mechanism, some active biological process is involved, because the metallic gold rapidly fades to a dull orange when the animal dies.

Watch these animals eat and mate and lay their eggs on bindweed and then watch their spiny larvae wave dark umbrellas over their heads. How many different kinds of leaf beetles can you find in the fields near your home or in your parents' garden? You can make a survey the next time you're pulling weeds. Perhaps it will make weed-pulling less of a chore and more of an adventure. Maybe you will discover the weed-eater that will make you a hero to gardeners everywhere!

ACTIVITIES

Beating the Bushes for Beetles

Materials needed: a sturdy insect net; a light-colored, flat tray (like a baking pan or a photographer's tray); collecting jars; tweezers; masking tape; your naturalist's notebook; a pencil or pen

Directions:

♦ Hold the insect net in one or both hands and sweep it quickly back and forth in front of you as you walk through foliage. After you've taken a dozen steps or so, quickly close off the top of the net with one hand, keeping the insects you've collected in the cone end of the net. Have someone else position the tray so you can turn the net upside down. Release your hold on the net and turn the net's cone inside out so that the contents fall into the tray.

♦ There should be lots of jumping, crawling, and squirming insects in the tray. Your goal is to find some leaf beetles, preferably the golden tortoise beetle, *Metriona bicolor*. They will be small (about ⅛ of an inch across), round or oval, and bright, metallic gold. They resemble small turtles with nearly transparent shells. Related species may appear clear or yellow-brown in color with dark spots. They can fly away, but beetles tend to be clumsy fliers, so if you work fairly quickly you can collect them before they escape.

♦ With your fingers or tweezers collect all of the small beetles you can see and put them in a collecting jar with some bindweed (or samples of the most common weeds in the area you sampled).

📖 IN YOUR NOTEBOOK

Write in your naturalist's notebook the time, location, and weather conditions at the time of sampling. Mark sample #1 in your book and on a piece of masking tape you put on your sampling jar.

Look also for the immature larval form of this beetle. It is about the same size as the adult but bright yellow with a fringe of spines (see fig. 14.3). Add the larvae to the same jar with the adults, if necessary. Have your teacher help with identification.

Make additional sweeps with your net if you are not successful the first time. If you try different areas, be sure to record the unique aspects of each site in your notebook.

Raising and Observing Tortoise Beetles

Materials needed: petri dishes or other clear containers that will fit on the stage of a dissecting microscope; a dissecting microscope; tweezers; your naturalist's notebook; pencil or pen; colored pencils

Directions:

♦ Sort out larvae and adults. Put all the adults in one petri dish and larvae in another. Look at them with a dissecting scope and watch their behavior for awhile.

📖 IN YOUR NOTEBOOK

Draw a picture of an adult beetle. What is its overall shape? Notice that part of its turtlelike "shell" is formed by the upper wings, called elytra, and part is formed by a shieldlike structure in front of the wings called the pronotum. Can you see the insect's black head beneath the pronotum? What do its antennae look like? Into how many segments are its legs divided? What's unusual about its "feet"? How might feet like this be useful to a tortoise beetle?

Pick up a tortoise beetle adult between the thumb and forefinger and gently squeeze. Place the beetle on the table and observe any color change. If it changed color, try the same thing with another beetle and have someone time how long it takes for the animal to change color.

Draw a picture of a larval beetle. Can you see its forked tail beneath all the excrement? Draw a bird's-eye view of the animal. Under a dissecting scope look for motion in its digestive tract through its transparent skin. What color are its eyes?

Observe adults and larvae over several days. If the larvae begin to form pupae, draw and describe them. Make a diagram showing the life cycle of a tortoise shell beetle.

TO KNOW A BEETLE IS TO LOVE A BEETLE

Notes on the Student Article

Well, if loving beetles is too great a leap, at least you can come to appreciate them. They may just be the most hardy creatures on Earth, numbering in the vicinity of 300,000 species with an ancestry stretching back 300 million years.

Beetles have six legs, three body parts, two pairs of wings, and an external skeleton like all other insects, but they have an order all to themselves that displays certain other characteristics. For example, the front wings (elytra) are leathery or hard without veins and meet in a straight line down the middle of the back. Beetles actually fly with more typical veined, translucent wings that lie under the elytra, but flying is a clumsy process in this group as the elytra hang out like a pair of shields and provide lots of drag. In addition, beetles have chewing mouth parts and a form of development called complete metamorphosis.

Metamorphosis is one of those neat Greek polysyllabic words meaning "change in form." Insects as a group display either no metamorphosis, simple metamorphosis, or complete metamorphosis like the beetles. The snow fleas we met in chapter 5 have no metamorphosis. They hatch from eggs, grow, molt occasionally, and become adults that are basically larger versions of the young insect. Grasshoppers, dragonflies, boxelder bugs, aphids, and other insects have young that are small, wingless versions of adults called nymphs. Nymphs and adults have similar habits and often feed together. After their last, molt nymphs get the wings of adulthood and fly off to mate somewhere.

Beetles, flies, ants, bees, and butterflies represent some of the insects that truly "change forms" (see chapters 7, 9, and 16). Wormlike creatures called larvae hatch from eggs and go through a series of molts. These larvae are referred to as instars. The first larvae out of the egg is the first instar, the one after the first molt is the second instar, and so on. They eat and behave differently from adults. Eventually, larvae stop eating and transition into a resting stage called a pupa. Pupae often wait out the winter while genes direct the total transformation of the insect body into its adult form.

One of the things so interesting about the golden tortoise beetle is the bizarre looks and behavior of its larva. If it were a larger beast, its weird spines alone would certainly garner it as least as much attention as a rhinoceros or a porcupine. The family of beetles to which it belongs is large, even if its physical size is diminutive. There are about 25,000 Chrysomelidae worldwide and 1,460 species in North America. Adults munch on an assortment of flowers and foliage.

Bindweed, also called *Convolvulus arvensis*, is native throughout the temperate regions of both hemispheres. It's common along ditches, roadways, and railroad tracks and is a persistent weed of cultivated areas. This perennial herb, with stout runners and stems that scramble or climb by twisting in an anti-clockwise fashion around the stems of other plants, should be easy to find. The flowers are pink or white, funnel-shaped, and often have five purplish stripes on the outside. Bees and various sorts of flies are the usual pollinators.

Notes on the Student Activities

Beating the Bushes for Beetles

You can purchase insect nets from biological supply houses like Carolina Biological Supply (offices in Burlington, NC 27215 or Gladstone, OR 97027) or make them fairly easily from nylon, nylon marquisette, scrim, organdy, or fine-mesh bolting cloth. The pattern shown in figure 14.4 is adapted from the book *How to Know the Insects*. You may also be able to buy a net that would serve the purpose at a local sporting goods store. Simply keep in mind that the mesh on the netting has to be fine enough to trap the small beetles yet sturdy enough to withstand being swept through the bushes.

Light-colored collecting trays make it easier to see small bugs. A large cake tray or photographer's developing tray with relatively high sides keeps insects in one place long enough to sort them out. Collecting jars can be any glass jars students can bring from home, preferably with some sort of screw-on top. If tweezers are limited or too hard to use, bugs could be scooped up on small pieces of white paper and "funneled" into jars.

Students should be kept busy making lots of sketches and records in their naturalist's notebooks of when and where things were captured. It is hoped, that by now, these notebooks are dog-eared with use.

Raising and Observing Tortoise Beetles

Petri dishes are very handy for classroom work. You can buy 50 or 100 plastic disposable ones from biological supply houses fairly cheaply. Students can make many observations with the naked eye and small magnifiers, but a dissecting microscope will definitely help if one or two are available.

When drawing pictures of adult bettles, have the students note those characteristics that separate insects from other arthropods (like the number of body segments and the number of legs) as well as those characteristics that distinguish beetles from other insects (kind and arrangement of wings, chewing mouth parts, and complete metamorphosis). The quick key in chapter 15 might also be useful here.

To observe color changes in the beetles, students will have to apply gentle pressure on the beetle long enough for spots to begin to appear. Then they can set the beetle down and time the complete changeover. The color change seems to happen symmetrically from the outside edges in.

The golden tortoise beetle's feet have large pads and clawlike projections for hanging on to leaf surfaces. You may notice when collecting, however, that beetles can drop to the ground quickly when something is after them.

Students who show an interest in entomology might be encouraged to contact the Young Entomologists' Society, Inc., 1915 Peggy Place, Lansing, MI 48910-2553. In addition to providing opportunities for contacting others with "buggy" interests, this is a good source of many books on different aspects of studying, raising, and working with insects as well as journal articles by teachers and students. The society also can provide sources of supplies for insect study. Sonoran Arthropod Studies, Inc. (SASI), P.O. Box 5624, Tucson, AZ 85703 is a conservation organization that promotes the understanding and appreciation of the role of arthropods in nature. It offers many educational programs for students and adults and publishes the magazine *Backyard Bugwatching*.

Notes on the References

How to Know the Insects by Roger G. Bland and H. E. Jaques and *A Field Guide to the Beetles of North America* by Richard E. White are probably your best general references, especially for fieldwork. H. F. Chu's *How to Know the Immature Insects* is good for identifying larvae when no adults are around. A few more technical pieces are included in the "References" section at the back of this book for those who become really enthralled with leaf beetles.

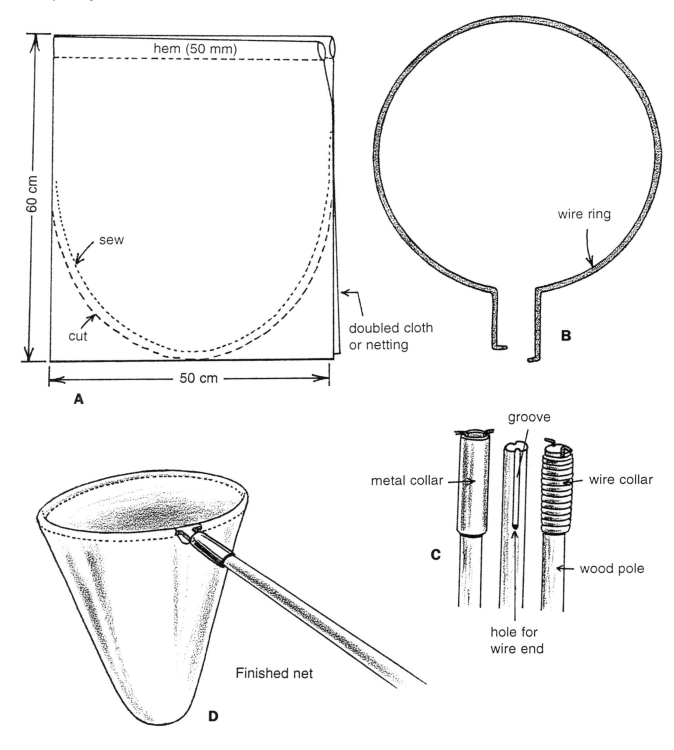

Fig. 14.4. How to make a sweep net. This simple design will give you a rugged field net for insect collecting. Use a piece of cloth or netting long enough to accommodate your wire ring. A 100-cm-long cloth (which folds in half to 50 cm as in the diagram) will fit a 30.5-cm (12") diameter ring of #6 or #8 wire. Sew a hem along one side of the cloth. Fold the cloth in half and sew the bottom of the net (*A*). Slip the net onto the wire ring. The arms and hooks of the wire ring (*B*) should fit into the grooves and holes on the handle (*C*). The ring/handle assembly is held together by a collar (two types are shown). The finished net should resemble the illustration (*D*). Adapted with permission from Roger C. Bland and H. E. Jacques, *How to Know the Insects*, 3d ed. Copyright © 1978 Times Mirror Higher Education Group, Inc. Dubuque, Iowa. All Rights Reserved.

Chapter 15

THE MILKWEED UNIVERSE

ONCE UPON A MILKWEED . . .

Once upon a milkweed, the biologist's story goes, there sat a monarch butterfly. She had lunch sipping nectar from the weed's pink flowers. Afterward, she laid her eggs on a milkweed leaf, then flapped her black-and-orange-trimmed wings and flew away. The eggs hatched into equally flashy orange and black caterpillars that ate the milkweed's leaves and thrived, even though the milkweed's creamy sap poisons most other creatures. Not only did the monarch's offspring survive, they took the plant's alkaloid-filled sap into their own bodies, which made them taste awful to frogs, birds, and other animals looking for a snack. Once made sick, birds and other animals avoid them in the future. After the caterpillars ate their fill, they found a nice spot beneath a milkweed leaf, each formed a hard case *(chrysalis)* around its body, and became a brownish pupa. As pupa, amazing changes took place. Some of their genes turned off and others turned on. Some tissues died or were transformed.

Finally, the adult butterfly cracked its brown case and emerged to start a new generation (see fig. 15.1).

THE END?

Well, not quite. Relationships in nature are rarely so simple. It's true that monarch butterflies and milkweed plants do interact as described, but the monarch's story is only one of many tales that could be told about the insects and spiders that make a living in the milkweed universe. Figure 15.2 shows just a few of the creatures that call the milkweed home. And what about the milkweed plant? What does it get from all the creatures that suck its nectar, eat its leaves, and nibble its seeds in the fall? You can bet when you see long-term relationships in nature that all the organisms involved gain some benefits and pay some prices for the lives they lead.

147

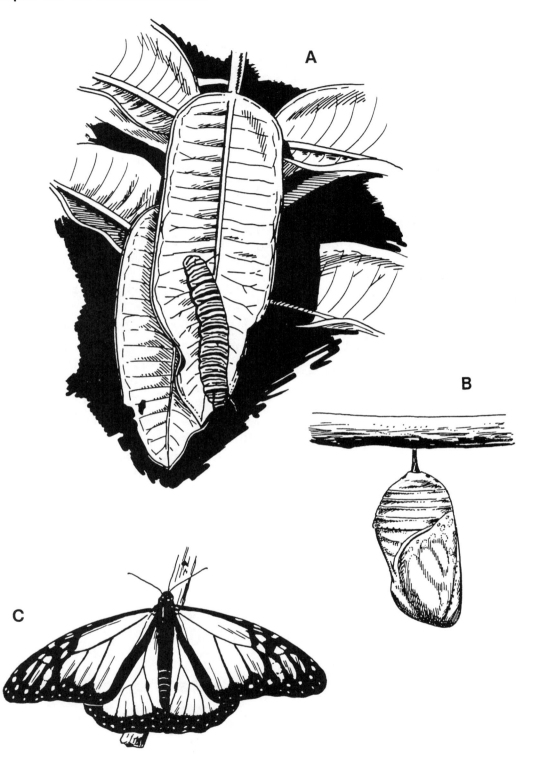

Fig. 15.1. The monarch life cycle. The monarch butterfly has complete metamorposis with larval (*A*), pupal (*B*), and adult (*C*) stages. All stages contain the alkaloid poisons of their milkweed host. Reprinted from *Dinosaurs in the Garden,* courtesy Plexus Publishing, Inc., Medford, NJ.

Fig. 15.2. The milkweed universe. This illustration shows several key inhabitants of the milkweed universe. Left center: bumblebee. Top: monarch adult. Bottom, on milkweed leaf: milkweed longhorn beetle. A cluster of milkweed flowers, both open and closed, dominate the center of the picture.

The Milkweed's Bargain

If a milkweed could run an ad in the newspaper it might look like this:

HELP WANTED
to take pollen to my relatives.
Will exchange for really good food.
Call 1-800-MLK-WEED.

Because the average milkweed has not discovered newspapers, it advertises with a particularly sweet-scented nectar. The insects that most often apply to this advertisement and that can best help the milkweed transfer its pollen are moths and bumblebees. They are big enough to haul away the milkweed's *pollen*. The pollen (the plant's male sex cells) is produced in "saddlebags" called *pollinaria* that straddle the *stigma,* or female part of the flower. (See fig. 15.3.) Each pollinarium is composed of two *pollinia* that are connected by a clip called the *corpusculum.* A bumblebee or moth will get a leg hooked on one or several clips and transports the pollen saddlebags from one milkweed to another. These insects even work in shifts: the bumblebee works daylight hours and moths take over at night.

Problems with Freeloaders

Other insects, including the monarch, are also attracted by the odor of nectar. Sometimes these freeloaders seem to get a "free lunch" because they can't benefit the milkweed for whatever nectar they consume. For example, scientists have shown that ants can significantly reduce pod production in milkweeds by hauling off large quantities of nectar, thus making the plants they infest less desirable to pollinating bees and moths. There are other types of freeloaders as well. In the fall, when milkweed seeds are ripening in their pods, milkweed bugs come to suck on seeds. Aphids, small insects that are sometimes garden pests, may infest the plant stems and suck on their sap. And our friends the monarch caterpillars sometimes eat entire seedpods.

Apparently, milkweeds can afford these costs in order to pay for getting pollen distributed and seeds fertilized. And the price "freeloaders" pay can sometimes be quite high. They may even pay with their lives.

From *Explorations in Backyard Biology.* © 1996. Teacher Ideas Press. (800) 237-6124.

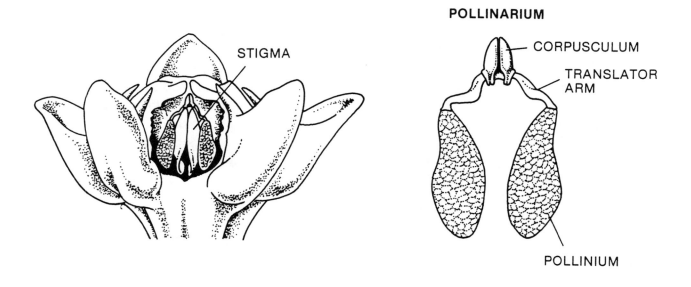

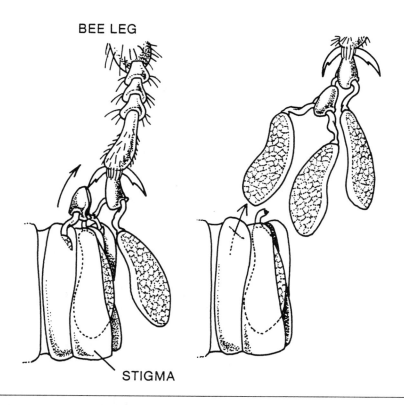

Fig. 15.3. The milkweed flower and pollination. The milkweed flower has an enlarged stigma (part of the female part of the flower) with a saddlebaglike structure called a pollinarium looped over it. Each saddlebag (pollinium) carries the male pollen grains. Bees and other large insects get their legs caught in the clip that holds the pollinarium together. If they don't get stuck, they carry one milkweed's pollen to another plant. Reprinted from *Dinosaurs in the Garden,* courtesy Plexus Publishing, Inc., Medford, NJ.

Dangers in the Milkweed Universe

As mentioned earlier, the milkweed's sap is dangerous. Even monarch caterpillars have developed an eating technique to minimize their contact with it. They start a meal by partially gnawing through the large central leaf vein. This causes the leaf to bleed sap and it droops. The caterpillar then chews from the leaf tip inward, often not pausing until it reaches the leaf base. The milkweed beetle (not the milkweed bug) uses a similar technique later in the season, nipping at several veins before munching in earnest near the leaf margin.

Freeloaders intent on sucking nectar from the flowers may not notice until too late the crab spider sitting on a petal with its long forelegs extended and its body colored a deceptive pink to match its background. Spiders in such high-traffic areas can increase their weight 10 times in a couple of weeks.

Bees and moths sometimes get their legs or mouths stuck in the pollinarium clips and hang there until they starve. Harvestmen—spider relatives often called daddy longlegs—serve as clean up crews by eating such insect corpses. Occasionally, harvestmen tussle with the crab spiders for their prey or may even eat the spiders, if possible.

Parasites make a nice living in the milkweed universe as well. Tachinid flies lay their eggs on monarch caterpillars. When they hatch, they eat the caterpillar from the inside out. Spider wasps paralyze adult spiders and carry them back to a nest where they lay their eggs on or in the luckless spiders.

All's Well That Ends Well

But for the most part, the associations in the milkweed universe serve everyone's interests. Over millions of years, the milkweed and the creatures that call it home have reached a balance whereby the animals are fed and have the energy to reproduce, and the milkweed produces enough mature seeds to replace itself the following year and perhaps extend its range into your backyard and beyond.

Is this then, THE END of the milkweed story?

Certainly not. There are many more stories in the milkweed universe and throughout nature. They only await a careful observer to find and tell them—perhaps a storyteller just like you.

ACTIVITIES

Observations and Drawings for Your Notebook

1. Make a list of arthropods observed on or near milkweeds. Use the "Quick Key for Creature Identification" provided by your teacher to identify major groups; use more detailed keys as much as possible to identify specific insects. Note such things as the season, time of day, and weather when observations are made. Is the milkweed plant in flower? Have seeds set? Do leaves appear to have insect damage? Is there a cluster of plants or only one?

2. Draw a milkweed leaf. Show its form and venation pattern. Sketch how the leaves are arranged on the plant. How does the plant look from above to a descending insect?

3. Dig up a cluster of milkweed plants and see if they are a clone by noting below-ground connections. How many separate plants in your cluster are actually the same genetic individual?

4. Are there any unusual swellings on plant stems or leaves? These swellings, called gauls, are a plant's attempt to combat an insect invader or heal a wound. If you cut open a gaul you can often find an immature insect (larva).

5. Collect insects or other arthropods on milkweed and draw them. What part of the plant were they on? Were there many individuals or only one or two? What role might you assign to each creature you found based on what you observed it doing? (Was it a leaf eater, a plant sap feeder, a seed eater, a nectar gatherer, a nectar gatherer and pollinator, a predator of insects, a parasite of spiders, a parasite of the monarch or some other insect, or a scavenger?)

6. What is the percentage of various kinds of insects trapped in milkweed flowers? Do the trapped insects tend to fall in the same size or weight range?

7. Examine milkweed flowers by making a careful drawing. With a pair of tweezers or wire pull out the "saddlebags" of pollen (called a pollinarium) and draw it. Are any dead bees or other insects "hooked" on a flower? Did small insects crawl out from the flower head while you were sketching it?

8. In the fall, break open a ripe seedpod. How are the seeds arranged? Draw a seed with its attached parachute. How would you suspect milkweed seeds are dispersed? Carefully pull out 10 seeds without damaging their parachutes. Release them, one at a time, from the same height. With a measuring tape determine how far each travels before it hits the ground. How many of the seeds fell in a spot where they might germinate?

9. Describe the smell of milkweed flowers. Make a list of all of the insects you can observe on the flower heads. Which of them seem to be nectar feeders? How can you tell? (Hint: Do they having sucking rather than biting mouth parts?)

10. Observe some milkweed plants after dark. The best way is to use a flashlight covered with red cellophane because most insects can't see red light. What kinds of insects show up at night that weren't there during the day?

11. Can you devise an experiment to test whether flower color, flower shape, or odor of nectar is most important in attracting insects? Does the same characteristic attract both day pollinators and night pollinators?

More Projects and Experiments

Breeding Milkweed Insects

Try and raise one of the species of insects found on milkweed and observe its life cycle. For seed eaters like the large milkweed bug, collect seeds in the fall for later use. You can keep the culture in a small fishbowl, covered with cloth held in place by rubber bands or string. Provide water in a small vial, moisten a cotton ball, and stopper the vial with it. Insects will suck moisture from the cotton and some water will evaporate in the container to provide humidity. Replenish water as necessary.

During the summer, you can place a small wire cage over outdoor plants to make a kind of vivarium. Keep in mind that some insect larvae need soil or twigs to complete their life cycle. Butterflies and moths survive on sugar water until they lay their eggs.

Lacewings—thin, green insects with delicate wings folded over their back—may come to milkweeds to eat aphids. To see their life cycle, capture adults and place them in a coffee can or cardboard ice cream container. Replace the cover with a piece of cheese-cloth held on with a rubber band. Place a moist cotton ball (or the vial and wick arrangement) in the bottom to provide moisture. Place the container out of direct sunlight at a temperature of 70 to 80 degrees Fahrenheit.

Adults will lay their eggs around the inside of the can and on the cheesecloth. The eggs are white, oblong, and mounted on the end of a thin, rigid stalk. Using something like an emery board, you can scrape the sides of the can to deposit the eggs on a piece of paper. Transfer the eggs to a shoe box lined with tissue and evenly distribute the eggs on several layers of the tissue. Cover the shoe box with cheesecloth.

Eggs hatch in about 5 days and the larvae will feed for about 12 more if you provide them with aphids or other soft-bodied insects. Some larvae may cannibalize others if there is not enough food. They pupate in fuzzy, ovoid cocoons and hatch into adults in 6 to 10 days.

Comparing Pollinators

Which insects are most important in the pollination of milkweeds? Test whether night pollinators or day pollinators are most important by covering flowers of one group of plants during the day with nylon netting and another group of plants at night. Count the number of flowers that produce seeds on each plant. (Morse found in his studies that bumblebees accounted for 75 percent to 90 percent of diurnal pollinations and that moths, which pollinate at night, were responsible for 5 percent to 25 percent of all pollinations.)

Testing Reactions to Milkweed Sap

Test the reaction of various insects to milkweed sap. For the approach described below, you will need the following materials:

> cotton swabs
>
> insect net
>
> plastic or enamel tray
>
> milkweed sap (either directly from a nearby plant or in a small vial)
>
> identification keys for insects and spiders
>
> jars to hold selected arthropods
>
> notebooks

1. Collect 6 to 10 different arthropods using a sweep net and tray similar to the ones described in chapter 14. Identify them as closely as you can from available identification keys and separate them, one creature to a jar.

2. List the animals in a column in your naturalist's notebook under the heading "Test Animals."

3. Head a second column "Reaction to Sap."

4. Place your first animal in a clean collecting tray. Dip a cotton swab in a sample of milkweed sap and place it near the head of the animal.

5. Put a plus (+) in the reaction column if the animal stays near the sap or tries to eat it. Put a minus (-) in the column if the animal runs away from the sap.

6. Try to explain the results in your notebook.

7. Repeat the experiment several times to see if you get similar results. Also collect arthropods that normally live on milkweed and compare their reactions to a more random collection of arthropods.

Is milkweed sap a good defensive weapon for milkweeds? Research other ways plants defend themselves from insects.

Germinating Milkweed Seeds

Test the germination rate of milkweed seeds under varying conditions of moisture and temperature.

Materials needed:

> milkweed seeds collected in the fall
>
> small plastic or peat pots to germinate seeds
>
> plastic sandwich bags
>
> water and potting soil
>
> grow light
>
> refrigerator space for one night
>
> notebooks

1. Divide the seeds into four groups. Keep two groups at room temperature and refrigerate two groups overnight.

2. Add equal amounts of potting soil to enough pots to accommodate all the seeds (one seed per pot). Add enough water to each pot to make the soil moist but not "soaked."

3. Plant the room temperature seeds. Cover half of these pots with plastic bags.

4. Plant the seeds that were refrigerated for a night. Cover half of the pots with plastic bags. Keep the room temperature seeds separated from the cold seeds.

5. Place all the pots, covered and uncovered, under the grow light.

6. Make four columns in your naturalist's notebook headed "Warm/dry," "Warm/moist," "Cold/dry," and "Cold/moist."

7. Down the length of the page enter dates for the next 14 days.

8. Water all pots equally once a day or as needed.

9. Record the total number of seeds germinated under each column category for each date.

Consider the following questions: Under what conditions do milkweed seeds germinate best? Do they need a period of cold to germinate effectively? Where do you find most of the milkweeds near your house? Are the conditions there similar to the best growth conditions in your experiment? If you have time, compare milkweed seed growth with that of other plants, either wild or ornamental.

EXPLORING THE MILKWEED UNIVERSE

Finding Milkweeds

The student article and the information presented here is based on the "Showy Milkweed" (probably called the "Obnoxious Milkweed" by some), *Asclepias speciosa*. The plant is a native, creeping perennial that reproduces both by sending out horizontal, subterranean shoots and by scattering seeds. Plants stand 1 foot to 5 feet high, and the main stem is erect, stout, and unbranched. The leaves are opposite, thick, oblong, gray-green in color, and 3-8 inches long. The milkweed is white-woolly all over with short, downy hairs. Flowers are pink to purple and borne in large umbels (clusters). Fruits are spindle-shaped and 3-5 inches long. Ripe seedpods yield brown, corky-margined seeds with tufts of silken hairs on the end. And, of course, if you break a leaf or a stem you get lots of milky white sap.

If you live in the western states you may also come across the western whorled milkweed, *Asclepias subverticulata*. It's a thinner and shorter plant with thin leaves 2-5 inches long emerging three or four at a time at each node of the stem. Flowers are greenish white and look a bit like onion blossoms. You'll find the same basic flower design, seed dispersal, and milky sap in this plant. The common name of this plant is poison milkweed because it can kill livestock if they eat much of it. It, too, however, would make a fascinating study in ecology if it is more common in your area.

I go into considerable detail on the milkweed community in chapter 11 of *Dinosaurs in the Garden* (see the "References" section at the back of this book). Douglass H. Morse's article in *Scientific American* is also quite valuable as is chapter 9 in Scott Camazine's *The Naturalist's Year*. The spin-off potential for studying a plant community like this one is limited only by your time and imagination.

A Quick Key for Creature Identification

I've attempted to develop a "Quick Key" to help kids (and teachers) sort out the major types of animals you're apt to find in your milkweed universes. It is not meant to be all inclusive, but it should let you know where to begin looking in more elaborate field guides if you want to track down some strange creature. This key is based on "counting legs" for a first-order separation and wing features and body segmentation for second-order discrimination. Let me know if it works for you!

QUICK KEY FOR CREATURE IDENTIFICATION
STEP 1: DETERMINE HOW MANY LEGS YOUR CREATURE HAS

1. NO LEGS?

Does the critter look slimy and have two antennae with dark eye spots on the end? If so, you probably have a slug, which is a land-living, shell-less snail. Slugs are in the phylum Molluska and are distant relatives of squids and octopuses.

2. TWO LEGS?

You probably have seen a classmate or a bird. For the former, check the class roster. For the latter, use a good bird field guide. Ruby-throated hummingbirds sometimes get nectar from milkweed flowers. Hawkmoths sometimes look like hummingbirds. See #1 under "Insects."

3. SIX LEGS?

Anything with six legs and three body parts (head, thorax, and abdomen) is an insect. See "Insects."

4. EIGHT LEGS?

If your creature has one body part with legs long in comparison to the body you probably have one of the spider relatives called HARVESTMEN. If the creature has two body parts, see the daddy longlegs reference under "Spiders."
If your creature has one body part and is roundish with short legs, see "Sow Bugs and Pill Bugs."

5. FOURTEEN LEGS (SEVEN PAIRS)?

If your creature has an oblong body, is gray or brownish in color, sometimes with white or yellow markings, and looks like a tiny armadillo, see "Sow Bugs and Pill Bugs."

6. MORE THAN FOURTEEN LEGS?

Does it move quickly and have a long, multisegmented body with one pair of relatively long legs on each segment? It's a CENTIPEDE. Be careful. These guys can bite.
Does it move slowly and have two pairs of relatively short legs per segment? It's a MILLIPEDE.

Quick Key continued on next page.

STEP 2: GO TO THE GROUP INDICATED BY YOUR LEG COUNT

SOW BUGS AND PILL BUGS
(Fourteen legs)

Both sow bugs and pill bugs are land-living crustaceans — relatives of lobsters and crayfish. Both are harmless and eat bits of organic material in soil. Occasionally they become garden pests. Birds and a certain group of spiders find them tasty.
If you poke at your creature and it can't roll up into a ball, it's a SOW BUG.
If you poke at your creature and it does roll up into a ball, it's a PILL BUG.

MITES AND TICKS
(Eight legs, one body part, small)

Very small, present in large quantity in soils, MITES are either free-living predators or parasites of other animals.
If the creature is up to an inch long with a hard, roundish shell it may be a TICK. Ticks are external parasites of birds, mammals, and reptiles and sometimes transmit diseases like Rocky Mountain spotted fever. If you are in a tick-infested area, check for ticks periodically. Because they wander around on an animal's body awhile before taking a blood meal, they can be picked off carefully with fingers or tweezers.

SPIDERS
(Eight legs, two body parts)

If the spider is in a WEB...

...and the web is basically round with a regular pattern of rings and spokes you probably have an ORB WEAVING SPIDER. These common spiders have poor vision but a good sense of touch. They create a web and settle down to wait for a victim to blunder into it.

...and the web is irregular and somewhat haphazard in design (a cobweb), you may have a BLACK WIDOW. Black widows are poisonous spiders with shiny black bodies. They hang upside down in the web and have a red hourglass marking on their abdomen. Leave these gals to their own business.

If the spider is not in a WEB...

...and it moves with quick, jerky motions and seems to be watching you with two large eyes, it is a JUMPING SPIDER. These spiders actually have eight eyes, but the front two are very large. They are active predators of other spiders and insects.

...and it holds its legs crablike out to the side and can walk forward, backward, or sideways, it's a CRAB SPIDER. These spiders are common on flowers like the milkweed flowers and can take on the background color of the flowers they are on.

...and it is a fairly large, fast-moving spider, possibly with dark stripes on a brownish background, it may be a WOLF SPIDER. These spiders are usually ground-based predators. They have a row of four small eyes below four larger eyes.

...and it has very long legs with flexible ends, it may be a DADDY LONGLEGS (family Pholcidae). They tend to be whitish or gray in color. (Don't confuse with the harvestman, which has one body part.)

Quick Key continued on next page.

INSECTS
(Six legs, three body parts)

If your insect has NO WINGS...

...and is small with a flattened body and piercing or sucking mouth parts it may be a LOUSE (Anoplura). These are parasites of birds and mammals and may carry diseases.

...and the body segments are distinct with a thin "waist" between thorax and abdomen, you probably have an ANT. Although ants have two pairs of wings, there are only certain individuals of a colony that display them at certain times in the season. Ants are relatives of BEES AND WASPS (Hymenoptera; see #2 below).

...but has what appears to be a hard covering on its back divided into two parts down the center, you may have a BEETLE or an EARWIG. One pair of a beetle's wings forms a hard case that covers the more delicate pair beneath them. Earwigs have short, leathery forewings and pinchers on their tail end (see #3 below).

If your insect has WINGS...

...and they are either broad and colorful or somewhat furry looking and brown and covered by a scaly coating that leaves a dusty residue on your fingers, go to #1 below.

...and they are thin and transparent like cellophane, go to #2 below.

...and they are hard, leathery, or opaque, whether brightly colored or not, go to #3 below.

#1 Scaly, large wings, order Lepidoptera: MOTHS AND BUTTERFLIES
These are medium to large insects with two pairs of scaly wings and sucking mouth parts.
If the antennae are smooth with knoblike endings you have a BUTTERFLY. Although the monarch butterfly caterpillars specialize in feeding on milkweeds, other butterflies, like the hairstreaks, enjoy the nectar of milkweed flowers.
If the antennae are feathery you have a MOTH. Noctuid moths, geometrid moths, and hawkmoths visit milkweeds. The hawkmoths or sphinx moths can be mistaken for hummingbirds because they hover around flowers, sucking at the nectar with their long mouth parts.
The immature stages of butterflies and moths are caterpillars, often with some elements of coloration found in the adults. Larvae of hawkmoths are called hornworms, and the larvae of geometrid moths are inchworms because of the way they move.

#2 Thin, transparent wings
If the insect has only two wings (one pair) and is small to medium in size with large eyes and sucking mouth parts, you have a FLY (Diptera). You may see tachinid flies, robber flies, or syrphid flies (they look like bees) on or near milkweeds.
If the insect is large and thin with big eyes and two pairs of wings held out to the side like a biplane, you have a DRAGONFLY. If the animal looks nearly the same as described but holds its wings straight up over its back when at rest it's a DAMSELFLY (Odonata).
If the insect is thin and delicate with a long, two- or three-pronged tail and holds its wings straight up over its body when at rest it's a MAYFLY (Ephemerata).
If the insect has two pairs of wings, about equal in size and netted with veins, and holds them folded over its back you have a LACEWING (Neuroptera). The larvae of lacewings are called aphid lions because they have large jaws and like to munch on aphids.
If the insect is small to medium in size with two pairs of unequally sized wings, a narrow waist between thorax and abdomen, chewing or sucking mouth parts, and possibly a stinger, you have a BEE, WASP, OR ANT (Hymenoptera). Common worker ants don't have wings, but those specialized for reproduction do.

Quick Key continued on next page.

#3 Hard, leathery, or opaque wings

If the insect is medium to large in size with leathery forewings and hindwings folded fanlike over the body you have a GRASSHOPPER, CRICKET, ROACH, or one of their kin (Orthoptera).

If the insect is small with stubby wings and a pincherlike tail you have an EARWIG (Dermaptera).

If the insect has two pairs of wings with the forewings partly thickened and jointed, and sucking mouth parts, you have a TRUE BUG (Hermiptera). From the top, the insect looks like it has a large *V* or *X* on its back. There are two milkweed bugs, both of which eat milkweed seeds in the fall. The larger is called *Oncopeltus fasciatus* and the smaller is *Lygaeus kalmii*. Both are red and black.

If the insect is small with two pairs of slender, spotted wings, long antennae and legs, and a scorpionlike rear end, it is a SCORPION FLY.

If the forewings are modified into thickened covers that form a shell-like case with a seam down the middle, you have a BEETLE (Coleoptera). Beetles have chewing mouth parts. There are more species of beetles than all other animals put together. The milkweed beetle is red with black spots and has two very long antennae.

Some Notes on the Quick Key

To avoid the confusion and difficulty of using more complete identification keys, I've tried to eliminate a lot of formal terminology and the usual two-part numbering choices. In step 1 have students do a leg count. This sorts out the phyla of Mollusks, Chordates, and Arthropods as well as the major subphyla of arthropods and a couple of the larger classes:

NO LEGS: Phylum Molluska (snails)

TWO LEGS: Phylum Chordata and then either Class Mammalia (mammals) or Class Aves (birds)

SIX LEGS: Phylum Arthropoda, Subphylum Mandibulata, Class Insecta

EIGHT LEGS: Phylum Arthropoda, Subphylum Chelicerata, Class Arachnida (spiders, mites, ticks, harvestmen)

FOURTEEN LEGS: Phylum Arthropoda, Subphylum Mandibulata, Class Crustacea (sow bugs and pill bugs)

MORE THAN FOURTEEN LEGS: Phylum Arthropoda, Subphylum Mandibulata, Classes Diplopoda (millipedes) and Chilopoda (centipedes)

The insects, because they are so numerous, are further sorted out into the major orders, which are given in parentheses in the key. Refer to some of the more detailed field identification guides to go into more depth, if desired.

Chapter 16

WHO'S A PEST?

Some bugs feed on rosebuds,
And others feed on carrion.
Between them they devour the earth.
Bugs are totalitarian.

—Ogden Nash

GYPSIES, SCAMPS, AND THEE

We all know that a pest is someone or something that is particularly annoying. In biological terms, a pest acquires its reputation by being a threat to human beings or their interests. If a critter eats the same things we do or makes us sick, or if a plant grows next to our corn or petunias, we try to get rid of it any way we can. When it grows or multiplies so fast that we have a hard time keeping it under control, it becomes a Pest with a capital "P." Some creatures— let's call them gypsies—become overly successful when they migrate or are moved from their home habitats, where other organisms can keep them in check. Others, the scamps, are opportunists who take advantage of some change in resources.

A Notable Gypsy

One famous "gypsy" is the gypsy moth, an insect that a young man from France, Etienne Leopold Trouvelot,

thought would make him a lot of money. In Trouvelot's time, many people looking for a way to get rich tried to find or breed a better silkworm, silk being an expensive and popular cloth. The gypsy moth was thought to be a relative of the domesticated Chinese silkworm, so Trouvelot brought some to his new home in Medford, Massachusetts. One thing led to another, and in either 1868 or 1869 some of his moths escaped and found Medford a nice place to breed. Sometimes the "street was black with them." In 1889 one man said, "They struck into the first apple tree in our yard, and the next morning I took four quarts of caterpillars off of one limb."[1]

The state legislature of Massachusetts declared war on the insects in 1890, in the first of many efforts to eliminate the gypsy moth, but it has eaten its fill of oaks and many other trees throughout the New England states and cross-country to the Pacific coast. The poison DDT was most effective in killing it, but it tended to kill and injure many other living things, too. Although the moth does strip trees during outbreaks, most trees survive. It would be fair to say that the gypsy moth is more a pest to people than it is to trees. People cringe at the sight of large numbers of squiggly caterpillars and bare tree limbs.

---

1. Sue Hubbell, *Broadsides from the Other Orders* (New York: Random House, 1993), 186-87.

161

A Notable Scamp

The Colorado potato beetle is a native American (with some Mexican ancestors) who found a good thing to eat and took advantage of it. This "scamp" was first described by the naturalist Thomas Say in 1823. He found individuals munching on a weed called buffalo bur along the Front Range of the Rocky Mountains. Buffalo bur pops up in disturbed areas where cattle and buffalo wallow as well as in fields where people plant crops. When people planted fields full of potatoes in the mid-1800s, the beetle successfully changed diets, which wasn't overly surprising because the buffalo bur plant is something of a country cousin of the potato.

With so much of a good thing to eat, the potato beetle followed farmers across the country. By the 1880s it could be found everywhere potatoes grew. Its population only tends to explode because farmers like large tracts of weedless fields. Various other "pests" earn their status by taking advantage of large, single-species expanses of farm crops.

Other Gypsies and Scamps

Disease-causing microorganisms can also be gypsies and scamps. Smallpox and other European diseases killed many Native Americans because human hosts in America had not had any time to develop any resistance to them. Many bacteria and viruses are also opportunists that multiply when human populations grow dense and transmission becomes easier.

The density of a population is defined as the number of individuals within a given area. The density of any population, whether of potato beetles or people, is determined by only four things: birth rate, death rate, emigration, and immigration. A greater number of births and individuals entering an area (immigration) increase population density. Deaths and emigration (individuals leaving an area) decrease density. Because a given area can only support a limited number of creatures, an increase in one population usually means a decrease in another. Also, if we consider the world as a closed system (with emigration and immigration impossible), only births and deaths affect overall density.

Humans as Pests

Human populations have increased dramatically in the last few hundred years. On a global scale, to a neutral observer, humans might appear to be a pest species. We have no natural predators of any consequence left, and we have learned enough of the tricks of microorganisms to keep many of them at bay—at least temporarily. Reducing our death rate would seem to be a good thing, but there are consequences. Humans can't live without the rest of a healthy mixture of plants and animals to maintain an ecological balance. The trouble is, we don't know enough about the complex interactions between organisms to know when we might destroy that balance with more people than the world can support.

Fortunately, unlike other creatures, we have a choice. Knowing that our numbers can't increase forever without exceeding the resources of our planet, we can choose to limit birth rates—the only other determiner of population density. All we need is the knowledge and will, both as individuals and as a species, to consistently make that choice. The only alternative is a nature-imposed "death tax" no one wants to pay.

ACTIVITIES

Controlling a Pest

Some Background

By looking at how an agricultural pest like the Colorado potato beetle is controlled, we can learn many things about how populations grow and what factors limit or change that growth.

All creatures tend to reproduce as effectively as they can. When an organism first enters a habitat, it may have all the food and space it could want. Pioneer potato beetles, invading potato fields for the first time, might have thought they had entered the promised land of unlimited food and breeding space. Under such conditions, populations grow rapidly, as can be seen from the graph in figure 16.1.

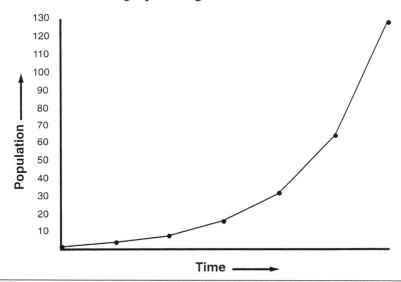

Fig. 16.1. A graph of exponential growth. A graph measuring time on the horizontal axis and population numbers on the vertical axis when the population increases by a series of doublings. This type of growth is called exponential growth.

This type of growth is called exponential growth because it results from a series of doublings that can be expressed as increasing exponents of 2: 2^1, 2^2, 2^3, 2^4, 2^5 (2, 4, 8, 16, 32), and so on.

Eventually, growth reaches limits because of certain factors, either living or nonliving. Living factors include food supply, other animals competing for the same space and resources, predators, and stresses caused by high population densities. Nonliving factors include limited livable space; weather, which includes changing temperature and moisture; minerals; pollutants; and unexpected disasters like volcanoes, earthquakes, and fires. During this phase of growth, populations may fluctuate considerably around some average value that might be considered "normal" for a given species under fairly constant conditions.

From *Explorations in Backyard Biology.* © 1996. Teacher Ideas Press. (800) 237-6124.

Over time, populations may decline to zero in a given area. If conditions are right elsewhere and some individuals can emigrate, the species survives. If all members of a species die, the species becomes extinct. An overall growth curve for a population with limited resources would look like that shown in figure 16.2.

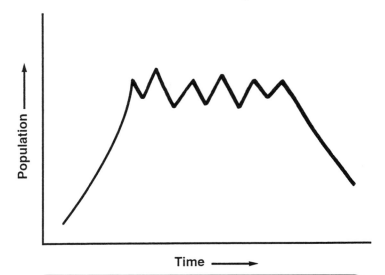

Fig. 16.2. A typical population growth curve. Organisms typically increase in numbers quickly (often showing exponential growth, if conditions are ideal), then their numbers fluctuate about some average number depending on food, predators, weather, and other factors. Populations with limited resources or populations that suffer some kind of disaster may go extinct.

Let's look at some real population studies of the Colorado potato beetle, both on buffalo bur and potato plants, then look at the factors involved in fluctuating beetle populations and how those factors have been used to control population explosions.

First, we need to know something about the potato beetle's life history. Figure 16.3 summarizes the stages, which are similar to the fruit fly's life cycle you've already studied, and shows at what point various predators and parasites may attack the beetle. Depending on the temperature and other weather factors, beetles may complete from one to three generations per season. Adult beetles overwinter by digging tunnels and going into a resting stage called diapause. Harsh winters kill more adults than mild winters, and adults survive winters better where soils are sandy enough for them to dig deeper tunnels. Because adult beetles are not particularly strong fliers, they don't travel far before laying eggs in the spring. Only 20 percent or fewer of potato beetles in a field are immigrants; 80 percent had parents in the same field the previous season.

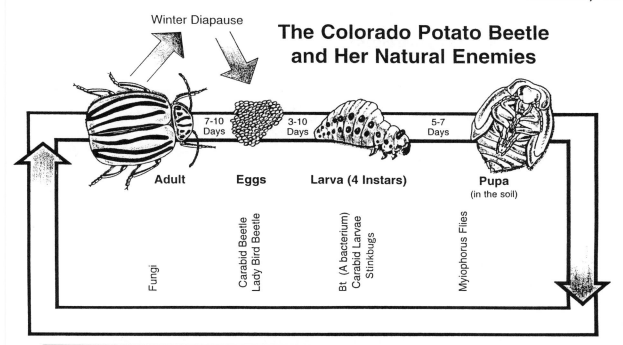

The Colorado Potato Beetle and Her Natural Enemies

Winter Diapause

Adult — 7-10 Days — Eggs — 3-10 Days — Larva (4 Instars) — 5-7 Days — Pupa (in the soil)

Fungi

Carabid Beetle
Lady Bird Beetle

Bt (A bacterium)
Carabid Larvae
Stinkbugs

Myiophorus Flies

Fig. 16.3. Potato beetle life cycle. This life cycle of the potato beetle shows the length of each life stage and the organisms that attack the beetle during these different stages. Controlling pests depends on knowing both what to do and when to do it.

📖 IN YOUR NOTEBOOK

Look at figure 16.4 on page 167, which contains graphs that show the population numbers of three life stages of the beetle at different times of the host plant growing season. Answer the following questions:

1. During what month do the numbers of eggs and larvae peak?

2. During what month do the numbers of adults peak?

3. During what month would you expect to find the greatest numbers of carabid beetles and stinkbugs? (Hint: Look at the life cycle chart of the potato beetle.)

4. If an insecticide were most effective at killing the first instar of the beetle, when would you want to apply it?

5. When might be the best time to apply a general insecticide that kills adult insects?

Continued on next page.

From *Explorations in Backyard Biology.* © 1996. Teacher Ideas Press. (800) 237-6124.

IN YOUR NOTEBOOK (continued)

6. Based on the habits of the adult beetle, how effective do you think crop rotation would be in controlling beetle populations?

   The graph in figure 16.5 on page 168 shows how well the potato beetle reproduces on two native "weeds" and the potato plant. Look at the graph and answer these questions:

7. On which plant does the beetle reproduce best?

8. If potato plants don't provide the best habitat for potato beetles, what factors may have caused them to become pests on potato plants?

Controlling Potato Beetles

Several techniques can control potato beetle populations with varying degrees of success: the use of insecticides, both chemical and bacterial; the use of natural enemies like stinkbugs, other beetles, and parasitic flies; scientific methods to make host plants more resistant; and crop rotation. Each technique has its own strengths and weaknesses.

Chemical insecticides have had mixed success, often depending on the part of the country in which they are used. Where populations go through several generations in one season and insecticides are used too often, the beetles become resistant to the chemicals. In addition, other insects and spiders that might help control the beetle population are also killed. Bt insecticides that infect young beetle larvae with a bacterium don't kill helpful insects but are only effective at a certain stage of the potato beetle life cycle; thus they must be applied at the right time to be effective.

Natural enemies of the potato beetle include fungi, predatory insects, and parasitic flies. Fungi tend to be killed by fungicides farmers use to control rusts and smuts. Insects may be killed by insecticides. Rearing and releasing large numbers of predators can be expensive and requires a sound knowledge of the biology of all species involved (see fig. 16.6 on page 168).

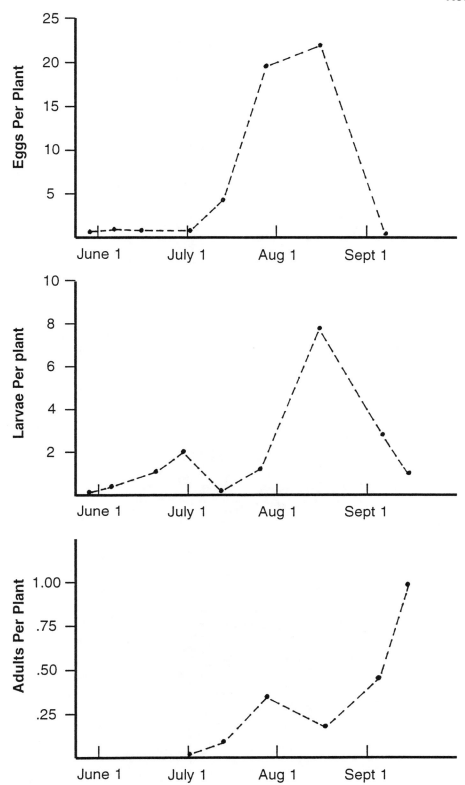

Fig. 16.4. Egg, larval, and adult beetle growth over three months. The numbers of potato beetle eggs, larvae, and adults found on potato plants over a four-month period have been plotted on these graphs. The data are a composite of records kept over a two-year period by David R. Horton (see "References").

From *Explorations in Backyard Biology*. © 1996. Teacher Ideas Press. (800) 237-6124.

Effect of Host Plant on Beetle Reproduction

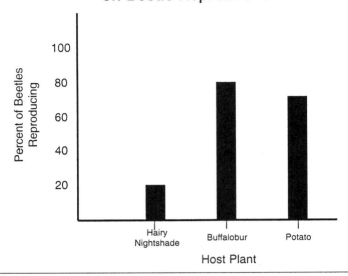

Fig. 16.5. Beetle population growth. The percentages of beetles reproducing on three different plants in the potato family are shown. Hairy nightshade and buffalo bur are native weeds often found near potato fields. Data are from the Ph.D. work of David R. Horton (see "References").

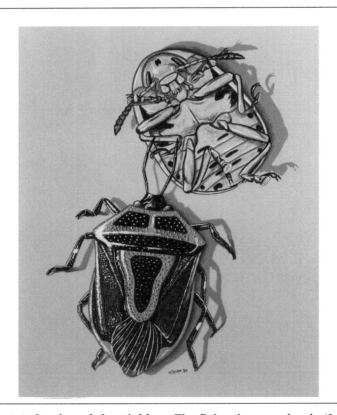

Fig. 16.6. The potato beetle and the stinkbug. The Colorado potato beetle (*Leptinotarsa decemlineata*), shown at the top of this illustration on its back, may find itself the victim of the eyed stinkbug (*Perillus bioculatus*). The stinkbug is an insect with striking black and red coloration. Reprinted from *Dinosaurs in the Garden,* courtesy Plexus Publishing, Inc., Medford, NJ.

From *Explorations in Backyard Biology.* © 1996. Teacher Ideas Press. (800) 237-6124.

Strains of plants that create chemicals that potato beetles don't like have been created, including plants that produce the bacterial endotoxins used in Bt insecticides. However, potato beetles are very adaptable. Because the natural plants they feed on also produce potent anti-insect chemicals, potato beetles have a history of changing their genetic makeup quickly to detoxify poisons.

Crop rotation is the single most effective means of control. Because adult beetles are poor fliers, they have a hard time infecting distant targets, and when they do, they don't have as much time to feed and reproduce. The more diverse the plant life in an area, the less chance any one creature will rise to "pest" status. Maintaining a healthy diversity of plants and animals is the single most effective way to ensure a healthy ecosystem.

Supplemental Activities

1. Invite a local farmer to discuss ways he or she controls pests.

2. Report on the history of a pest like the gypsy moth, starling, or English sparrow.

3. Research the story of the eradication of smallpox or report on recent advances in the control of AIDS.

4. Plot the growth of human populations over the last few centuries and analyze the growth curve. What stage of population growth are we in worldwide?

LOOKING AT ANIMAL POPULATIONS

Notes on the Student Article

Pests are usually defined in human terms. The student article attempts to show that we might profitably expand the meaning of the term to include any organism, including *Homo sapiens*, that threatens the stability of its ecosystem. Although the gypsy moth and Colorado potato beetle are given as examples of pests, this chapter gives you the opportunity to introduce any local beastie that students might be more familiar with. The book *The Alien Animals* by George Laycock describes the history of many game or "pleasure" animals that were brought into this country; Sue Hubbell, in *Broadsides from the Other Orders,* details the gypsy moth problem.

Notes on the Student Activity

Controlling a Pest

The information provided about potato beetles will give students an opportunity to think about the complexity of interactions in the living world as well as some experience working with actual scientific data. The information provided in the graphs was adapted from the Ph.D. work of David Horton (whose dissertation is listed in the "References" section at the back of this book). Horton's work asked the question "How did the Colorado potato beetle become a pest species?" To answer the question, he studied beetles living on both natural food plants (buffalo bur and nightshade) and potato plants to see how their growth patterns differed.

"In Your Notebook" Questions:

1. Egg and larval numbers peak in early August.

2. Adult numbers peak in September.

3. Carabid beetle and stinkbug populations should peak in August when their food, the larval potato beetles, is most plentiful.

4. The insecticide for first instars would be most effective if applied in June when eggs are hatching. The Bt insecticides are most effective on first and second instars. *Bt* stands for *Bacillus thuringiensis,* a bacterium that affects the beetle larvae's midgut and causes starvation. Because the bacterium kills most of the first and second instars, but only 50 percent of older larvae, it should be applied soon after egg hatch but before the second instar molt. Because it needs to reach the beetle's gut, it should be applied in the warmth of midday when the larvae are actively feeding.

5. Adult insecticides would be best applied in September when adult populations are high and when it won't matter as much if other beneficial insects are killed.

6. Crop rotation is very effective at control because 80 percent of the beetles that infect a field come from adults who lived there the previous year.

7. The beetles reproduced best on buffalo bur.

8. David Horton believed that four things turned the potato beetle into a pest: (a) because people don't like prickly weeds like buffalo bur growing near crops, they destroy the beetle's natural host; (b) potatoes and other crops are planted in high-density monocultures, providing a vast food source for the beetles; (c) fertilization, irrigation, and weed control reduce the effects of natural variations in water and competition that would regulate beetle numbers by regulating the number of host plants; and (d) by planting

potatoes in the same place each year the beetle's life cycle can become more easily synchronized with its host plant.

Some Things to Emphasize

A pest doesn't have to be exterminated to be controlled. Its numbers just have to be reduced so that the damage it causes is relatively small. Completely destroying any species could result in many long-term problems not immediately obvious because of the complexity of ecosystems.

No control measure is necessarily all bad or all good. As in many things, timing is everything. Insecticides applied too often or at the wrong time result in the death of many important nontarget insects and increase resistance in the target insect. Manipulating natural enemies can be expensive and requires a sound knowledge of the interrelationships in an ecosystem.

We need to think of ourselves as part of, rather than above or exempt from, the natural world. We are unique in two respects: 1) our learning and culture allow us to live in almost every conceivable habitat, so we have spread globally and multiplied greatly; and 2) we have the intelligence to be able to anticipate the consequences of what we do. We must use this latter ability to save ourselves from the consequences of a runaway population whose numbers will some day soon stretch the resources of our planet to its limits.

Chapter 17

DRAWING STRENGTH
FROM NATURE

BUILDING GREEN CASTLES

You've spent an hour building an elaborate block castle. Big towers rise in several places. You can almost see the knights and well-dressed ladies peeking from the windows or walking through long, elaborate corridors. Now, you think, I wonder what would happen if I take out this block right *here*. You carefully slide the block out. Parts of the castle tremble, but the walls hold. Then you try another, perhaps near the bottom of a large tower. This time, the castle sways, then crashes quickly in a tumble of bouncing and rolling blocks.

The block you chose to remove may have been just a fraction of your castle, but because it was in a critical spot, its removal destroyed your entire building. Similar things happen in the complex structures of living communities. Animals or plants that have a huge impact on the communities in which they live are called *keystone species.*

The Importance of Keystone Species

Sea otters along the Pacific coast of the United States turned out to be such a keystone species, but people discovered that the hard way. When European settlers first arrived, otters lived by the millions all along the coast, from Alaska to southern

California. These whiskered, 85-pound relatives of weasels lived in lush forests of marine algae called kelp. The kelp sheltered numerous other animals and plants, including sea urchins, crustaceans, squid, numerous fish, and gray whales, which fed on rich soups of microscopic organisms collectively called plankton.

Unfortunately for the sea otters, they possessed beautiful, thick brown pelts of fur that people liked to wear. Europeans hunted them so successfully that 120,000 pelts were taken during a 50-year period from just one small area near the Commander Islands in the Bering Sea. When the otters disappeared, many unforeseen things happened. The otter's main food, the sea urchins, exploded in number and fed like an army of lawn mowers on the kelp beds. With the kelp gone, the shallow coastal areas became underwater deserts, with few of the fish and other creatures that had lived within the kelp.

Fortunately, people realized what was happening before it was too late. They reintroduced otters at various spots along the coast using individuals from scattered remnant populations. Otters are still rare and endangered, but are making a comeback. So are the kelp forests. The intricate otter-kelp castle is being rebuilt to something close to its original richness and beauty.

172

Sometimes we aren't so lucky. In the Philippine Islands, fishermen lived for thousands of years off a rich harvest of fish and other marine life that existed as part of a large coral reef community. Looking for short-term solutions to feeding an increasing human population, the Philippine government encouraged a policy of fishing with dynamite. The explosions killed huge quantities of fish, allowing the fishermen to scoop them up easily as they floated to the surface. Fishermen prospered for awhile. But the explosions damaged the reef organisms themselves. Without the corals, the reef ecology collapsed. Because corals grow much more slowly than kelp, it could take hundreds or even thousands of years for them to rebound.

Nature's Impact on Living Systems

Time is very important in building large, strong castles. If your baby brother or sister comes in every five minutes and takes a swat at your castle, it won't get very big or complex. You also need a level place that's not moving or shaking a lot. Living ecologies are similar in this respect, too. Most complex, living systems have self-assembled over thousands, sometimes millions, of years under conditions of climate, temperature, and geology that have remained relatively constant.

Once in awhile, all of our planet's living systems get shaken up drastically. Scientists know this from the fossil record, which sometimes goes from being very rich to very poor in just a few thousand or a few million years of deposits. Fifteen times since the days of *Anomalocaris* (see chapter 8) large fractions of Earth's living creatures have become extinct quickly. During five of these, more than 50 percent of the species

alive at the time died. On two occasions, complex Earth life narrowly escaped total destruction.

The reasons for severe extinctions vary. The slow drifting of continents that alter the number of marine and land habitats, increased volcanism that cools Earth's overall temperature, long-term cycles in Earth's orbit about the sun that affect climate, and impacts of large hunks of rock from outer space have all played roles in the past. Over the past 200,000 years another factor has appeared: the rise and flourishing of our species, *Homo sapiens*.

The Role of Humans in Ecology

Look at a graph of human population growth over the last 300 years and compare it to a graph of animal extinctions over the same period (see fig. 17.1). The similarity in the curves is striking. Sometimes people destroy keystone species like the otter, without knowing how important they are in their communities. Other times people destroy habitat, like clear-cutting jungle forests, which destroys millions of forest-living creatures by default, many of them unknown.

In the past, when human numbers were small and nature seemed endless and scary, people thought of nature as an opponent that should be beaten. Now we know that we are a part of the natural world and if we destroy it, either intentionally or because we are ignorant of how it works, we will only end up hurting or destroying ourselves. We can admire and live in nature's living castles for thousands of years to come if we learn to keep in place the cornerstones that hold up her beautiful, green walls.

Billions

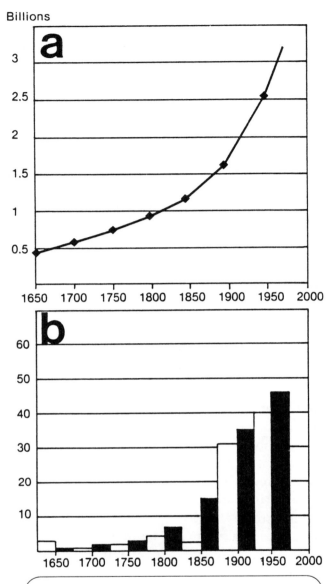

Fig. 17.1. Human population growth and animal extinction. Comparison of growth curve for human population (*a*) with the number of extinctions (*b*) of mammals (white bars) and birds (black bars) over the last 300 years. Reprinted from *Dinosaurs in the Garden,* courtesy Plexus Publishing, Inc., Medford, NJ.

ACTIVITIES

A Look at the Valley of Contentment

The Indians that lived along the Front Range of northern Colorado knew a spot near the foothills they called the Valley of Contentment because of its beauty and wealth of wild animals. Much of this area is still preserved as Lory State Park, west of Fort Collins, Colorado. An unusual mix of animals and plants share this spot and call it home. This is possible because of the unique geology of the area, which places it at the boundary between mountains and plains. By observing how geology and climate affect this community, you can look for similar patterns where you live.

The modern Rocky Mountains formed about the same time the Age of Dinosaurs came to an end, 65 million years ago. Before that, the area that would become the Valley of Contentment was at various times ocean bottom, beach, and windblown desert. These incarnations left their traces as sediments that later turned to rock. When geological forces deep in the Earth became active 65 million years ago, dense igneous rocks called granite and pegmatite that had been created a billion years earlier during a similar geologically active period were thrust upward through the softer sedimentary rock like a knife poking through a crust of dried mud.

The "granite knife" is now called Arthur's Rock. The ridges of relatively hard sand-stones on the eastern side of the valley are called hogbacks because their knobby contours look like an animal's backbone. Hogbacks here and elsewhere along the Front Range run in several parallel ribbons that trend north and south like the rising Rockies that created them. Softer sedimentary rocks, mostly shales and mudstones, eroded faster and became the floor of the valley between the hogbacks and Arthur's Rock. Streams draining from the top of Arthur's Rock cut draws that serve as pathways for people and animals. In a couple of hours you can climb the 1,000-foot vertical rise between valley floor and foot-hills peak. Let's take a short verbal climb. The path is marked in figure 17.2.

Temperature and moisture largely control the patterns of life here. "Semiarid" describes the region as a whole because average annual rainfall is 14 inches. Summer temperatures range from 85°F to 55°F, and the average minimum temperature in winter is 12°F. Warm winds called chinooks often blow from the west. But the change in elevation from valley floor to granite peak also affects temperature, and the streams provide moisture in places that would otherwise be dry. We'll start our trip in the warm, dry Grassland Community on the valley floor and along the base of the hogbacks.

Stay on the path and listen for the rattle of a diamondback rattlesnake that might be out hunting deer mice. Notice that large tracts of long-stemmed grasses are punctuated here and there with yellow-topped rabbit brush and gnarled mountain mahogany bushes. Meadowlarks sing to each other, and black-and-white magpies may glide from perch to perch. Watch for mule deer early in the morning or at dusk, but don't step on the prickly pear cactus if you're walking in soft-soled shoes.

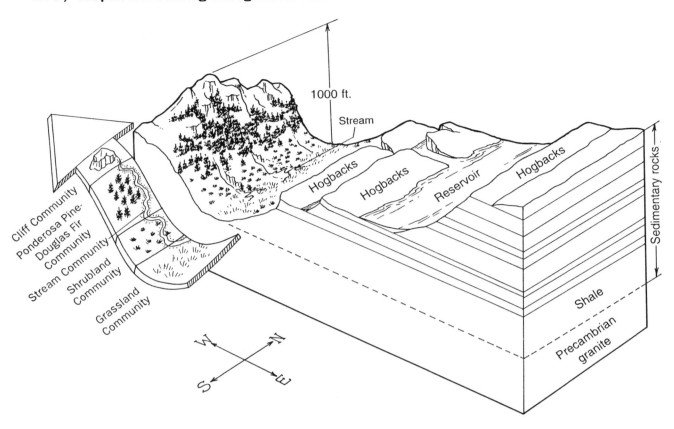

Fig. 17.2. Geological cross section of the Valley of Contentment. The Valley of Contentment was created when ancient granite rock poked through layers of sedimentary rock as the result of volcanic activity 65 million years ago. The softer shales and mudstones eroded away, quickly forming several valleys. Harder sedimentary rocks form ridges called hogbacks that stretch north and south. The 1,000-foot change in elevation from granite peak to valley floor creates temperature and moisture differences that support different groupings of plants and animals. Humans filled one valley with water to create a reservoir for irrigation purposes. The living and nonliving elements of our planet interact in complex and sometimes poorly understood ways.

As you get higher, the temperature cools and shrubs take hold on rocky slopes. Look for mountain maple, wild berry bushes, and a tall, soft-leaved plant called wooly mullein that Indians are said to have used for toilet paper. You'll see chipmunks now and then, possibly a skunk, and, on rare occasions, black bear. Mountain bluebirds flit from bush to bush or from bush to scattered ponderosa pine. You are now in the Shrubland Community.

Ponderosa pine get more numerous as you climb and are joined by Douglas firs. These two species define the Ponderosa Pine-Douglas Fir Community. Abert's squirrels feed on ponderosa needles and may complain about your company. Snowberry bushes, larkspurs, wild roses, and juniper dot the landscape. You may see where porcupines have gnawed on bark or have to step over the droppings of deer or elk. If you stop for lunch, a Stellar's jay will probably beg for a handout. A goshawk may cruise overhead on a warm updraft.

Special living communities develop near flowing water, which you may find in several places along the way. Look for willows, cottonwood trees, bluebells, pea flowers, raccoons, and shrews. Look up to see turkey vultures flying overhead in search of a tasty rodent.

If you're puffing when you reach the top of Arthur's Rock, you either hurried too much or just aren't used to the 6,500-foot elevation. You may see a long-tailed weasel or wood rat among the raspberry bushes and wild roses. Cliff swallows perch on ragged rock faces, and you may get a glimpse of a golden eagle. Bobcats and an occasional mountain lion find their way here in search of food.

From the top of Arthur's Rock look east. Beyond the hogbacks, blue sky reflects from the surface of the 6.5-mile-long Horsetooth Reservoir, completed in 1956, which holds water used for crop irrigation. Before then a dry canyon separated the hogbacks from the plain on which the city of Fort Collins was built. A railroad once ran to the town of Stout, now a drowned relic beneath the reservoir's water. Indians that climbed this rock would have seen a sea of native grasses in the distance. Today, a city of 100,000 people stretches north and south. Numerous cottonwoods and other trees line many of the streets. On some days a haze of pollution blurs the details.

📖 IN YOUR NOTEBOOK

On our verbal journey through the Valley of Contentment you saw five communities of living things: a Grassland Community, a Shrubland Community, a Ponderosa Pine-Douglas Fir Community, a Mountain Meadow/Stream Community, and a Cliff Community. Copy the illustration in figure 17.2 into your notebook and label where you can find each of these communities. Based on the names of the first three communities, what are their keystone species? Which community would you expect to have the coldest average temperature? Which community would you expect to be the driest? How does the Mountain Meadow/Stream Community differ from low to higher elevations?

Because our valley is at a latitude of about 41° N, slopes that face south will get more heat from the sun than slopes that face north. If you are walking up a draw from valley floor to Arthur's Rock, which side of the trail will have more snow left in the spring? What differences might you expect to see in the plants found there? Going from valley floor to the top of Arthur's Rock, would you expect there to be sharp divisions between the different communities or considerable overlap? Why?

How have human beings changed the living and nonliving environment in the last few hundred years? Which changes would you consider improvements and which changes have decreased the diversity of life here? How should people manage this land in the future?

From *Explorations in Backyard Biology.* © 1996. Teacher Ideas Press. (800) 237-6124.

Landforms, Life-Forms, and Devilish Details

Take a field trip to a nearby federal or state park where natural habitats have been preserved. If such a park is not nearby, visit any outdoor spot in your town, city, or community, but plan to look at it in a new way.

1. Before your trip, get maps of the area that show elevation, streams, rivers, lakes, and other waterways, as well as human-made structures like quarries, buildings, roads, and so forth.

2. Plan to hike or drive to the highest spot in the area.

3. Get out your trusty naturalist's notebook and sketch the landforms you see around you. Where are the hills and valleys? Where are streams and lakes? Make four rough sketches, one facing toward each of the compass points: north, east, south, and west.

4. Now look for life-forms. Where are the trees? Where are bushes? Where are grass-lands? Where are cities, roads, and other human constructions? On your first sketches, color areas with trees dark green, areas with mostly bushes light brown, and grassy areas light green. Color waterways blue and human constructions red.

   What factors seem most important in determining where life-forms (including human settlements) are located? Do you think you have a proper balance of living things, human and nonhuman, in your area to support a healthy community?

5. Find something alive near you—a plant or insect will do, perhaps even another student—and sketch him, her, or it in your notebook. Ask yourself: How does this creature survive here? Will it be here in the future? What can I do to help make sure that it will be?

From *Explorations in Backyard Biology*. © 1996. Teacher Ideas Press. (800) 237-6124.

DRAWING THE BIG PICTURE

Notes on the Student Article

I mentioned in the student article that there were two extinction events in the history of Earth where a large fraction of life on our planet was destroyed. One was 250 million years ago at the end of the Paleozoic era. An event so distant in time is hard to reconstruct, but global cooling, associated with increased glaciation, seems to have been the key element in the wholesale destruction that occurred then.

The other severe extinction happened 65 million years ago, about the time the Rockies were rising, and killed off the last of the dinosaurs (except birds) and most other large land vertebrates. Increased volcanism, leading to a cooler climate, played a role, but the evidence is also strong that one or more large asteroids pelted the Earth, raising huge clouds of sun-blocking dust and creating firestorms that filled the skies with smoke. Mammals in general and *Homo sapiens* in particular benefited from this extinction. Our hairy forebears inherited a nearly empty world of opportunity and diversified to fill it.

Scientists like Peter Ward (author of *The End of Evolution*) and Edward O. Wilson (author of *The Diversity of Life*) believe we are now in the midst of a third great extinction whose beginnings go back 2.5 million years to the start of a new period of glaciation. The advent of humans some 200,000 years ago, however, may have accelerated the process. Everywhere people have gone, species have perished. Historical and fossil records validate species extinction on every island habitat discovered. Some scientists assert that the flourishing of the Clovis culture in North America 11,000-12,000 years ago and the loss of most of the megafauna here (lions, short-faced bears, saber-toothed tigers, giant ground sloths, camels, etc.) is no coincidence.

Although it's easy to get depressed about this state of affairs, it is not a situation without hope. Humans have also made deserts bloom with new life and are capable of creating clever solutions to many problems. The key is education and understanding, two things that educators strive to promote. When we understand a problem, we have a better than even shot of solving it. As in many things, attitude is critical. We have to realize our role and our responsibilities as a part of the natural world.

Notes on the Student Activities

A Look at the Valley of Contentment

I used this spot as an example because I visit it many times in the course of a year, both for recreation and renewal. Boating and camping, as well as hiking, biking, and horseback trails, provide lots of recreational possibilities. Having a natural area within 30 minutes of where I live and work allows me to reconnect with the natural world and regain perspective. I hope you have access to similar places and can introduce them to your students.

If you and your students have allowed yourself to experiment with the drawing techniques I've tried to encourage in this book, perhaps you have discovered that this activity can be relaxing and satisfying, too. There is no reason why drawing skills shouldn't be developed at an adult level, just as we strive to help people develop their mathematical and writing skills. Tapping the intuitive, creative, right brain helps us integrate the confusing multiplex messages of the modern world.

"In Your Notebook" Questions: Grasses are keystone species in the Grassland Community, mountain maples and other shrubs in the Shrubland Community, and ponderosa pines and Douglas firs determine the nature of their community. The Cliff Community is coldest by virtue of being the highest and most exposed. The Grassland Community is driest. At lower elevations, the Mountain Meadow/Stream Community is more likely to support the growth of aspens and cottonwoods along its banks. At higher elevations, wildflowers and grasses take advantage of the added moisture.

More snow will remain on north-facing slopes. Because moisture is retained better here, you will find trees on these slopes and often shrubs or grasses on warmer, drier, south-facing slopes. Communities have considerable overlap, and creatures like mule deer may migrate up and down through communities depending on the time of year. Microhabitats vary in moisture, temperature, and soil character based on topography, exposure, and the mineral content of nearby rocks.

Filling a canyon with water eliminated some desert/grassland communities and created new associations in and near the water. Most of the water is used for irrigation. Increased plant growth adds more water to the air, which may affect local climate to a certain extent. Better farming and opportunities for recreation encouraged population growth. Population growth brings with it problems of waste disposal and pollution. Drinking water in semiarid regions is often "borrowed" from wetter, less developed areas where its removal has consequences for those communities as well. Each community must wrestle with the good and bad aspects of earlier decisions and plan for the futures they want to see for themselves and their children.

Landforms, Life-Forms, and Devilish Details

Materials for a successful field trip will vary somewhat, depending on your local conditions, but here is a partial list:

notebooks

regular and colored pencils

hand pencil sharpeners

erasers

water

sack lunches

daypacks

comfortable hiking shoes or boots

sunscreen

hat

jackets or sweaters for variable weather

You may also want to carry a camera to record events for classroom work or future trips. Slides can now be put on CD-ROM disks easily, and students could work on extended projects in school or even at home.

Use this activity as an opportunity for students to see their own surroundings as part of a larger picture—a picture that includes more than just human beings, but one where human beings are making ever bigger brush strokes.

FINAL THOUGHTS

Someone once said, "The devil is in the details," meaning that many ideas or concepts look great overall but become difficult to put into practice when it comes to dealing with the specifics of bringing about change. This is very true when discussing the effects of human growth on nature, because everything communities do affects the way people live and work.

In this book you've had a chance to look at many individual plants and animals and some of their "devilish details." The details can be fascinating and exciting, but it is easy to get lost in them. Because we possess an intelligence that gives us a unique perspective on all life around us and allows us to learn how everything works together, we are not at the total mercy of the forces that have buffeted life in the past. We can choose to control events to our liking and must struggle to keep the machinery of an ancient and complex living world working properly.

Drawing is one tool that allows us to tap the creative side of our brain—the side that allows us to synthesize a confusing mass of facts and use them to solve new problems. I hope you will find ways to further use drawing skills to enjoy and learn about science and to create personal satisfaction in exploring the natural world around you.

References

Chapter 1: Drawing as a Tool in Science: The Naturalist's Notebook

Diagram Group. *The Brain: A User's Manual.* New York: Berkley Books, 1983.

Edwards, Betty. *Drawing on the Right Side of the Brain.* Los Angeles: J. P. Tarcher, 1979 (Distributed by Houghton Mifflin Co., Boston).

Johnson, Cathy. *The Sierra Club Guide to Sketching in Nature.* San Francisco: Sierra Club Books, 1990.

McKim, Robert H. *Experiences in Visual Thinking.* Boston: PWS Publishers, 1980.

Restak, Richard M. *The Brain.* New York: Bantam Books, 1984, pp. 237-70.

———. *The Mind.* New York: Bantam Books, 1988, pp. 26-29.

Shaw, John M. *Lab-Top Book for Writing in Science.* Access through NASA Spacelink, a public archive of NASA resources. (With modem, call 205-895-0028. With Internet connectivity, use Telnet to spacelink.msfc.nasa.gov or use IP address 192.149.89.61 and follow login prompts.)

Chapter 2: Let's Get Small

Boeke, Kees. *Cosmic View: The Universe in 40 Jumps.* New York: John Day, 1957.

Hertzberg, Hendrik. *One Million.* New York: Random House, 1993.

McGowan, Chris. *Diatoms to Dinosaurs: The Size and Scale of Living Things.* Washington, DC: Island Press/Shearwater Books, 1994.

McMahon, Thomas A., and Bonner, John Tyler. *On Size and Life.* New York: Scientific American Books, 1983.

Morrison, Philip, and Morrison, Phylis. *Powers of Ten.* New York: Scientific American Books, 1982.

Wells, H. G.; Huxley, Julian S.; and Wells, G. P. *The Science of Life.* New York: Book League of America, 1936.

Identification/Culturing Guides

Jahn, T. L. *How to Know the Protozoa.* Dubuque, IA: William C. Brown, 1949.

James, Daniel E., and Kylander, Jackie E. *Culturing Bacteria and Fungi.* Burlington, NC: Carolina Biological Supply Company, 1982.

Klots, Elsie B. *The New Field Book of Freshwater Life.* New York: G. P. Putnam's Sons, 1966.

Margulis, Lynn, and Schwartz, Karlene V. *Five Kingdoms: An Illustrated Guide to the Phyla of Life on Earth.* San Francisco: W. H. Freeman and Company, 1982.

Prescott, G. W. *How to Know the Freshwater Algae.* Dubuque, IA: William C. Brown, 1964.

Sagan, Dorian, and Margulis, Lynn. *Garden of Microbial Delights.* New York: Harcourt Brace Jovanovich, 1988.

Chapter 3: Microwars

Barron, G. L. "Structure and Biology of a New *Harposporium*-Attacking Bdelloid Rotifers." *Canadian Journal of Botany* 61 (1983): 1875-1878.

Bold, Harold C. *Morphology of Plants*. 2d ed. New York: Harper & Row, 1967.

Cooke, Roderic. *The Biology of Symbiotic Fungi*. New York: John Wiley & Sons, 1977.

James, Daniel E., and Kylander, Jackie E. *Culturing Bacteria and Fungi*. Burlington, NC: Carolina Biological Supply Company, 1982.

Margulis, Lynn, and Schwartz, Karlene V. *Five Kingdoms: An Illustrated Guide to the Phyla of Life on Earth*. San Francisco: W. H. Freeman and Company, 1982.

Morholt, Evelyn; Brandwein, Paul F.; and Alexander, Joseph. *A Sourcebook for the Biological Sciences*. 2d ed. New York: Harcourt Brace Jovanovich, 1966.

Pirozynski, K. A., and Hawksworth, D. L., eds. *Coevolution of Fungi with Plants and Animals*. New York: Academic Press Limited, 1988.

Raham, R. Gary. *Dinosaurs in the Garden: An Evolutionary Guide to Backyard Biology*. Medford, N. J.: Plexus, 1988.

Science News Staff. "Attack of the Worm-Eating Mushrooms." *Science News* 125 (14) (April 7, 1984): 129.

———. "'Peacekeeper' Fungus: Rotifers Beware." *Science News* 123 (2) (January 8, 1983): 23.

Tzean, S. S., and Barron, G. L. "A New Predatory Hyphomycete Capturing Bdelloid Rotifers in Soil." *Canadian Journal of Botany* 61 (1983): 1345-1348.

Chapter 4: Monsters in the Mud Puddle

Brock, Thomas D., and Brock, Louise M. *Life in the Geyser Basins*. Yellowstone Library and Museum Association, 1971.

Dobell, Clifford, ed. *Antony van Leeuwenhoek and His "Little Animals."* New York: Dover Publications, 1960.

Gould, James L., and Gould, Carol Grant. *Life at the Edge*. New York: W. H. Freeman and Company, 1989.

Jahn, T. L. *How to Know the Protozoa*. Dubuque, IA: William C. Brown, 1949.

Klots, Elsie B. *The New Field Book of Freshwater Life*. New York: G. P. Putnam's Sons, 1966.

Margulis, Lynn, and Schwartz, Karlene V. *Five Kingdoms; An Illustrated Guide to the Phyla of Life on Earth*. San Francisco: W. H. Freeman and Company, 1982.

Prescott, G. W. *How to Know the Fresh-Water Algae*. Dubuque, IA: William C. Brown, 1964.

Raham, R. Gary. *Dinosaurs in the Garden: An Evolutionary Guide to Backyard Biology*. Medford, NJ: Plexus, 1988.

Sagan, Dorian, and Margulis, Lynn. *Garden of Microbial Delights*. New York: Harcourt Brace Jovanovich, 1988.

———. *Micro-cosmos*. New York: Summit, 1986.

Schopf, William J. *Major Events in the History of Life*. Boston: Jones and Bartlett, 1992.

Tappan, Helen. *The Paleobiology of Plant Protists.* San Francisco: W. H. Freeman and Company, 1980.

Chapter 5: Before Insects Could Fly

Bland, Roger G., and Jaques, H. E. *How to Know the Insects.* Dubuque, IA: William C. Brown, 1978.

Bodanis, David. *The Secret Garden.* New York: Simon & Schuster, 1992.

Evans, Howard Ensign. *Life on a Little Known Planet.* New York: Dell, 1968.

Holldobler, Bert, and Wilson, Edward O. *Journey to the Ants.* Cambridge, MA: Belnap Press, 1994.

Levi, Herbert W., and Levi, Lorna R. *A Guide to Spiders and Their Kin.* New York: Golden Press, 1968.

Morholt, E.; Brandwein, P.; and Alexander, J. *A Sourcebook for the Biological Sciences.* 2d ed. New York: Harcourt Brace Jovanovich, 1966.

O'Toole, Christopher, ed. *The Encyclopedia of Insects.* New York: Facts on File, 1986.

Stokes, Donald W. *A Guide to Observing Insect Lives.* Boston: Little, Brown, 1983.

Zim, Herbert S., and Cottam, Clarence. *Insects: A Guide to Familiar American Insects.* New York: Golden Press, 1951.

Chapter 6: The Eyes Have It

Brusca, Richard C., and Brusca, Gary J. *Invertebrates.* Sunderland, MA: Sinauer Associates, 1990.

Downer, John. *Supersense: Perception in the Animal World.* New York: Henry Holt, 1988.

Foelix, Rainer F. *Biology of Spiders.* Cambridge, MA: Harvard University Press, 1982.

Levi-Setti, Ricardo. "Ancient and Wonderful Eyes." *Fossils* 1 No. (1) (May 1976): 24-36.

Raham, R. Gary. *Dinosaurs in the Garden: An Evolutionary Guide to Backyard Biology.* Medford, NJ: Plexus, 1988.

———. "Through Arthropod Eyes." *Backyard Bugwatching* (13) (1991): 9-12.

———. "Through Raptor's Eyes." *On the Wing* 6 (Spring/Summer 1991): 4, 6.

Time-Life Editors. *The Camera.* New York: Time-Life Books, 1976.

Chapter 7: Pond Dragons

Corbet, Philip S. *A Biology of Dragonflies.* Chicago: Quadrangle Books, 1963.

Dalton, Stephen. *Borne on the Wind.* New York: Reader's Digest Press, 1975.

Durrell, Gerald. *A Practical Guide for the Amateur Naturalist.* New York: Alfred A. Knopf, 1983.

Evans, Howard Ensign. *Life on a Little Known Planet.* New York: Dell, 1968.

Farb, Peter. *The Insects.* New York: Time, 1962.

Klausnitzer, Bernhard. *Insects—Their Biology and Cultural History.* New York: Universe Books, 1987.

Klots, Elsie B. *The New Field Book of Freshwater Life.* New York: G. P. Putnam's Sons, 1966.

Nowak, Mariette. "Can Dragons Teach Us to Fly?" *National Wildlife* 29 (3) (April/May 1991): 14-17.

O'Toole, Christopher, ed. *The Encyclopedia of Insects*. New York: Facts on File, 1986.

Raham, R. Gary. *Dinosaurs in the Garden: An Evolutionary Guide to Backyard Biology*. Medford, NJ: Plexus, 1988.

Stokes, Donald W. *A Guide to Observing Insect Lives*. Boston: Little, Brown, 1983.

Stolzenburg, William. "Hunting Dragons: On Safari for the Big Game of the Insect World." *Nature Conservancy* 44 (3) (May-June 1994): 24-29.

Chapter 8: Stories in Stone: The First Predators

Briggs, Derek E. G.; Erwin, Douglas H.; and Collier, Frederick J. *The Fossils of the Burgess Shale*. Washington, DC: Smithsonian Institution Press, 1994.

Briggs, Derek E. G., and Whittington, Harry B. "Terror of the Trilobites." *Natural History* 94 (12) (December 1985): 34-39.

Gore, Rick. "The Cambrian Period: Explosion of Life." *National Geographic* 184 (4) (October 1993): 120-36.

Gould, Stephen J. "Treasures in a Taxonomic Wastebasket." *Natural History* 94 (12) (December 1985): 22-33.

Gould, Stephen Jay. *Wonderful Life*. New York: W. W. Norton, 1989.

Horner, John R. *Digging Dinosaurs*. New York: Workman Publishing, 1988.

Lanham, Url. *The Bone Hunters*. New York: Dover, 1973.

Lichter, Gerhard. *Fossil Collector's Handbook*. New York: Sterling, 1993.

MacFall, Russell P., and Wollin, Jay C. *Fossils for Amateurs: A Handbook for Collectors*. New York: Van Nostrand Reinhold, 1972.

McMenamin, Mark A. S. "The Emergence of Animals." *Scientific American* 256 (4) (April 1987): 94-102.

McMenamin, Mark A. S., and McMenamin, Dianna L. Schulte. *The Emergence of Animals*. New York: Columbia University Press, 1990.

Parker, Steve. *The Practical Paleontologist*. New York: Simon & Schuster, 1990.

Rogers, Katherine. *The Sternberg Fossil Hunters: A Dinosaur Dynasty*. Missoula, MT: Mountain Press, 1991.

Sternberg, Charles H. *The Life of a Fossil Hunter*. Bloomington, IN: Indiana University Press, 1990.

Walker, David, and Ward, David. *Eyewitness Handbooks Fossils*. New York: Dorling Kindersley, 1992.

Chapter 9: Robbers, Copycats, and Opportunists

Chu, H. F. *How to Know the Immature Insects*. Dubuque, IA: William C. Brown, 1949.

Dethier, Vincent G. *To Know a Fly*. Oakland, CA: Holden-Day, 1962.

Evans, Howard Ensign. *Life on a Little Known Planet*. New York: Dell, 1968.

Hubbell, Sue. *Broadsides from the Other Orders*. New York: Random House, 1993.

Morholt, Evelyn; Brandwein, Paul F.; and Joseph, Alexander. *A Sourcebook for the Biological Sciences*. 2d ed. New York: Harcourt Brace Jovanovich, 1966.

Oldroyd, Harold. *The Natural History of Flies*. London: Weidenfeld and Nicolson, 1964.

O'Toole, Christopher, ed. *The Encyclopedia of Insects*. New York: Facts on File, 1986.

Stokes, Donald W. *A Guide to Observing Insect Lives*. Boston: Little, Brown, 1983.

Chapter 10: Spiders Say the Darndest Things

Bristowe, W. S. *The World of Spiders*. London: Collins Clear-Type Press, 1971.

Crompton, John. *The Spider*. New York: Nick Lyons Books, 1987.

Foelix, Rainer F. *Biology of Spiders*. Cambridge, MA: Harvard University Press, 1982.

Forster, Lyn. "Visual Communication in Jumping Spiders (Salticidae)." In *Spider Communication Mechanisms and Ecological Significance*, Peter N. Witt and Jerome S. Rovner, eds. Princeton, NJ: Princeton University Press, 1982, 161-210.

Jackson, Robert R. "The Behavior of Communicating in Jumping Spiders (Salticidae)." In *Spider Communication Mechanisms and Ecological Significance*, edited by Peter N. Witt and Jerome S. Rovner. Princeton, NJ: Princeton University Press, 1982, 213-45.

Kaston, B. J. *How to Know the Spiders*. Dubuque, IA: William C. Brown, 1978.

Levi, Herbert W., and Levi, Lorna R. *Spiders and Their Kin*. New York: Golden Press, 1968.

Peckham, G. W., and Peckham, E. G. "Additional Observations on Sexual Selections in Spiders of the Family Attidae." *Occasional Papers of the Wisconsin Natural History Society,* Vol. 1 (1889), pp. 3-60.

Preston-Mafham, Rod, and Preston-Mafham, Ken. *Spiders of the World*. New York: Facts on File, 1984.

Raham, R. Gary. *Dinosaurs in the Garden: An Evolutionary Guide to Backyard Biology*. Medford, NJ: Plexus, 1988.

Chapter 11: Sneaky Creatures

Bland, Roger G., and Jaques, H. E. *How to Know the Insects*. Dubuque, IA: William C. Brown, 1978.

Dixon, Dougal. *After Man: A Zoology of the Future*. New York: St. Martin's Press, 1981.

———. *Man After Man: An Anthropology of the Future*. New York: St. Martin's Press, 1990.

———. *The New Dinosaurs: An Alternative Evolution*. Topsfield, MA: Salem House Publishers, 1988.

Greene, Erick; Orsak, Larry J.; and Whitman, Douglas W. "A Tephritid Fly Mimics the Territorial Displays of Its Jumping Spider Predators." *Science* 236 (1987): 310-12.

Mather, Monica H., and Roitberg, Bernard D. "A Sheep in Wolf's Clothing: Tephritid Flies Mimic Spider Predators." *Science* 236 (1987): 308-10.

Raham, R. Gary. *Dinosaurs in the Garden: An Evolutionary Guide to Backyard Biology*. Medford, NJ: Plexus, 1988.

Science News Staff. "Bait and Capture by an Insect in Disguise." *Science News* 122 (24) (December 11, 1982): 379.

———. "Flashtrack: Firefly Plays Hawk." *Science News* 124 (20) (November 12, 1983): 379.

————. "Spider's Perfume Fatal for Moth." *Science News* 131 (22) (May 30, 1987): 340.

Chapter 12: What the Birds Say

Carey, John. "Lifestyles of the Rich and Famous." *National Wildlife* 33 (1) (1995): 44-49.

Feare, Christopher. *The Starling*. New York: Oxford University Press, 1984.

Marsh, Peter. *Eye to Eye*. Topsfield, MA: Salem House Publishers, 1988.

Perrins, Christopher, and Harrison, C. J. O. *Birds, Their Life, Their Ways, Their World*. Pleasantville, NY: Reader's Digest, 1979.

Raham, R. Gary. *Dinosaurs in the Garden: An Evolutionary Guide to Backyard Biology*. Medford, NJ: Plexus, 1988.

Robbins, Chandler S.; Bruun, Bertel; and Kim, Herbert S. *A Guide to Field Identification, Birds of North America*. New York: Golden Press, 1966.

Stokes, Donald W. *A Guide to Bird Behavior, Volume I*. Boston: Little, Brown, 1979.

Stokes, Donald W. and Stokes, Lillian Q. *A Guide to Bird Behavior, Volume II*. Boston: Little, Brown, 1983.

————. *A Guide to Bird Behavior, Volume III*. Boston: Little, Brown, 1989.

Weatherhead, Patrick J. "The Bird's Communal Connection." *Natural History* 94 (2) (1985): 35-41.

Wernert, Susan J., ed. *North American Wildlife*. Pleasantville, NY: Reader's Digest, 1982.

Chapter 13: Good Bee-Havior

Barth, Friedrich G. *Insects and Flowers*. Princeton, NJ: Princeton University Press, 1991. (chapters 12-17 and chapter 27)

Gould, James L., and Gould, Carol G. *The Honey Bee*. New York: Scientific American Library, 1988.

Kirchner, Wolfgang H., and Towne, William F. "The Sensory Basis of the Honeybee's Dance Language." *Scientific American* 270 (6) (June 1994): 74-80.

Meeuse, Bastiaan, and Morris, Sean. *The Sex Life of Flowers*. New York: Facts on File, 1984. (chapter 2)

Minton, Sherman A., Jr., and Minton, Madge Rutherford. *Venomous Reptiles*. New York: Charles Scribner's Sons, 1969, pp. 15-16.

Chapter 14: Of Beetles and Bindweed

Balsbaugh, E. V., Jr., and Hayes, K. L. "The Leaf Beetles of Alabama." *Agricultural Experiment Station Bulletin* [Auburn University] 441 (1972): 1-223.

Barrow, E. M. "Life Cycles, Mating, and Colour Changes in Tortoise Beetles (Coleoptera, Chrysomelidae, Cassidinae)." *Coleopterists' Bulletin* 33 (1) (1979): 9-16.

Bland, Roger G., and Jaques, H. E. *How to Know the Insects*. 3d ed. Dubuque, IA: William C. Brown, 1978.

Chu, H. F. *How to Know the Immature Insects*. Dubuque, IA: William C. Brown, 1949.

Jolivet, P. J.; Petitpierre, E.; and Hsiao, T. H., eds. *Biology of the Chrysomelidae*. Boston: Kluwer Academic Publishers, 1988.

Mason, C. W. "Transient Colour Changes in Tortoise Beetles (Coleoptera, Chrysomelidae)." *Entomological News* 40 (2) (1929): 52-56.

Raham, R. Gary. "Of Bindweed and Beetles." *Backyard Bugwatching* (10)(1990): 3,17.

White, Richard E. *A Field Guide to the Beetles of North America.* Boston: Houghton Mifflin, 1983.

Chapter 15: The Milkweed Universe

Camazine, Scott. *The Naturalist's Year.* New York: John Wiley & Sons, 1987.

Cranshaw, Whitney. *Pests of the West.* Golden, CO: Fulcrum, 1992.

Garber, Steven D. *The Urban Naturalist.* New York: John Wiley & Sons, 1987.

Mayer, Daniel F., and Mayer, Connie. *Bugs: How to Raise Insects for Fun and Profit.* South Bend, IN: and books, 1983.

Morse, Douglass H. "Milkweeds and Their Visitors." *Scientific American* 253 (1) (July 1985): 112-19.

Raham, R. Gary. *Dinosaurs in the Garden: An Evolutionary Guide to Backyard Biology.* Medford, NJ: Plexus, 1988.

Stokes, Donald W. *A Guide to Observing Insect Lives.* Boston: Little, Brown, 1983.

USDA Forest Service. *Range Plant Handbook.* New York: Dover, 1988.

Zimdahl, Robert L. *Weeds of Colorado.* Fort Collins, CO: Colorado State University Cooperative Extension Service, 1983.

Field Identification Guides

Bland, Roger G., and Jacques, H. E. *How to Know the Insects.* 3d ed. Dubuque, IA: William C. Brown, 1978.

Chu, H. F. *The Immature Insects.* Dubuque, IA: William C. Brown, 1949.

Levi, Herbert W., and Levi, Lorna R. *A Guide to Spiders and Their Kin.* New York: Golden Press, 1968.

White, Richard E. *A Field Guide to the Beetles of North America.* Boston: Houghton Mifflin, 1983.

Zim, Herbert S., and Cottam, Clarence. *Insects.* New York: Golden Press, 1956.

Chapter 16: Who's a Pest?

BSCS Green Version High School Biology. Chicago: Rand McNally, 1963.

Horton, David R. "Evolution into a Pest Niche by the Colorado Potato Beetle." Colorado State University, Ph.D. diss., 1987.

Hubbell, Sue. *Broadsides from the Other Orders.* New York: Random House, 1993.

Laycock, George. *The Alien Animals.* Garden City, NY: The Natural History Press, 1966.

Raham, R. Gary. *Dinosaurs in the Garden: An Evolutionary Guide to Backyard Biology.* Medford, NJ: Plexus, 1988.

Rowe, Randall C., ed. *Potato Health Management.* St. Paul, MN: APS Press, 1993.

Chapter 17: Drawing Strength from Nature

Foster, Norman H., and Beaumont, Edward A. "Creative Thinking in the Earth Sciences." *Geotimes* (August 1994): 16-18.

Jordan, Celeste Adele. "Teacher's Guide to the Arthur's Rock Trail." Available by request for copying fee from Lory State Park, Bellvue, CO.

Raham, R. Gary. *Dinosaurs in the Garden: An Evolutionary Guide to Backyard Biology.* Medford, NJ: Plexus, 1988.

Stanley, Steven M. *Extinction.* New York: Scientific American Books, 1987.

Ward, Peter. *The End of Evolution.* New York: Bantam Books, 1994.

Wilson, Edward O. *The Diversity of Life.* Cambridge, MA: Harvard University Press, 1992.

Index

About the Author

If there is such a thing as a teaching gene, Gary Raham suspects he has it. Although he only taught high school biology and physics for two years before beginning a career as a graphic artist, writer, and illustrator, he finds great enjoyment sharing his excitement about natural history with others—especially young people.

Gary received B.S. and M.S. degrees in biology from the University of Michigan and has done additional postgraduate work at Colorado State University. He is a member of the Society of Children's Book Writers and Illustrators and the Guild of Natural Science Illustrators. *Explorations in Backyard Biology* is his second book on natural history. He has written and illustrated for a variety of commercial and educational science markets including *Highlights for Children, The American Biology Teacher*, and *Earth Magazine*. Gary wrote the script for the Scott Resources video "Fossils: Uncovering Clues to the Past," which won an Award of Excellence from the Denver Video Festival in 1993.

Gary and his wife, Sharon, have two great daughters and live in Wellington, Colorado. He and his family enjoy wandering about the Rocky Mountain west searching for spectacular scenery. Gary likes to arrange for interesting fossils and/or bugs to be part of the scenery whenever possible.

from **Teacher Ideas Press**

BEYOND THE BEAN SEED: Gardening Activities for Grades K–6
Nancy Allen Jurenka and Rosanne J. Blass

Gardening provides a dynamic springboard for learning with these engaging book-based lessons that integrate gardening, children's literature, and language arts through creative activities. **Grades K–6**.
Spring 1996 ca.225p. 8½x11 paper ISBN 1-56308-346-7 $26.00 ($31.00 outside North America)

CULTIVATING A CHILD'S IMAGINATION THROUGH GARDENING
Nancy Allen Jurenka and Rosanne J. Blass

Lead children to literacy and learning along the garden path with books and activities designed to spark interest and imagination. A great companion to *Beyond the Bean Seed*. **Grades K–6**.
Fall 1996 ca.125p. 8½x11 paper ISBN 1-56308-452-X $19.50 ($21.50 outside North America)

THE WORLD'S REGIONS AND WEATHER: Linking Fiction to Nonfiction
Phyllis J. Perry

Use the power of fiction and the imagination to draw students into the world of climate and weather. **Grades 5–9**.
Literature Bridges to Science Series
1996 xvi, 157p. 8½x11 paper ISBN 1-56308-338-8 $22.00 ($26.50 outside North America)

INTERMEDIATE SCIENCE THROUGH CHILDREN'S LITERATURE: Over Land and Sea
Carol M. Butzow and John W. Butzow

Focusing on earth and environmental science themes and activities, each chapter centers on a work of literature and provides hands-on and discovery activities that implement scientific concepts. **Grades 4–7**.
1995 xxv, 193p. 8½x11 paper ISBN 0-87287-946-1 $23.00 ($27.50 outside North America)

GLUES, BREWS, AND GOOS: Recipes and Formulas for Almost Any Classroom Project
Diana F. Marks

This invaluable source pulls together hundreds of practical, easy recipes and formulas for classroom projects that span the curriculum. **Grades K–6**.
1996 xvi, 179p. 8½x11 paper ISBN 1-56308-362-0 $23.00 ($27.50 outside North America)

SIMPLE MACHINES MADE SIMPLE
Ralph E. St. Andre

Present scientific principles and simple mechanics through hands-on cooperative learning activities that use *inexpensive* materials (e.g., tape, paper clips). **Grades 3–8**.
1993 xix, 150p. 8½x11 paper ISBN 1-56308-104-0 $20.00 ($24.00 outside North America)

CIRCUIT SENSE FOR ELEMENTARY TEACHERS AND STUDENTS:
Understanding and Building Simple Logic Circuits
Janaye Matteson Houghton and Robert S. Houghton

Your classroom will be literally buzzing, flashing, and whirring with the simple and affordable activities generated by this handbook! **Grades K–6**.
1994 xi, 65p. 8½x11 paper ISBN 1-56308-149-0 $13.00 ($15.50 outside North America)

BLAST OFF! Rocketry for Elementary and Middle School Students
Leona Brattland Nielsen

You'll launch excitement in the classroom with this complete teaching package of fascinating facts and motivational activities on rocketry. **Grades 4–8**.
Winter 1997 ca.110p. 8½x11 paper ISBN 1-56308-438-7 $18.00 ($21.50 outside North America)

For a FREE catalog, or to order any of our titles, please contact us with your address:
Teacher Ideas Press
Dept. B7 · P.O. Box 6633 · Englewood, CO 80155-6633
1-800-237-6124, ext. 1 · Fax: 303-220-8843 · E-Mail: lu-books@lu.com